MW01120661

Population Ageing, Pensions and Growth

Population Ageing, Pensions and Growth

Intertemporal Trade-offs
and Consumption Planning

John Creedy

*Department of Economics, The University of Melbourne,
Australia*

Ross Guest

Griffith Business School, Griffith University, Australia

Edward Elgar
Cheltenham, UK · Northampton, MA, USA

Published by
Edward Elgar Publishing Limited
The Lypiatts
15 Lansdown Road
Cheltenham
Glos GL50 2JA
UK

Edward Elgar Publishing, Inc.
William Pratt House
9 Dewey Court
Northampton
Massachusetts 01060
USA

A catalogue record for this book
is available from the British Library

Library of Congress Control Number: 2009921840

ISBN 978 1 84844 531 4

Printed and bound by MPG Books Group, UK

Contents

III   Pensions and Taxation

IV   Population Ageing

List of Tables

List of Figures

Acknowledgements

This book makes substantial use of a number of journal articles, though they have been considerably revised and rearranged. We are grateful to the editors and publishers for permission to use the material here. We should again like to thank the anonymous referees for their constructive comments. In Part II, Chapter 2 is based on Creedy and Guest (2008a); Chapter 3 is based on Creedy (2007); Chapter 4 is based on Creedy and Guest (2008e). In Part III, Chapter 5 is based on Creedy and Guest (2008c); Chapter 6 is based on Creedy and Guest (2008d); Chapter 7 is based on Creedy and Guest (2008b). In Part IV, Chapter 8 is based on Guest (2006); Chapter 9 is based on Guest (2007a) and Chapter 11 is based on Guest (2007b).

Part I

Introduction

Chapter 1

Introduction

Many areas of economics require the evaluation of time streams of costs and
benefits, whereby a flow of net consumption or income over a number of
periods must be compressed into a single measure for comparison purposes.
They may involve decisions at the individual level, for example in the context
of educational choice where the costs are incurred early in the life cycle
whereas the returns accrue over the working life. They may involve decisions
at the firm level, relating to investment projects. Importantly they also
involve plans and decisions at the local and national level. The latter issues
may relate to plans, for example, regarding the building of roads, schools and
hospitals where in each case additional complications arise from decisions
regarding the method of finance (in particular the structure of taxation, the
burden of which can fall on different generations of individuals).

At the national level, societies also face long-term phenomena that impose
costs and benefits far into the future. Demographic change and climate
change are currently two such phenomena. Dealing with them requires policy
prescriptions that typically distribute costs and benefits unevenly over time
and among people at any given time. This presents challenges for economic
policy makers in the planning of intertemporal aggregate consumption, not
least in balancing objectives of efficiency and equity. An exploration of these
issues – with respect to population ageing in particular – is the primary

motivation for this book.

The demography of population ageing is well understood. Population ageing occurs in the latter stages of the demographic transition that accompanies economic development. The demographic transition starts with declining infant mortality and increases in adult life expectancy and is followed by declining fertility rates. Countries are at different stages in this process of demographic transition. In most developed countries the population aged over 60 is expected almost to double between between 2005 and 2050 while the population under 60 is expected to decrease.[1] However, many developing countries are at least 50 years behind countries such as Japan and those of Western Europe in the sense that their population share of over 65 year olds will be the same in 2050 as those in Japan and Western Europe today. Nevertheless, the demographic transition is developing economics appears in some cases to be progressing more rapidly than it did in industrialised countries.

The economics of population ageing is, by contrast, a far less settled field of enquiry. This applies both to the economic effects of ageing and the appropriate policy prescriptions. The vast literature in the macroeconomic modelling of population ageing that has developed mainly since the early 1980s reveals some vexacious modelling issues. A critical issue is how to value the welfare of future generations. Other issues include: whether long-run productivity growth is independent of demographic change; the degree to which agents can be assumed to optimise intertemporally and; the relative merits of the social planner paradigm versus the decentralised model of overlapping generations of representative agents.

The responses to questions such as these partly determine whether population ageing can be regarded as an economic crisis, or a more managable problem, or even an opportunity. In any case, it is widely accepted that

---

[1]Median Variant Projections in United Nations (2007) World Population Prospects 1950-2050. Database (2006 Revision). United Nations Population Division, New York.

ageing will have at least some macroeconomic implications in terms of living standards, economic welfare, government budgets, intergenerational equity and labour markets. The aim of this book is to evaluate some of these effects with a particular focus on the role of concepts, assumptions and value judgements.

The substantive chapters of this book are divided into three parts. Part II is concerned with discounting and time preference, and begins in chapter 2, which reviews the central concept of discounting and evaluating alternative time streams. Some of the issues discussed in this chapter are taken up again in more detail later in the book. This long-standing problem is inevitably controversial, partly because there is no escape from fundamental value judgements. The chapter begins by considering social evaluations based on the concept of a social welfare function which, as well as attaching different weights to different levels of consumption irrespective of their timing, discounts future flows using a 'pure time preference rate'. In order to consider the nature of judgements implied by time preference, an axiomatic approach is discussed. The chapter then turns to decisions regarding the optimal allocation of resources over time, involving the planning, by an independent judge, of optimal saving and consumption patterns. Situations giving rise to the use of decreasing discount rates over time are examined, including the use of an alternative formulation of the social welfare function involving 'sustainable preferences' and the effect of uncertainty. This chapter also introduces some complications arising from attempts to allow for the fact that income units differ in size and composition, and examines some approaches to measurement.

The latter topic is then considered in further detail in chapter 3, which reviews a number of frameworks in which the concept of the 'elasticity of marginal valuation', in the context of evaluating a social welfare function, is central. It is argued that this central elasticity concept cannot in fact be measured objectively but necessarily involves value judgements, so that economists should examine the implications of adopting alternative value judgements.

Chapter 4 takes up another topic first introduced in chapter 2, that of a social welfare function with value judgements reflecting 'sustainable preferences', whereby neither the present nor the future is favoured over the other. Alternative forms of social welfare function are used to examine, within the framework of a simple growth model, the resulting optimal time path of consumption. A policy designed to reduce some form of damage, arising in the long term, is examined. This abatement policy imposes costs on current and future generations in order to reduce damages that are expected to increase over a long time horizon and emphasis is on trying to understand the nature and implications of adopting alternative value judgements.

Chapter 5 examines the optimal path of aggregate consumption in the context of population ageing, where older age groups are considered to have relatively greater 'needs', resulting for example from additional health costs. These differences give rise to the concept of the 'equivalent number of persons', as distinct from the population size. Many models in this context employ the concept of a hypothetical representative agent who is assumed to be infinitely lived and who has the characteristics (or 'needs') of an average person in the population in each year. Chapter 5 compares the representative agent approach with an alternative in which the optimal aggregate consumption stream is determined by a social planner who maximises a social welfare function defined over the same time horizon. Individuals are considered to differ only by age and hence the planner is not concerned with inequality. One important issue relates to the choice of consumption unit in weighting the consumption per equivalent person in each period. Two cases are examined – the use of individuals and of equivalent persons. Each of these cases has sensible, but possibly inconsistent, welfare rationales. The difference between the representative agent and social planner paradigms turns out to depend on whether the social planner is concerned with individuals or equivalent persons in evaluating social welfare.

Part III of this book turns to the topic of pensions and taxation. Chapter 6 examines the labour supply and savings effects of a change in superannuation taxation. The labour supply effects of taxes on superannuation can take several forms because of the existence of three separate stages at which superannuation is taxed, including the contributions to a superannuation fund, the earnings obtained by the fund, and the income withdrawn from the fund after retirement. For example, a system is of the TTT variety if tax is imposed in all three stages. When compulsory superannuation was introduced in Australia, the TTT structure was adopted, making it the only OECD country with this form. But in the 2006 Australian Government Budget, benefits after retirement were made exempt from taxation. Chapter 6 provides a preliminary analysis using a simplified model of lifetime labour supply and consumption and investigates the extent to which the direction of some changes can be anticipated *a priori*, without the need for detailed empirical estimates. The lifetime is modelled as consisting of just three stages, the last of which is retirement.

Chapter 7 uses a more complex overlapping generations general equilibrium model to examine unanticpicated policy changes. The government budgetary implications of a tax change may be non-trivial given population ageing because the government, by eliminating tax during the retirement stage, has cut off a revenue stream that would otherwise have grown with the increasing proportion of households who are self-funded retirees. The fact that tax policy changes are almost always unanticipated by households means that they have the potential to affect saving plans with resulting implications for intergenerational equity, macroeconomic variables and economic welfare. The initial effects are likely to be stronger than the long run effects because the unanticipated nature of the policy causes relatively large adjustments immediately following the shock as middle-aged households, in particular, adjust their behaviour over a short time frame.

Part IV turns to the subject of population ageing, around which much concern has been expressed in popular debates. First, chapter 8 analyses the implications for intergenerational equity and social welfare of smoothing the fiscal costs of population ageing. This is done by simulating an overlapping generations computable general equilibrium (CGE) model, calibrated to the Australian economy, and using historical and projected demographic data along with projections of demographically sensitive government spending. The effects of tax smoothing on intergenerational equity are found by comparing the effects on lifetime utility of different generations; and the effects on social welfare are evaluated using a social welfare function. The overlapping generations framework allows winners and losers from tax smoothing to be identified. The fact that some generations lose and some win as a result of tax smoothing implies the need for a social evaluation of tax smoothing. This is done using a social welfare function under a range of alternative value judgements regarding the choice of parameters.

Chapter 9 assesses the effect of population ageing on national living standards by taking account of emerging evidence of potential dividends from demographic change. This is not an exercise in the general equilibrium modelling of population ageing, but it has the advantage of simplicity and transparency at the cost of ignoring behavioural feedback effects.

The effect of population ageing on labour productivity is a critical relationship because labour productivity growth could potentially offset – indeed swamp – the economic burden caused by a falling employment to population ratio. Chapter 10 explores a link between population ageing and labour productivity that has received little attention – that is, the effect on labour productivity via capital intensity which in turn is affected by sectoral shifts in demand in response to population ageing. The method is to apply a calibrated simulation model using data for two OECD countries, the United States and Australia. Broadly speaking there are two sources of labour productivity growth: technical progress and increases in the average capital-labour ratio. Labour productivity affects economic welfare via consumption.

In the analyses of population ageing in Chapters 8, 9 and 10, various non-conventional assumptions were adopted. The purpose of chapter 11 is to revisit these assumptions in order to investigate the sensitivity of the results to variations in the key parameters. Four assumptions are chosen for the sensitivity analysis: the parameters of the production function used in modelling imperfect elasticity of substitution between of workers of different ages (chapter 9); sectoral capital intensities and the effect of ageing on sectoral demands (chapter 10); rule-of-thumb consumers (chapter 10); and an upward sloping supply price of foreign capital (chapter 8).

Part II

Discounting and Time Preference

Chapter 2

Discounting and Time Preference

The aim of this chapter is to review a central issue in the evaluation of alternative time streams – that of discounting. The context is one in which evaluation of a public project is made by a disinterested judge, that is someone who has no personal interest in the outcomes. Investment projects typically involve a present cost incurred in order to achieve future benefits. These might be in the context of investments in health technology, civil engineering projects, or environmental protection. It is therefore necessary to evaluate alternative outcomes, involving different time streams of net benefits. In any exercise of this kind there are obviously huge problems associated with measurement issues and uncertainty about the future. But these are not the focus of attention here.

Despite the long-standing nature of the problem, it remains controversial and even the basic issues are far from being settled.[1] One of the problems concerns a lack of clarity over the concepts. Another difficulty arises from the fact that there is no escape from fundamental value judgements, while protagonists on different sides of debates often conceal their value judgements.

---

[1] For example, the controversial nature of discounting is demonstrated by the debate over the *Stern Report* (2007) on climate change; see, for example, Carter *et al.* (2006), Dasgupta (2006), Nordhaus (2006) and Varian (2006).

Hence it is important to be clear about precisely how they enter the calculations and how they may be specified. Emphasis is placed on the analytical issues rather than providing a comprehensive literature review.

Section 2.1 sets the scene by considering social evaluations based on the concept of a social welfare function: this is dominant in the literature concerned with evaluating public projects. This form of welfare function involves, as well as attaching different weights to different levels of consumption irrespective of their timing, the discounting of future flows using what is called a 'pure time preference rate'. There are alternative views about the way to proceed. One approach is simply to say that the social welfare function is meant to represent alternative value judgements and therefore results should be reported for alternative time preference rates. Some economists attempt to impose their own value judgements, using rhetorical arguments suggesting for example that pure time preference is in some sense 'ethically indefensible'. Thus Ramsey (1928, p.543) stated that discounting utility over time is 'a practice which is ethically indefensible and arises merely from the weakness of the imagination'. Pigou (1932, p. 25) also argued that time preference implies that 'our telescopic faculty is defective'. More recently an objection to discounting has been made in terms of overlapping generations, the criticism being that it is 'unethical' to impose the preferences of the current generation on the utility of people who are not yet born (Padilla, 2002).[2]

However, it is desirable to have a clear understanding not only of what is implied by pure time preference – or its absence – but what specific value judgements may lie behind it. That is, it is useful to appreciate how time preference can arise from more basic axioms stating value judgements in a clear way. Section 2.2 discusses an axiomatic approach to time preference,

---

[2]It is a small step to the argument that it is unethical to impose a constant discount rate over the lifetime of an individual because an individual's life can be divided into the current self and the future self who are effectively two different persons; see Caplin and Leahy (2000).

based on the argument of Koopmans (1960).

Section 2.3 turns from social evaluations of exogenous time profiles to decisions regarding the socially optimal allocation of resources over time. It therefore concerns the planning, again by an independent judge, of optimal saving and consumption patterns. However, it uses the same kind of social welfare function. Section 2.4 returns to the evaluation of alternative streams in the context of cost–benefit analyses. It discusses the concept of the social time preference rate and highlights a problem with its application. Situations giving rise to the use of decreasing discount rates over time are examined in section 2.5, including the use of an alternative formulation of the social welfare function involving 'sustainable preferences' and the effect of uncertainty. Section 2.6 introduces some complications arising from attempts to allow for the fact that income units differ in size and composition. Some approaches to measurement are examined in section 2.7. The interpretation of orders of magnitude regarding one aspect of value judgements is discussed in section 3.4. Brief conclusions are in section 2.9.

2.1 Social Evaluations

Suppose it is required to evaluate a time stream $C = [c_1, c_2, ...]$ of consumption. For simplicity, it is assumed that the population consists only of individuals (rather than families), that the size of the population remains unchanged over time, and that consumption is the only economic variable considered to be relevant by the judge. These assumptions are relaxed in section 2.5.1 below. The term c_t refers to aggregate consumption in period t. Hence there is, by assumption, no concern for within-period inequality among individuals. An evaluation cannot avoid the use of value judgements. Hence, the usual approach is to examine the implications of adopting a range of value judgements.

2.1.1   A Social Welfare Function

Consider social evaluations based on additive Paretian social welfare functions. These are functions for which social welfare, $W(C)$, is a weighted sum of consumption values in each period and an increase in consumption in one period, without a reduction in any other period, is regarded as an improvement. There are two components to such functions, involving first a weight, $U(c_t)$, to be attached to each c_t, irrespective of the time period, t, and second a view about the timing of consumption, reflected in a constant rate of pure time preference, ρ. The use of falling discount rates with time is considered below. The presentation here uses a discrete time framework, but conversion to continuous time would not affect the results.

Social welfare functions of this class take the form:

$$W(C) = \sum_{t=1}^{T} U(c_t) \left(\frac{1}{1+\rho}\right)^{t-1} \tag{2.1}$$

The effects of discounting alone can be seen in Figure 2.1, which plots the discount factor, $\left(\frac{1}{1+\rho}\right)^{t-1}$, against t, for several alternative values of ρ; in other words it shows how the present value of \$1 falls as the time period increases. This rate of decline is clearly highly sensitive to the choice of ρ.

The weighting function U – a cardinal measure of the contribution to W, before discounting, of period t's consumptionis – is sometimes called a utility function. Hence the pure time preference rate is sometimes also called a 'utility discount rate'. However, this terminology is somewhat misleading unless it refers to a single-person framework. The social welfare function W does not represent the wellbeing of society: above all, it does not represent 'society's views', but those of an independent judge. Indeed, it is known from Arrow's Impossibility Theorem that there is no consistent way of aggregating preferences, such that certain axioms are satisfied.

It is usual to consider the implications of types of $U(c)$ which reflect a decreasing marginal valuation, $dU(c)/dc$. The rate at which the marginal

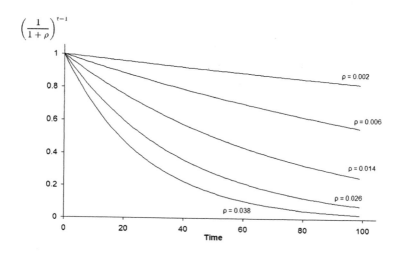

Figure 2.1: The Discount Factor and Time Period

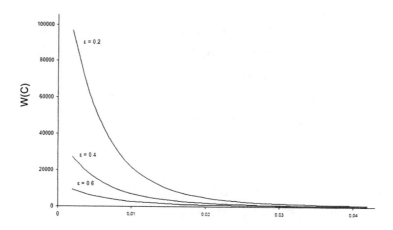

Figure 2.2: Sensitivity of $W(C)$ to Choice of Epsilon (Less Than 1)

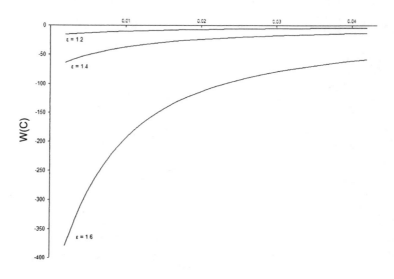

Figure 2.3: Sensitivity of $W(C)$ to Choice of Epsilon (Greater Than 1)

valuation falls as c increases is described by the 'elasticity of marginal valuation', $d\log(dU(c)/dc)/d\log c_t$. This elasticity is negative for concave U.
This value judgement therefore reflects adherence to a multi-period 'principle
of transfers' whereby (in the absence of discounting) a transfer of consumption from high to low consumption periods, so long as their relative ranks do
not change, is considered an improvement.

Consideration of alternative value judgements regarding U is simplified
by the use of constant-elastic functions. This means that U takes the form:

$$U(c_t) = \frac{c_t^{1-\varepsilon}}{1 - \varepsilon} \tag{2.2}$$

where the term ε is the absolute value of the elasticity of marginal valuation,
since $dU(c)/dc = c_t^{-\varepsilon}$ and $\log(dU(c)/dc) = -\varepsilon\log c_t$. Another way of describing ε is that it measures the judge's degree of constant relative aversion
to variability over time: in the absence of discounting the judge would prefer
to see a smooth consumption stream.

The implications of adopting different value judgements can therefore be examined, for a given consumption stream, by calculating W for alternative values of ε and ρ. Consider a consumption stream over 250 periods, where the initial value is 30 units and there is smooth growth at the constant rate of 2.3 per cent per period. The values of $W(C)$ are highly sensitive to the choice of ε, as shown in Figures 2.2 and 2.3, where each profile shows the variation in the present value of $W(C)$ as ρ is increased, for a given value of ε. Figure 2.2 shows the reduction in the present value as ε is increased from 0.2 to 0.6, while Figure 2.3 shows variations for values of $\varepsilon > 1$, for which $W(C)$ is negative.

The introduction of the terms ρ and ε in the social welfare function makes it clear that these reflect the value judgements of a hypothetical judge or decision maker. However, there are studies attempting to 'estimate' values using a variety of methods. These are discussed in section 2.7. Some authors decompose ρ to include a term depending on the perceived probability of extinction: see Pearce and Ulph (1998) and Stern (2007).

2.1.2 Comparing Alternative Time Streams

In view of the sensitivity of present values, it cannot be expected that alternative projects have the same ranking, independent of the choice of elasticity of marginal valuation and time preference rate. Consider the two profiles A and B in Figure 2.4, where B has the fastest constant growth rate of 1.6 per cent, compared with A of 0.9 per cent, but the starting value of B is 5 while that of A is 15. The profiles intersect only once. Time profile B is expected to dominate A only for relatively low values of ρ, though the particular value of ρ for which the ranking changes depends crucially on the choice of ε. Present values, $W(C)$, are shown in Figure 2.5 for $\varepsilon = 0.6$, showing that profile B is preferred for low values of ρ. However, it is found that for elasticity of marginal valuation, that is higher aversion to variability (values of $\varepsilon > 0.88$),

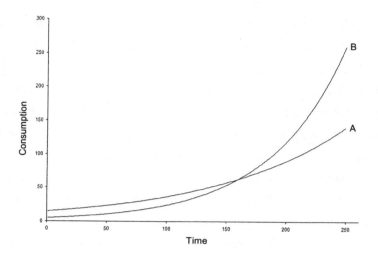

Figure 2.4: Two Consumption Profiles With One Intersection

the flatter profile A is preferred to B for all ρ varies.

More complex comparisons may result from more variable time profiles, making the choice of alternative streams more sensitive to the choices of ε and ρ. Consider Figure 2.6, where time stream A results from a constant growth rate of 2.3 per cent (starting from 10 units), but profile B results from a fixed trend rate of growth of 1.8 per cent (starting from 4 units) combined with a cyclical growth component having an amplitude of 5 per cent and a wavelength of 165 periods. The consumption profiles intersect twice, so it is likely that stream A has the highest value of $W\left(C\right)$ for both low and high values of ρ, while stream B is likely to dominate (that is have a higher $W\left(C\right)$ value) for intermediate values, though the precise values are again likely to be sensitive to the choice of ε. An example is given in Figure 2.7 for $\varepsilon = 0.2$, where project A is indeed preferred for high and low values of ρ.

The welfare function in (2.1) represents a particular set of value judgements, as well as those giving rise to pure time preference: the evaluation function is additive and Paretian. Alternative views about the desirable

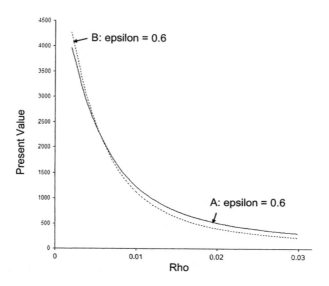

Figure 2.5: Present Value, $W(C)$, of Consumption Profiles for $\varepsilon = 0.6$ and Alternative ρ

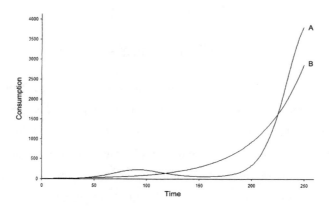

Figure 2.6: Two Consumption Profiles With Two Intersections

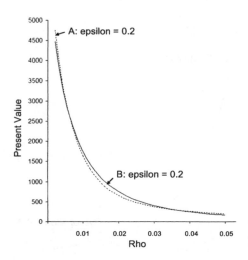

Figure 2.7: Present Value, $W(C)$, of Consumption Profiles for $\varepsilon = 0.2$ and Alternative ρ

evaluation of a time stream of consumption are obviously possible, and professional economists cannot make prescriptions about the form to be used, but can only investigate the implications of adopting alternative forms. An alternative approach is discussed in section 2.5.1.

2.2   Existence of Time Preference

The social welfare function in (2.1) simply starts from the position that the independent judge whose value judgements are examined has positive pure time preference. However, the precise nature of the value judgements underlying time preference are not immediately obvious. The question considered here is whether time preference is implied by a clear set of axioms describing an independent judge's or social planner's value judgements about time profiles of consumption. This makes it easier to identify precisely why judges may differ in their attitudes towards time preference. The following discussion is a simplified version of the argument put forward by Koopmans (1960).[3] This is not in any sense a proof that time preference does exist or is necessary: rather, it seeks to understand the nature of the axioms required and thus to make more transparent the nature of time preference.

2.2.1 An Axiomatic Approach

Consider an independent judge with an ordinal evaluation function, given by $P(C) = P(c_1, c_2, c_3, ...)$ and defined over a time stream of consumption represented by the vector, $C = [c_1, c_2, c_3, ...]$. It is simply assumed that this function has the usual properties of evaluation functions, such as monotonicity and transitivity. For simplicity, it is assumed that the population consists only of individuals (rather than families), that the size of the population remains unchanged over time, and that consumption is the only economic variable considered to be relevant by the judge. The term c_t refers to aggregate consumption in period t. Hence there is, by assumption, no concern for within-period inequality among individuals.

Stated informally, the *continuity* axiom states that any slight variation in C does not lead to big changes in the valuation of C, while a *boundedness* axiom states that paths C_A and C_B exist such that $P(C_A) \leq P(C) \leq P(C_B)$. If alternative paths were to produce unbounded values of P, they could not be ranked.[4]

The *sensitivity* axiom says that if paths C_0 and C_1 differ in only the first period, then $P(C_0) \neq P(C_1)$. Essentially this is stating that the first period matters, in that it cannot be swamped by all other periods. Without the

---

[3] Other demonstrations are available. Marini and Scaramozzino (2000, p.6) provided an interesting analysis of growth in an overlapping generations framework. They stated that, 'a social rate of pure time preference is justifiable on purely ethical grounds'. A clearer statement of what the authors showed is that *if* the objective of maximising average steady-state consumption per capita is adopted, then *an implication* of this *ethical value judgement*, combined with a model containing productivity and population growth, is that positive time preference exists that does not reflect myopia.

[4] Alternative (positive) time streams of consumption over an infinite period could not be compared in the absence of time preference, because they would be unbounded.

sensitivity axiom, a small gain to each of an infinitely large number of future periods, achieved at the expense of reducing consumption in the present period to zero, would be regarded as acceptable.

A *non-complementarity* (or *independence*) axiom states that if two time streams differ only by the first period, their ranking does not depend on the form of the remaining stream. Here, it is convenient to introduce the notation $C^{[2]} = (c_2, c_3, c_4, ...)$, so that $C = (c_1, C^{[2]})$. Hence, for two time profiles $C_0 = [c_{0,1}, c_{0,2}, c_{0,3}, ...]$ and $C_1 = [c_{1,1}, c_{1,2}, c_{1,3}, ...]$, where $c_{k,t}$ refers to consumption in the tth time period and the kth time stream, independence implies that if:

$$P\left(c_{0,1}, C_0^{[2]}\right) \geq P\left(c_{1,1}, C_0^{[2]}\right) \tag{2.3}$$

then:

$$P\left(c_{0,1}, C_1^{[2]}\right) \geq P\left(c_{1,1}, C_1^{[2]}\right) \tag{2.4}$$

and vice versa.

Finally, a *stationarity* axiom states that if paths C_0 and C_1 have the same consumption in the first period, so that $c_{0,1} = c_{1,1} = c_1$, then the ranking:

$$P\left(c_1, C_0^{[2]}\right) \geq P\left(c_1, C_1^{[2]}\right) \tag{2.5}$$

implies also that:

$$P\left(C_0^{[2]}\right) \geq P\left(C_1^{[2]}\right) \tag{2.6}$$

Hence the rankings of the alternative streams (with a common first element) remain unchanged if they are simply moved earlier one period in time.

Having stated the axioms, consider two time paths C_1 and C_2 such that $c_{1,t} > c_{2,t}$ for all t, and all $c_{k,t}$ are positive consumption levels ('all goods are good'). It must therefore be the case that $P(C_1) \geq P(C_2)$. Suppose there are two other time streams, $C_3 = (c_{3,1}, C_1)$ and $C_4 = (c_{4,1}, C_2)$ where $c_{3,1} = c_{4,1}$. Hence streams C_3 and C_4 have a common first period's consumption level, and thereafter have precisely the same streams, respectively, as C_1 and C_2. The stationarity axiom therefore implies that $P(C_3) \geq P(C_4)$.

By definition, the paths C_3 and C_4, by having a common first element, are less different than C_1 and C_2. Since, from above, each period matters, this implies that:

$$P(C_1 - C_2) > P(C_3 - C_4) \qquad (2.7)$$

This property implies that the difference is smaller, the more distant in time it is: this is referred to as 'time perspective'; see Koopmans, Diamond and Williamson (1964).

Next, consider alternative streams such that C_1 and C_2 differ only in the first time period, such that $c_{1,1} - c_{2,1} = 1$. Hence the streams C_3 and C_4 differ only in their second period, by the same amount. Using (2.7) it can be seen that:

$$P(1, 0, 0, 0, 0, ...) > P(0, 1, 0, 0, 0, ...) \qquad (2.8)$$

Hence, with only one unit of consumption available, there is a preference for having this in the first period, rather than having nothing in the first period and waiting to consume the unit in the second period. There is therefore a preference for bringing the consumption forward from the second to the first period. This result clearly implies pure time preference.

2.2.2 A Measure of Pure Time Preference

It is necessary to have a measure of the extent of this pure time preference. Consider for simplicity the two-period case. Time preference can be interpreted in a diagram with period 2's consumption on the vertical axis and period 1's consumption on the horizontal axis, using the concept of social indifference curves, along which P is constant. In general, the absolute slope of the social indifference curve, the marginal rate of substitution of period 1's consumption for period 2's consumption, MRS_{c_1,c_2}, is given by:

$$MRS_{c_1,c_2} = -\left.\frac{dc_2}{dc_1}\right|_P = \frac{\partial P/\partial c_1}{\partial P/\partial c_2} \qquad (2.9)$$

Where a social indifference curve passes through the point where consumption is the same in each period, the curve must be steeper than a downward sloping 45 degree line, which has an absolute slope of 1. This is because time preference implies that the social planner is prepared to give up one unit in the second period in order to get less than one extra unit in the first period. Hence:

$$MRS_{c_1,c_2}|_{c_1=c_2} = \frac{\partial P/\partial c_1}{\partial P/\partial c_2} > 1 \qquad (2.10)$$

A precise measure of pure time preference can be based on the extent to which the absolute slope of the social indifference curve at $c_1 = c_2$ exceeds 1, as follows. Suppose the evaluation function P is additively separable, so that $P(c_1, c_2) = P_1(c_1) + P_2(c_2)$. In the case where $c_1 = c_2 = c$ and consumption is the same in both periods, time preference implies that $P_1(c) > P_2(c)$. Writing $P_1(c) = U(c)$, it must be possible to write $P(c, c) = U(c) + \gamma U(c)$, where $\gamma < 1$, and hence when $c_1 = c_2 = c$:

$$MRS_{c_1,c_2}|_{c_1=c_2} = \frac{1}{\gamma} \qquad (2.11)$$

To express the fact that $\gamma < 1$, write $\frac{1}{\gamma} = 1 + \rho$. Clearly ρ reflects the extent to which the social indifference curve at $c_1 = c_2 = c$ is steeper than 45 degrees. Hence ρ measures the rate of pure time preference of the social planner, and $\gamma = 1/(1 + \rho)$.

In general it can be shown that if $P(C_0) > P(C_1)$, for two streams C_0 and C_1, then it is possible to write:

$$\sum_{t=1} \left(\frac{1}{1+\rho}\right)^{t-1} U(c_{0,t}) \geq \sum_{t=1} \left(\frac{1}{1+\rho}\right)^{t-1} U(c_{1,t}) \qquad (2.12)$$

where, as above, $U(c_t)$ represents an evaluation function defined over a single period, t, in contrast with the multi-period P. Hence, the ranking according to $P(C)$ is the same as the ranking according to:

$$W(C) = \sum_{t=1} \left(\frac{1}{1+\rho}\right)^{t-1} U(c_t) \qquad (2.13)$$

The evaluation function $W(C)$ has the same form as the welfare function in (2.1). The difference is that in the latter case, pure time preference is simply assumed to be a feature of the social planner, who uses the cardinal weighting function $U(c)$ in each period. It is necessarily cardinal because the values are added in (2.13). However, following Koopman's axiomatic approach, time preference is seen to be implied by a set of basic axioms, where evaluation of a time stream is based on an ordinal evaluation function, P.

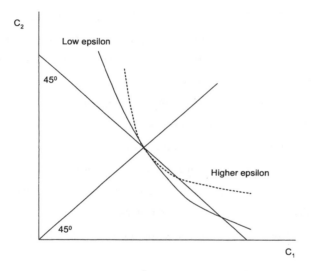

Figure 2.8: Social Indifference Curves and Time Preference

In general, the absolute slope of a social indifference curve associated with the social welfare function in (2.13) is:

$$MRS_{c_1,c_2} = -\left.\frac{dc_2}{dc_1}\right|_W = \left(\frac{1}{\gamma}\right)\frac{\partial U/\partial c_1}{\partial U/\partial c_2} = (1+\rho)\frac{\partial U/\partial c_1}{\partial U/\partial c_2} \qquad (2.14)$$

This may be compared with the special case of an iso-elastic weighting function, where:

$$MRS_{c_1,c_2} = \left(\frac{c_2}{c_1}\right)^{\varepsilon}(1+\rho) \qquad (2.15)$$

Examples of two indifference curves are shown in Figure 2.8. Consumption in each period is equal along the upward sloping 45 degree line from the origin. If, along this ray, each indifference curve has a downward slope of 45 degrees, it means that an increase in period 1's consumption by one unit must be matched by precisely the same fall in period 2's consumption. This would reflect an absence of pure time preference. A positive time preference means that giving up one unit in period 2 requires an increase in period 1 of less than one unit: hence the associated indifference curve is steeper than a downward sloping 45 degree line. In Figure 2.8, each indifference curve shown is steeper than the downward sloping 45 degree line. The degree of pure time preference is thus reflected in the difference between the slope of the indifference curve and the 45 degree line.

It can also be seen that the elasticity of marginal valuation, reflecting the concavity of U (the extent to which the slope, the marginal valuation, falls as consumption increases), is also a measure of the convexity of indifference curves. The solid curve in Figure 2.8 reflects a lower value of ε than the broken curve. The welfare function is also homothetic, whereby the marginal rate of substitution depends on only the ratio of consumption levels (the slopes of indifference curves are the same along any ray from the origin).

2.3   Choice of Optimal Time Stream

Instead of comparing given time streams, consider a planner, with value judgements represented by the social welfare function in (2.1), who must decide on the optimal consumption and saving path of the economy. The welfare function is maximised subject to an intertemporal budget constraint which can be written in the form:

$$\sum_{t=1}^{T} \left(\frac{1}{1+r} \right)^{t-1} c_t = Y \qquad (2.16)$$

where Y represents a measure of the present value of resources available for consumption over the period, and r is the rate of interest in a perfect capital market. The Lagrangean for this problem is:

$$L = W + \lambda \left\{ Y - \sum_{t=1}^{T} \left(\frac{1}{1+r} \right)^{t-1} c_t \right\} \qquad (2.17)$$

Hence first-order conditions, for $t = 1, ..., T$, are:

$$\frac{\partial L}{\partial c_t} = \left(\frac{1}{1+\rho} \right)^{t-1} \frac{dU}{dc_t} - \lambda \left(\frac{1}{1+r} \right)^{t-1} \qquad (2.18)$$

so that for two periods t and $t+1$:

$$(1+\rho) \frac{dU/dc_t}{dU/dc_{t+1}} = 1 + r \qquad (2.19)$$

Convenient analytical results can be obtained where U again takes the isoelastic form $U(c) = \frac{c^{1-\varepsilon}}{1-\varepsilon}$, discussed above, so that the absolute value of the elasticity of marginal valuation, $\left(\frac{c}{dU/dc} \right) \frac{d}{dc} \left(\frac{dU}{dc} \right)$, is constant and equal to ε. Hence (2.19) becomes:

$$(1+\rho) \left(\frac{c_{t+1}}{c_t} \right)^{\varepsilon} = 1 + r \qquad (2.20)$$

Defining $g_t = \frac{c_{t+1}}{c_t} - 1$, taking logarithms and using the approximation $\log(1+x) = x$, gives:

$$g_t = \frac{1}{\varepsilon} (r - \rho) \qquad (2.21)$$

This expression is the Euler equation for optimal consumption: it describes the optimal time path of consumption. In this simple problem, if the various rates are constant, consumption either grows or declines at a constant rate, depending on the value of $r - \rho$. If the pure time preference rate is equal to the market rate of interest, consumption smoothing is implied, with $g_t = 0$.

Rearrangement of (2.21) gives:

$$r = \rho + \varepsilon g_t \qquad (2.22)$$

This is often referred to the Ramsey equation. It means that at the optimal position, the market rate of interest is equated with $\rho + \varepsilon g_t$. It may therefore be said that along the optimal path, the planner equates the marginal return from saving, represented by the market rate of interest, r, with the marginal cost of saving, represented by $\rho + \varepsilon g_t$.

This analysis of optimal consumption is often used in macroeconomic models of optimal saving; see, for example, Blanchard and Fischer (1989) and Barro and Sala-i-Martin (1995). In such models macroeconomic behaviour is assumed to be captured by the behaviour of a single individual described as a 'representative agent', rather than a social planner as discussed here. There is therefore no consideration of aggregation requirements. In some growth models, the representative individual is assumed to be infinitely lived. The introduction of population growth and other complications can produce a different Euler equation from that given in (2.21), as discussed in section 2.6 below.

2.4   The Social Time Preference Rate

Previous sections have involved the use of the pure time preference rate, ρ, of a hypothetical judge in the context of a social welfare function to discount the weighted values $U(c_t)$ for each period. However, in cost–benefit analyses it is common to compare present values of time streams of money values of consumption, using a 'consumption discount rate', rather than the so-called 'utility discount rate' (the pure time preference rate), ρ. Following (2.22), the consumption discount rate, δ, is defined as:

$$\delta = \rho + \varepsilon g_t \qquad (2.23)$$

This rate, δ, is also widely referred to as the 'social time preference rate'. In the context of cost–benefit analyses where money values of an exogenous consumption stream are evaluated, (2.23) is the fundamental equation that

takes a central role when discussing social time preference rates to be used.[5]
The social time preference rate can therefore be positive even for $\rho = 0$.
However, it is possible, if the growth rate of consumption, g_t, is negative, for
δ to be negative, if ε is relatively large and ρ is small.

The use of the social time preference rate, δ, to evaluate a consumption
stream c_t (rather than the use of ρ to evaluate a weighted consumption stream
$U(c_t)$), involves an evaluation using W^*, where:

$$W^* = \sum_{t=1}^{T} c_t \left(\frac{1}{1 + \rho + \varepsilon g_t} \right)^{t-1} \tag{2.24}$$

It is usually taken for granted that this welfare function gives the same ranking of projects as does the function in (2.1). However, this is not guaranteed,
as can be seen from the following comparisons.[6]

It is convenient to begin with the most favourable case, that is where
consumption does in fact grow at a constant proportional rate, $g_t = g$ for all
t. Hence $c_t = c_1 (1 + g)^{t-1}$ and substitution into (2.1) gives:

$$W = \sum_{t=1}^{T} \frac{\{c_1 (1 + g)^{t-1}\}^{1-\varepsilon}}{1 - \varepsilon} \left(\frac{1}{1 + \rho} \right)^{t-1} \tag{2.25}$$

Rearrangement of this expression, and using the approximation $(1 + \rho)(1 + g)^\varepsilon = 1 + \rho + \varepsilon g$, gives:

$$W = \frac{c_1^{-\varepsilon}}{1 - \varepsilon} \sum_{t=1}^{T} c_t \left(\frac{1}{1 + \rho + \varepsilon g} \right)^{t-1} \tag{2.26}$$

and:

$$W = \frac{c_1^{-\varepsilon}}{1 - \varepsilon} W^* \tag{2.27}$$

---

[5]In this context δ does not need to be set equal to the market rate of interest. This
contrasts with determination of the optimal growth path, as in the previous section, where
δ must be equal to the market rate of interest, r. The latter is determined by, for example,
the marginal product of capital – depending on the precise nature of the growth model
considered.

[6]For a more detailed treatment, see Creedy (2007).

This final result demonstrates that W^*, obtained by discounting money values of consumption at the social time preference rate, does not necessarily coincide with W, obtained by discounting $U(c_t)$ at the pure time preference rate ρ. For given ε, W^* automatically gives the same ranking as W only if $\varepsilon < 1$ and two consumption streams, with different growth rates, have the same initial value of consumption. Otherwise, inconsistencies can arise. Hence it is advisable to use the basic form of welfare function in (2.1), with an explicit form for $U(c_t)$, rather than discounting the stream c_t using the rate $\rho + \varepsilon g$.

2.5   Time Varying Discount Rates

Previous sections have concentrated on the use of constant discount rates. The expression for the social time preference rate allows for some variation via differences in the growth rate, but it is usual to impose a constant rate. This section considers two cases which give rise to the use of a discount rate which decreases as the time period increases. In subsection 2.5.1, an alternative approach to specifying the welfare function is examined, while subsection 2.5.2 briefly discusses uncertainty.

2.5.1   An Alternative Welfare Function

Attention has so far been restricted to examining value judgements which can be summarised by the social welfare function in (2.1), in which weighted consumption values, $U(c_t)$, are discounted using a pure time preference rate. When considering an axiomatic derivation of time preference in section 2.2, the importance of the sensitivity axiom was stressed.[7] This ensures that the

---

[7] As stressed above, the axiomatic approach does not pretend to prove that time preference must exist, but rather clarifies the value judgements involved. As pointed out by Heal (1998), the independence axiom implies that the trade-off between events today and events in the distant future is independent of what happens in the meantime: not everyone would take this view.

infinite future is not allowed completely to dominate the present. With this kind of welfare function, there is a basic tension in that, for very long periods, discounting implies that the present dominates the future. Given that the role of the economist is to examine the implications of adopting alternative value judgements, there is clearly a challenge to specify an alternative formulation of a social welfare function – one which does not imply dominance by either the present or a far distant future period.

Ramsey (1928) realised that without discounting, infinite streams would be non-convergent and therefore could not be ordered using a welfare function like (2.1). His solution was to measure utility over time as a cumulative sum of the distance from a 'bliss' level of utility, but the main problem with this approach is the arbitrariness of the level of 'bliss'. An alternative value judgement, which has received much attention in the literature concerning income inequality, is a variation of the maxi-min rule discussed by Rawls (1971). In the present context this form of welfare function selects the alternative which maximises the value of the lowest time stream of consumption. But this criterion also fails to rank all the other streams. Similarly, an objective function that ranks the satisfaction of basic needs above all other outcomes fails to rank other outcomes.

One way of achieving a partial ordering of infinite utility streams without discounting is the overtaking criterion suggested by von Weizacker (1965). According to this welfare function, utility stream A is preferred to B if, after some finite time period, T, the cumulative utility of stream A is greater than stream B for all time $t > T$. However this is only a partial ordering of utility streams because one stream may oscillate above and below another stream indefinitely – it may never permanently overtake. Also, rather than replacing the need for discounting, the overtaking criterion comes close to Koopmans's axiomatic defence of discounting, because it implies that, for example, utility stream A:$\{0, 1, 0, 0, \ldots\}$ is preferred to stream B:$\{0, 0, 1, 0, 0, \ldots\}$. Stream B is stream A lagged by one period. Hence stream A 'overtakes' stream B in period 1 but is identical thereafter. The preference for the overtaking stream therefore reflects a time preference; see also Heal (1998) who made this point.

An alternative form of social welfare function was proposed by Chichilnisky (1997), who was concerned by the fact that choice of a constant discount rate versus a zero rate involves a choice between a 'dictatorship of the present' versus a 'dictatorship of the future', referred to above. She suggests a solution based on axioms that aim for equity and efficiency in intertemporal resource allocation (the axioms are not discussed in detail here). Her approach is to take an arbitrarily very long time horizon and assign weights to future utility that decline over time and then to assign some extra weight to the utility in the last period. The social welfare function then consists of a weighted average of two terms: the sum of discounted utility where the discount rate declines over time, and the (undiscounted) utility in the final period. Hence:[8]

$$W = \theta \sum_{t=1}^{T} (1 + \rho_t)^{1-t} U_t (C_t) + (1 - \theta) U_T (C_T) \tag{2.28}$$

with $\rho'_t < 0$ and $0 < \theta < 1$. Chichilnisky (1997, p. 468) describes the value judgements reflected in this form of social welfare function as 'sustainable preferences' because neither the present nor the future is favoured over the other. She cites Solow's (1992) term 'intertemporally equitable preferences' as an alternative description. This welfare function therefore involves choice of an additional parameter, the weight θ.

In justifying the declining discount rate in equation (2.28), Chichilnisky refers to a large body of experimental evidence that the relative weight that people give to two subsequent periods in the future is inversely related to

---

[8]Chichilnisky's function differs from (2.28) in that in her model utility is derived from both consumption, c, and a flow of services from the stock of natural capital, s. This implies an optimal combination of c and s at any time t. However, dropping s from the utility function, as here, does not affect the notion of sustainable preferences, the key ingredients of which are a declining discount rate applied to $U(.)$ and the second additive term in (2.28).

their distance from today. To give a simple example, if a person prefers to receive \$90 today than \$100 in one year's time, but prefers to receive \$100 in 5 years' time rather than \$90 in 4 years' time, then their discount rate from year 4 to 5 is lower than that from year zero to 1. Of course, the finding that some people have such preferences does not imply that they *should* be used in social evaluations. Such preferences have been called hyperbolic preferences (Laibson, 1996). In addition, a hyperbolic discount rate is found to be a necessary condition for an optimal path to exist in maximising (2.28) in the limit as T approaches infinity – a constant discount rate would not yield a solution. The second term in (2.28) justifies the term 'sustainable preferences' because it gives explicit recognition to the very long run (at time T). Taking a weighted average of the two terms implies a trade-off between the present and the future, yet neither need dominate completely.

These preferences are subject to the standard criticism of time inconsistency that applies to hyperbolic preferences since these are reflected in the first term in (2.28). But this criticism is weak when the objective is a socially optimal consumption path. From a social choice perspective there is nothing natural or desirable about time consistency, a point made forcefully by Heal (1998). His point is that as new generations arrive and older ones drop out of the choice process, there is no reason why the preferences of generations who have dropped out should be imposed on new generations in the name of time consistency. Chichilnisky's sustainable preferences cannot of course resolve the debate because they still imply a trade-off between the present and the future which is fundamentally an ethical judgement.

A variation on this type of welfare function reflecting sustainable preferences was introduced by Li and Lofgren (2000). Briefly, society is assumed to be composed of two representative individuals who have utility functions specified over a very long period which spans several generations, on the argument that individuals care about their offspring. One individual discounts the future at a constant rate and the other does not discount at all. The social welfare function is specified as a weighted average of the utilities of the two individuals, with the weights depending on value judgements. It can be shown that the implied time preference rate in this welfare function declines over time.[9] This approach also differs from the welfare function discussed in Sections 3 to 5, where per capita consumption in each period is subject to a weight reflecting the independent judge's value judgements (involving the elasticity of marginal valuation). The Li and Lofgren approach involves an assumed 'representative' form of utility function and the constant pure time preference rate also reflects the properties of the individual who discounts, rather than the judge. The earlier approach took the view that, however individuals in society may actually discount the future in their private consumption decisions, and whatever the degree of concavity of their utility functions, the welfare function embodies only value judgements. The approach here allows the preferences of individuals in the society to carry much more weight.

The advantage of the social welfare specifications discussed here is that they do offer alternative forms in which 'sustainable preferences' arise, in contrast to the extremes arising from (2.1), with either $\rho > 0$ or $\rho = 0$, in which either the present or the future dominates when very long periods are considered. Consistent with the basic approach recommended in this chapter, involving the comparison of alternative value judgements rather than an attempt to impose investigators' own values, the availability of specifications allowing for a wider range of views is to be welcomed.

2.5.2   Uncertainty

The models of Chichilnisky and Li and Lofgren generate a declining consumption discount rate through a declining pure rate of time preference. Alternatively, a declining consumption discount rate could be imposed from

---

[9]For further details see Li and Lofgren (2000) and Chapter 4 below.

the outset as an ad hoc way of taking account of uncertainty regarding the growth rate; see Weitzman (2007). Suppose the growth rate of consumption is assumed to be constant, but uncertain, giving rise to a distribution of possible values of the consumption discount rate, δ. If the possible values are δ_i, for $i = 1, ..., D$, and they have associated probabilities of p_i, Weitzman (2007) showed that the effective consumption discount rate, δ'_t, applying to period t is obtained not as a simple weighted average of the δ_is but of the discount factors. Thus the required relationship is:

$$(1 + \delta'_t)^{-t} = \sum_{i=1}^{D} (1 + p_i\delta_i)^{-t} \tag{2.29}$$

so that, by taking logarithms and using the approximation, $\log(1 + x) = x$:

$$\delta'_t = -\frac{1}{t} \log \sum_{i=1}^{D} (p_i\delta_i)^{-t} \tag{2.30}$$

It is clear from (2.30) that this declining rate weakens the 'dictatorship of the present' that arises with a constant discount rate, as do the models of Chichilnisky and Li and Lofgren. Weitzman actually gave the continuous time version of the above result. He also discussed the use of certainty equivalent discount rates and the implications of what Arrow and Hurwitz (1972) called 'pure uncertainty'. On alternative approaches to uncertainty see, for example, Shilizzi (2007) and Woodward and Bishop (1997).

2.6 The Choice of Unit of Analysis

The previous discussion has assumed that there are no relevant non-income differences between individuals and that population size is constant. Suppose instead that the number of individuals at time t is N_t and that individuals of age i have an equivalent adult size of s_i, for example because they may have special age-related needs. The discussion in this section assumes that population size is exogenous. However, taking a wider perspective means that judgements about population size and composition are themselves involved in social welfare comparisons. This raises important issues that are beyond the scope of the present chapter.

The equivalent size of the population at t is $P_t = \sum_i s_i N_{i,t}$ and the average equivalent size is $\bar{s}_t = P_t/\!/N_t$. The question then arises as to the variable, or 'welfare metric' to enter the social welfare function. One approach is to write U, the weighting function, as a function of the ratio of average consumption to average equivalent size, $\bar{c}_t/\bar{s}_t = C_t/P_t$, where C_t denotes aggregate consumption in period t. It should be recognised that this is not equal to average consumption per equivalent person, the average value of c/s in the population at year t. The two terms are equal either if $c_{i,t}/s_{i,t}$ is constant for all i, or if $s_{i,t}$ and $c_{i,t}$ are uncorrelated.

Given a distinction between individuals and equivalent persons, a further decision must be made about the unit of analysis in a welfare function. This decision again involves value judgements. The question of choice of units has been considered in the literature on inequality measurement, but has received little attention in multi-period contexts; for an exception, see Chapter 5. Statements about comparisons between households, in the context of inequality, can easily be converted to statements about comparisons between time periods. On the choice of units in the context of inequality include Shorrocks (2004), Decoster and Ooghe (2002), Glewwe (1991) and Ebert (1997). The use of different units can lead to opposite conclusions about the effects on inequality of a tax policy change. Examples of such conflicts using tax microsimulation models are given by Decoster and Ooge (2002) and Creedy and Scutella (2004).

One approach to defining a unit of analysis is to use the 'adult equivalent person'. In the multiperiod context, there are P_t adult equivalent persons at time t, and so the social welfare function becomes:

$$W = \sum_{t=1} P_t \left(\frac{C_t}{P_t}\right)^{1-\varepsilon} \frac{(1+\rho)^{t-1}}{1-\varepsilon} \qquad (2.31)$$

The resulting Euler equation for optimal growth at t is:

$$g_t = \frac{1}{\varepsilon}(r - \rho) + (p_t - n_t) \tag{2.32}$$

where g_t, p_t and n_t are respectively the proportional rates of change of C_t, P_t and N_t. In this way, the 'income' concept and the unit of analysis are treated consistently, ensuring that each individual's contribution depends on the demographic structure of the time period to which they belong. An alternative approach is to treat the individual as the basic unit of analysis. As there are N_t individuals at time t, the social welfare function can be written as:

$$W = \sum_{t=1} N_t \left(\frac{C_t}{P_t}\right)^{1-\varepsilon} \frac{(1+\rho)^{t-1}}{1-\varepsilon} \tag{2.33}$$

For the optimal consumption path problem, the Euler equation is found to be:

$$g_t = \frac{1}{\varepsilon}\{r - \rho + (\varepsilon - 1)(p_t - n_t)\} \tag{2.34}$$

so that although the difference between the social welfare functions (2.31) and (2.33) concerns only the choice of weights in each period, that is a choice between P_t or N_t, the resulting optimal consumption paths can differ substantially. This is because the choice between individuals and adult equivalents as the basic unit of analysis can in principle lead to different conclusions about the effects of transferring consumption between time periods, which has implications for the path of optimal consumption.

2.7 Measurement Attempts

It has been stressed that the elasticity of marginal valuation, ε, is not an objective measure relating to individuals in society, but reflects the subjective value judgements of a fictional judge who is evaluating alternative policies or outcomes. However, a superficially similar-looking concept of the 'elasticity of marginal utility' plays a central role in some consumer demand systems, particularly where directly additive utility functions are involved; this was first clarified by Frisch (1959). Define the elasticity of the marginal utility of total expenditure with respect to total expenditure as ξ. If $\delta_{\ell j}$ denotes the Kroneker delta, such that $\delta_{\ell j} = 0$ when $\ell \neq j$, and $\delta_{\ell j} = 1$ when $\ell = j$, and e_ℓ is the total expenditure elasticity for good ℓ, and w_j is the budget share of good j, Frisch showed that the price elasticities, $e_{\ell j}$, can be written as:

$$e_{\ell j} = -e_\ell w_j \left(1 + \frac{e_j}{\xi} \right) + \frac{e_\ell \delta_{\ell j}}{\xi} \tag{2.35}$$

This can be used to obtain ξ, given independent values of the elasticities. In the special case of the Linear Expenditure System, the elasticity of marginal utility has a convenient interpretaion. It is the ratio of total expenditure to supernumerary expenditure, that is, expenditure above a 'committed' amount. The use of the LES in empirical demand studies therefore necessarily involves an (absolute) elasticity value which is well above unity, and studies typically obtain a value of around 2.

In view of the entirely different contexts of welfare comparisons involving social evaluation functions and empirical studies of household consumption behaviour, there is no relationship whatsoever between ε and ξ. In other words, there is no reason why a value of ε, to be imposed in making comparisons, could be 'estimated' using information from studies of household budgets. Nevertheless, this suggestion is sometimes made; for example, elasticities obtained on the basis of the Linear Expenditure System are discussed by Evans (2005, pp. 204-206).

In considering alternative values of ε, it is useful to ensure that they are within a range that is considered appropriate by potential users of the results. For example there is little point in reporting values of, say, $\varepsilon > 10$ if the vast majority of readers would regard them as extreme. Hence questionnaire studies have been designed to elicit information about individuals' value judgements. Early questionnaire studies were carried out by Glesjer et al. (1977), and Gevers et al. (1979), although no attempt was made to estimate precise specifications of distributional preferences. It was in this spirit that the questionnaire study of Amiel *et al.* (1999) was carried out. Nevertheless, there was no suggestion that questionnaires can produce any single value that should be used in policy evaluations.[10] A substantial number of respondents did not adhere to the constant relative inequality aversion form. In addition, Amiel and Cowell (1994) have found that a large number of questionnaire respondents do not actually share the value judgements that are explicit in the most common forms of social welfare function used in evaluation work, such as the one discussed here. This presents a challenge to produce alternative flexible specifications.

2.7.1 Taxation and Equal Absolute Sacrifice

A different approach to the 'estimation' of ε involves attempts to estimate the implicit value judgements revealed by tax and transfer policies. Some authors, including Stern (1977), Cowell and Gardiner (1999) and Evans (2005), have suggested that such estimates provide a guide to ε values which should be applied in policy evaluations. Other attempts to infer value judgements include Brent (1984), Christiansen and Jansen (1978), Mera (1969) and Moreh (1981).

There are two steps to such an approach. The first step attempts to infer, from tax policy decisions, value judgements which are not otherwise made explicit. Such an attempt can be defended – provided of course that the model used to make inferences is plausible. For example, such estimates may be useful in checking whether there is in fact any correspondence between policies and basic value judgements of policy makers. Given the complexities involved in tax policy design, it may be useful to know if a particular structure is associated with implicit judgements that may actually be very different from those held (though seldom made explicit). This is the view taken by van

---

[10]There is sometimes confusion about this, as in Evans (2005).

de Ven and Creedy (2005) when examining adult equivalence scales implicit
in tax and transfer systems.

The second step is the illegitimate one of suggesting that estimates of
implicit value judgements 'should' be used in making social evaluations. This
criticism applies even in the most unlikely case where implicit views can be
identified precisely.

This subsection considers the first 'positive' step taken by the authors
mentioned above, and suggests that the model used is inadequate. The
approach is based on the assumption that income tax policy makers aim to
achieve equal absolute sacrifice. It assumes that incomes are exogenously
given, rather than arising from endogenous labour supply behaviour (subject
to endowments and education which give rise to individual productivities).
Suppose x represents income and the tax function is $T(x)$. Equal absolute
sacrifice requires, for all x, that the absolute difference between pre-tax and
post-tax utility is the same for all individuals. Hence:

$$U(x) - U(x - T(x)) = k \tag{2.36}$$

where $U(.)$ represents a utility function which is considered to be the same
for all individuals. The parameter k depends on the amount of revenue
per person. This differs from an alternative view that would replace $U(x)$
with $W(x)$. Thus, as with inequality measurement, a judgement is made
regarding the welfare metric, and then a view is taken about variations in x.
This judgement is quite separate from the way individuals may themselves
view such variations.

The combination of equal absolute sacrifice with the iso-elastic function,
$U(x) = x^{1-\varepsilon_\tau} / (1 - \varepsilon_\tau)$ for $\varepsilon_\tau \neq 1$, gives, from (2.36) above:[11]

$$\frac{x^{1-\varepsilon_\tau}}{1-\varepsilon_\tau} - \frac{(x - T(x))^{1-\varepsilon_\tau}}{1-\varepsilon_\tau} = k \tag{2.37}$$

---

[11] Young (1987) actually showed that the iso-elastic form is required if an indexation
requirement is imposed on the tax structure in addition to equal sacrifice. But of course
fiscal drag is a common, indeed almost universal, feature of income tax structures.

Differentiation and simplification gives, as in Evans (2005, p.207), the result that:

$$\log\left(1 - T'\left(x\right)\right) = \varepsilon_\tau \log\left(1 - \frac{T\left(x\right)}{x}\right) \tag{2.38}$$

where $T'\left(x\right)$ and $T\left(x\right)/x$ are marginal and average tax rates. This expression has been used to carry out ordinary least squares regressions using income tax schedules, so that ε_τ and its standard error are obtained as a regression coefficient. There is some difference of opinion over whether to include a constant in the regression: compare Cowell and Gardiner (1999) and Evans (2005), who also use different income measures. Alternatively, (3.20) can be rearranged to get $\varepsilon_\tau = \log(1 - MTR)/\log\left(1 - ATR\right)$, and 'estimates' of ε_τ are obtained and compared using simply the marginal and average tax rates at different income levels.

This approach automatically produces a value of ε_τ in excess of unity for a progressive tax system, for which the marginal tax rate exceeds the average tax rate. This feature was first discussed by Edgeworth (1897) and formally shown by Samuelson (1947). The values of ε_τ obtained in this way are thus severely constrained by the specification of the objective of equal absolute sacrifice. Furthermore, those using the approach to 'estimate' ε ignore the objections raised by Edgeworth and others concerning the various interpretations of sacrifice theories. This does not apply to those, such as Richter (1983) and Young (1987) who were interested only in deriving the implications of various axioms.

For $\varepsilon_\tau > 1$, equation (3.19) can be rearranged as:[12]

$$T\left(x\right) = x - \left\{x^{1-\varepsilon_\tau} - k\left(1 - \varepsilon_\tau\right)\right\}^{1/(1-\varepsilon_\tau)} \tag{2.39}$$

which gives smooth and increasing marginal and average rate schedules. Of course, in practice tax functions are multi-step functions with ranges where the marginal rate is constant. In some structures there is a 'standard rate'

---

[12]In stating this result, Young (1987, p. 212) rewrote $-k\left(1 - \varepsilon\right)$ as $\lambda^{1-\varepsilon}$, so that the tax function campares with a constant elasticity of substitution form.

which applies over a wide range of taxable income, so this function obviously has difficulty capturing this range. The imposition of $\varepsilon > 1$ is highly restrictive. Furthermore, the model applies only to positive taxes. It can thus relate at best to a small component of a much broader set of taxes and transfers. If equal absolute sacrifice is combined with a welfare function displaying constant absolute inequality aversion, α, such that $W = 1 - \exp(-\alpha x)$, a tax function of the form $T(x) = x + \frac{1}{\alpha} \log \{k + e^{-\alpha x}\}$ arise. This can be made to display rate schedules similar to those illustrated here. Dalton (1954, pp. 68-70) discussed several examples using alternative utility functions and sacrifice principles, and showed that if equal absolute sacrifice produces progression, equal proportional sacrifice produces a more progressive tax structure. In an early study, Preinreich (1948) considered the form of the utility schedule consistent with the US tax legislation, without imposing a specific functional form over the whole income range. He assumed equal proportional sacrifice.

Hence some scepticism must be attached to interpretations of estimates obtained using this model as implicit value judgements. It seems most likely that the approach has been chosen largely – or indeed only – for its simplicity. On the other hand, the optimal tax framework has demonstated the considerable complexity involved in the link between value judgements and the tax structure and, importantly, progression can arise with values of $\varepsilon < 1$. But of course even if the estimation of implicit preferences were considered plausible, they cannot qualify as value judgements which should be imposed. There is no alternative to accepting that value judgements are required and the best attitude of professional economists is to report a range of results based on alternative value judgements. In reporting results, readers need to appreciate precisely what is implied about value judgements by different values of ε, since it is not immediately obvious whether, for example, a value of $\varepsilon = 0.5$ indicates a high or low aversion to inequality. This is considered in the following section.

2.8   Interpreting Orders of Magnitude

In using ε values to compute values of social welfare functions, or carry out cost–benefit evaluations, there is no alternative but to consider a range alternative values, implying different degrees of aversion to inequality. In some cases, 'dominance' results may be obtained. In other words one policy may be judged to give rise to a higher value of social welfare than another policy for all values of ε. In other situations, readers can make up their own minds given the reported computations. It is therefore important to appreciate the precise nature of the comparisons being made. When the link between a social welfare function and a measure of inequality was introduced by Atkinson (1970), he recognised the difficulty of forming views about the orders of magnitude of ε using the welfare function $W = \sum_{h=1}^{H} \frac{y_h^{1-\varepsilon}}{1-\varepsilon}$. In order to help interpretation, he used the idea of a 'leaky bucket' experiment, which considers the extent to which a judge is prepared to tolerate some loss in making a transfer from one person to another.[13]

Consider two individuals, so that from the welfare function, setting the total differential equal to zero gives:

$$-\frac{dy_1}{dy_2}\bigg|_W = \left(\frac{y_1}{y_2}\right)^{\varepsilon} \tag{2.40}$$

The welfare function is thus homothetic, as the slopes of social indifference curves are the same along any ray drawn through the origin. Consider two individuals and, using discrete changes, suppose a dollar is taken from the richest, such that $\Delta y_2 = -1$. The amount to be given to the other individual to keep social welfare unchanged is thus:

$$\Delta y_1 = \left(\frac{y_1}{y_2}\right)^{\varepsilon} \tag{2.41}$$

For example, if $y_2 = 2y_1$ and $\varepsilon = 1.5$, it is necessary to give person 1 only

---

[13]Okun (1975) examined a slightly different kind of leaky bucket experiment involving transfers between groups of individuals.

35 cents – a leak of 65 cents from the original dollar taken from person 2 is tolerated. If $\varepsilon = 1$, a leak of 50 cents is tolerated.

This type of experiment, and thus the sensitivity of the tolerance for a leaking bucket, is well-known in the literature on inequality measurement. But in other contexts in which the same kind of iso-elastic function is used, relatively large values of ε are often adopted without, it seems, consideration of such implications.[14] For example, in the intertemporal literature, a value of $\varepsilon = 2$ is often used. Suppose that total income (or consumption) in the first period is 100 and this grows at a rate of 0.02 per period. In period 10 it is thus 119.5, and a judge with $\varepsilon = 2$ would be prepared to take a dollar from period 10, and give only \$0.70 to period 1. By period 20 total income would be 145.7, and the same judge would reduce period 20's income by \$1 while adding only \$0.47 to the first period. The social time preference rate is thereby increased significantly above the pure time preference rate. The leaky bucket experiment therefore provides a useful illustration of the implications, in terms of value judgements, of adopting particular values of ε in any policy evaluation.

2.9   Conclusions

This chapter has provided an analytical review of problems arising in the evaluation of alternative time streams of consumption using the concept of time preference. The potential sensitivity of comparisons, especially to the choice of time preference rate and elasticity of marginal valuation, was stressed. The nature of time preference, based on an axiomatic approach, was examined. The analysis of individual optimisation over time then led to the concept of the social time preference rate, and a difficulty with using this rate was highlighted and complications introduced by non-income differences between individuals were examined. Attempts to measure the elasticity of marginal

---

[14]However, it is discussed by Pearce and Ulph (1998, pp. 280-281).

valuation were critically discussed.

A basic theme of this chapter is that ultimately, evaluations cannot avoid value judgments, so the role of the economist is to examine the implications of adopting alternative value judgements. As argued by Varian (2006), 'Exploring the implications of alternative assumptions is likely to lead to better policy than making a single blanket recommendation. At least at this stage of our understanding, exploration beats exhortation'. Much earlier, Robbins (1935, p. 149) argued that 'this is not to say that economists may not assume as postulates different judgments of value, and then on the assumption that these are valid enquire what judgment is to be passed upon particular proposals for action.'

In view of the fact that, in the formulations discussed here, there are few parameters representing value judgements, sensitivity analyses do not present any problems computationally. There is no excuse for computing and presenting only one set of values. However, care is needed regarding presentation of results. First, it is useful to investigate whether 'dominance' results can be obtained: that is, is one policy option judged superior to others for all, or at least a very wide range, of parameter value combinations? When clearly specified alternative policies are being considered, it is more useful to report critical values of parameters, and their combinations, for which a particular policy dominates, rather than using an arbitrary range of values. For example if there are just two alternative consumption streams, a diagram showing combinations of ε and ρ (where the relevant social welfare function is involved) which 'divide' the two policies can be constructed. Above all, the nature of the comparisons must be explained as clearly as possible to policy makers. Here the type of leaky bucket experiment discussed above can be useful. Above all, economists have a duty to make it clear that there is no observable 'social time preference rate' or 'elasticity of marginal valuation' which 'should' be imposed in any policy analysis.

Chapter 3

The Elasticity of Marginal Valuation

The aim of this chapter is to review and critically examine a number of frameworks in which the concept of the 'elasticity of marginal valuation', in the context of evaluating a social welfare funciton, is central. This arises particularly in assigning welfare weights in inequality comparisons and in cost–benefit analyses involving discounting, for example in discussions of population ageing or environmental policy. Stress is placed on the need to distinguish these contexts and models clearly, in order to avoid the possible inappropriate 'transfer' of a value from one context to another. It is argued that this central elasticity concept cannot in fact be measured objectively but necessarily involves value judgements. Hence the role of economists is not to propose the use of particular values, which is equivalent to imposing judgements, but to examine the implications of adopting alternative value judgements. The view put forward here is in line with – and is indeed intended as a reminder of – that of Robbins (1935, p.148) when he famously argued, 'between the generalisations of positive and normative studies there is a logical gulf fixed which no ingenuity can disguise and no juxtaposition in space or time bridge over.'

Social welfare functions are used both in static contexts, involving a distribution over appropriately defined units, and in dynamic contexts, involving a distribution over time periods. Decisions must be made regarding the 'welfare metric' (for example, income, consumption, or utility) and the unit of analysis (for example, households, individuals or equivalent adults). Both of these decisions also involve value judgements, but they are not the concern of the present chapter. The emphasis here is on the fact that, in attaching 'welfare weights' to each unit or time period, the concept of the elasticity of the marginal valuation of the chosen welfare metric plays an important role. For example, it is prominent in the current fierce debate on the economics of climate change: see, for example, Stern (2007) and criticisms of the discount rate used by Stern which include Nordhaus (2006), Dasgupta (2006) and Carter et al. (2006).

Many contributions to the literature appear to regard this elasticity as something that can be objectively measured. For examples of the use of various approaches to 'measuring' this elasticity, extensive references and a range of 'estimates', see Pearce and Ulph (1998), Cowell and Gardiner (1999) and Evans (2005). In fact, the UK Treasury recommends a value for the elasticity of around unity, based on empirical estimates. Evans (2005) argued that the Treasury recommendation, when forming distributional welfare weights or computing a social time preference rate in cost–benefit studies, is too low. Pearce and Ulph (1998, p. 282) argued that the earlier UK Treasury recommended discount rate at the time was too high, saying that 'we find it impossible to support the continued use of rates in the region of 6% for the UK. Such rates are far too high.' In each of these examples, the view was presented as an objective finding, rather than a value judgement.

Section 3.1 briefly introduces the form of social welfare function and welfare weights widely adopted in the literature on policy evaluation in the single-period context. The concept of the elasticity of marginal valuation is defined and the use of 'estimates' based on empirical information about a sample of individuals' consumption behaviour is criticised. Section 3.2 turns to the multi-period context and its additional complications. Much emphasis has been placed on the estimation, and adoption, of a value of the elasticity that is thought to be implicit in an income tax structure. Attempts to impute such a value include Mera (1969), Stern (1977), Christiansen and Jansen (1978), Moreh (1981), Brent (1984), Cowell and Gardiner (1999) and Evans (2005). This approach, based on an assumption of equal absolute sacrifice as a policy objective, necessarily produces for a progressive tax a value of the elasticity of marginal valuation in excess of unity. Section 3.3 considers, first, whether this approach can actually provide reliable evidence of implicit judgements and, second, whether it could legitimately be used as the foundation of an argument in favour of using those values. Section 3.4 briefly gives some idea of the implications, in terms of value judgements, of adopting alternative values of the elasticity. This involves the idea, familiar from the literature on inequality measurement, of the 'leaky bucket' experiment, which makes explicit the tolerance of losses when making income transfers between individuals.

Given the need to make value judgements, economists have no special qualifications or authority to impose their own judgements on others, and cannot use 'estimates' as support for their views. Economists have an obligation to make value judgements explicit, and their role is to examine the implications of adopting a range of such judgements. Having been presented with alternative results, readers can then form their own opinions. Ultimately, this chapter aims to make clear some important distinctions which are often confused in the literature.

3.1 Social Evaluations: A Single Period

Any attempt to answer the question, 'when is a change an improvement?', faces the fundamental difficulty that it cannot avoid the use of value judgements. Hence complete agreement in any particular context – say the effect of a proposed change to a tax and transfer system – is most unlikely, even if there are no losers. The Pareto criterion has little practical use as it refuses to pass judgement where losers exist, and is certainly not a value-free criterion. There are also well-known problems with the use of 'potential Pareto improvements'. The approach adopted in economics is to specify explicit value judgements in a formal manner, using a social evaluation function or, following Samuelson (1947), a 'Social Welfare Function'. Crucially, this function formally expresses the value judgements of a fictional judge or policy maker. It is not, despite the use of the term 'social', intended to represent any kind of aggregate or representative views of society.[1] Indeed the judge is considered to be an independent person who is not affected by the outcomes. This section discusses the form of social welfare function commonly used and the associated elasticity of marginal valuation.

3.1.1   The Welfare Function

Some simple properties of welfare functions are typically specified, with the hope that while they cannot be expected to represent any kind of consensus, they are at least likely to appeal to a large number of people. It is in this spirit that the form of evaluation function widely adopted reflects adherence to value judgements such as the 'principle of transfers', whereby a transfer from a richer to a poorer person is judged to produce an 'improvement', This is conditional on the transfer being such that the transferee does not become richer than the transferor. In addition, it is individualistic, additive and Paretian.[2]

The first choice is to select a welfare metric, say x_h for unit h, and to define the unit of analysis itself, with both choices involving value judgements. The definition of x, the welfare metric, is problematic and usually depends on the context. It is variously defined as income, consumption, utility or money

---

[1] The extreme case of a 'representative agent', mentioned below, is the exception where the welfare function corresponds to the utility function of the fictional representative.

[2] However, other approaches are widely used. For example, the welfare function implicit in the use of the Gini inequality measure involves quite different value judgements.

metric utility, where each concept may, in addition, be expressed in 'adult equivalent' terms, and such equivalence scales themselves involve difficult value judgements. The choice of unit of analysis, between for example individuals and adult equivalents, also involves incompatible value judgements. This important issue is not discussed here, and for simplicity the unit is referred to below simply as the individual; on this issue, see Chapter 5.

An additive social welfare function is typically formed as an appropriate weighted sum. Thus the problem is to specify precisely how those weights, referred to as 'welfare weights', are formed. For 'classical utilitarians', the evaluation criterion was simply the sum, over all individuals, of utilities. The welfare weights were thus all unity. Define the contribution to social welfare of individual h as $W(x_h)$. Social welfare, W_S, is thus defined as:

$$W_S = \sum_{h=1}^{H} W(x_h) \tag{3.1}$$

Importantly, $W(x_h)$ is *not* individual h's utility function. Indeed, the welfare metric may itself be utility (or some money metric measure of utility), as in the optimal tax literature. In the marginal indirect tax reform literature it represents indirect utility. In that literature, W is defined in terms of (indirect) utilities, V_h, so that $W = \sum_{h=1}^{H} W(V_h)$ and the effect of a change in the price of good i, p_i, say arising from a tax change, is:

$$\frac{\partial W}{\partial p_i} = \sum_{h=1}^{H} \frac{\partial W(V_h)}{\partial V_h} \frac{\partial V_h}{\partial p_i} \tag{3.2}$$

From Roy's Identity, $x_{hi} = -(\partial V_h/\partial p_i)/(\partial V_h/\partial m_h)$, where m is total expenditure, and:

$$\frac{\partial W}{\partial p_i} = \sum_{h=1}^{H} \left(\frac{\partial W}{\partial V_h} \frac{\partial V_h}{\partial m_h} \right) x_{hi} \tag{3.3}$$

In specifying the term in brackets, W is usually re-interpreted in terms of total expenditures, with $W(m_h) = m_h^{1-\varepsilon}/(1-\varepsilon)$ and so the term in brackets becomes $m_h^{-\varepsilon}$.

3.1.2   The Elasticity of Marginal Valuation

Any change – which may be induced by a policy reform to an income or indirect tax structure – gives rise to a total change in social welfare of:

$$dW_S = \sum_{h=1}^{H} \frac{\partial W\left(x_h\right)}{\partial x_h} dx_h \tag{3.4}$$

Letting $v_h = \frac{\partial W\left(x_h\right)}{\partial x_h}$ denote the 'marginal valuation', the contribution to the change in W_S of a change in x_h, (3.4) becomes:

$$dW_S = \sum_{h=1}^{H} v_h dx_h \tag{3.5}$$

The term v_h represents the 'welfare weight' attached to the hth individual. An aversion to inequality on the part of the hypothetical judge is specified by an assumption that $W\left(.\right)$ is concave, so that it satisfies the 'principle of transfers'. A measure of relative inequality aversion, R, is therefore based on the concavity measure:

$$R = -\frac{x d^2 W\left(x\right)/dx^2}{dW\left(x\right)/dx} \tag{3.6}$$

This is equivalent to the 'elasticity of marginal valuation', $\left(\frac{dv}{dx}\right)\left(\frac{x}{v}\right)$. This elasticity plays an important role in what follows. Importantly, the term 'marginal valuation' is used here rather than using 'marginal utility' since, as stated above, $W\left(x\right)$ is not a utility function. The function $W\left(x\right)$ represents the contribution to social welfare (that is to the social evaluation function) of the hth person, however x is defined.

3.1.3   Choice of Values

The function $W\left(x\right)$ is specified in the vast majority of studies as:

$$W\left(x\right) = \frac{x^{1-\varepsilon_s}}{1-\varepsilon_s} \tag{3.7}$$

for $\varepsilon_s \neq 1$, and $W(x) = \log x$, where $\varepsilon_s = 1$. In this case, substitution in (3.6) gives $R = \varepsilon_s$ and ε_s thus reflects a constant degree of relative inequality aversion of the judge or policy maker.

Importantly, ε_s is not an objective measure relating to individuals in society, but reflects the subjective value judgements of a fictional judge who is evaluating the effects of alternative policies or outcomes. However, a superficially similar-looking, but very different, concept of the 'elasticity of marginal utility' plays a central role in some consumer demand systems, particularly where directly additive utility functions are involved; this was first clarified by Frisch (1959). Define the elasticity of the marginal utility of total expenditure with respect to total expenditure as ξ. If $\delta_{\ell j}$ denotes the Kroneker delta, such that $\delta_{\ell j} = 0$ when $\ell \neq j$, and $\delta_{\ell j} = 1$ when $\ell = j$, and e_ℓ is the total expenditure elasticity for good ℓ, and w_j is the budget share of good j, Frisch showed that the price elasticities, $e_{\ell j}$, can be written as:

$$e_{\ell j} = -e_\ell w_j \left(1 + \frac{e_j}{\xi} \right) + \frac{e_\ell \delta_{\ell j}}{\xi} \tag{3.8}$$

This can be used to obtain ξ, given independent values of the elasticities. In the special case of the Linear Expenditure System, the elasticity of marginal utility has a convenient interpretaion: it is the ratio of total expenditure to supernumerary expenditure, that is, expenditure above a 'committed' amount. The use of the LES in empirical demand studies therefore necessarily involves an elasticity value of, say ε_{LES}, which is well above unity, and studies typically obtain a value of around 2.

In view of the entirely different contexts, of welfare comparisons involving social evaluation functions and empirical studies of household consumption behaviour, there is no relationship whatsoever between ε_s and ε_{LES}. In other words, there is absolutely no reason why a value of ε_s, to be imposed by economists in making comparisons, could be 'estimated' using information from studies of household budgets. Nevertheless, this suggestion is sometimes made; for example, elasticities obtained on the basis of the Linear

Expenditure System are discussed by Evans (2005, pp. 204-206).

In using ε_s values to compute values of social welfare functions, or carry out cost–benefit evaluations, there is no alternative but to consider a range alternative values, implying different degrees of aversion to inequality. In some cases, 'dominance' results may be obtained. In other words one policy may be judged to give rise to a higher value of social welfare than another policy for all values of ε_s. In other situations, readers can make up their own minds given the reported computations.

In considering alternative values of ε_s, it is clearly useful to ensure that they are within a range that is considered appropriate by a reasonable number of users of the results. Hence questionnaire studies have been designed to elicit information about individuals' value judgements. It was in this spirit that the questionnaire study of Amiel *et al.* (1999) was carried out. Nevertheless, there was no suggestion that questionnaires can produce any single value that should be used in policy evaluations. A substantial number of respondents did not adhere to the constant relative inequality aversion form. In addition, Amiel and Cowell (1992, 1994) have found that a large number of questionnaire respondents do not actually share the value judgements that are explicit in the most common forms of social welfare function used in evaluation work, such as the one discussed above. This presents a challenge to produce alternative flexible specifications.

3.2   Multi-Period Contexts

Evaluations are also made in a multi-period context. Some models use a representative individual, and hence subsection 3.2.1 begins by looking at a single individual optimisation in a multi-period framework. Subsection 3.2.2 then considers social evaluation functions.

3.2.1 A Single Individual

Consider a single individual where C_t represents consumption in period t. An additive utility function defined over T periods, where ρ is the 'pure time preference' rate of the individual is thus:

$$U_T = \sum_{t=1}^{T} \left(\frac{1}{1+\rho} \right)^{t-1} U\left(C_t\right) \tag{3.9}$$

Consider periods 1 and 2. The pure time preference, or impatience, rate measures the extent to which the slope of an indifference curve, at a point where $C_1 = C_2$, deviates from a downward sloping (from left to right) 45 degree line.[3] It reflects impatience, or an 'aversion to waiting' on the part of the individual, whereby faced with a constant consumption stream the individual is prepared to give up more than one unit of C_2 in order to obtain one more unit of C_1. For any combination of C_1 and C_2, the marginal rate of substitution between consumption in the two periods, MRS_{c_1,c_2}, is the absolute value of the slope of the individual's indifference curve, and is thus $\frac{\partial U_T / \partial C_1}{\partial U_T / \partial C_2}$.

The discount rate, r, at any combination of C_1 and C_2, is defined as:

$$1 + r = MRS_{c_1,c_2} \tag{3.10}$$

Supposing that $U\left(C_t\right)$ is the iso-elastic form:

$$U\left(C_t\right) = \frac{C_t^{1-\varepsilon_p}}{1 - \varepsilon_p} \tag{3.11}$$

where ε_p is the absolute value of the individual's elasticity of the marginal utility of consumption. It is also the absolute value of the elasticity of the

---

[3]The terminology is not universally accepted. For example, Pearce and Ulph (1998), refer to this simply as the 'rate of time preference (the rate at which *utility* is discounted', and decompose it into a 'pure rate' and a term reflecting the rate of growth of life chances. They refer to what is below called the 'social time preference rate' as the 'consumption rate of interest'.

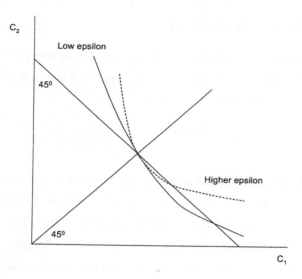

Figure 3.1: Time Preference

marginal rate of substitution with respect to the ratio of consumption levels. Then:

$$MRS_{c_1,c_2} = \left(\frac{C_2}{C_1}\right)^{\varepsilon_p} (1 + \rho) \tag{3.12}$$

An example is shown in Figure 3.1. At the point of intersection with the 45 degree line from the origin, along which consumption is equal in both periods, the solid indifference curve shown is steeper than the downward sloping 45 degree line, indicating a degree of pure time preference. The convexity of the indifference curve is affected by the value of ε_p, so that the solid curve reflects a lower value than the broken curve. If $\varepsilon_p = 0$, the indifference curves are straight lines and the individual's optimal position would be a corner solution, consuming everything either in period 1 or 2, depending on whether the market rate of interest (assuming equal borrowing and lending rates) is less than or greater than the pure time preference rate. In general the individual's optimal position is a tangency where the market rate of interest equals the discount rate.

A convenient expression for the discount rate can be obtained using an approximation which holds when the various rates are small. Let g denote the (constant) growth rate of consumption, so that $\frac{C_2}{C_1} = 1 + g$ and:

$$r = (1 + g)^{\varepsilon_p} (1 + \rho) - 1 \qquad (3.13)$$

Expanding $(1 + g)^{\varepsilon_p}$ and neglecting squared and higher-order powers gives $(1 + g)^{\varepsilon_p} \approx 1 + \varepsilon_p g$. Hence $r = (1 + \varepsilon_p g)(1 + \rho) - 1$, and making the further assumption that $\varepsilon_p g \rho \approx 0$, the individual's discount rate is:

$$r = \rho + \varepsilon_p g \qquad (3.14)$$

Hence the discount rate is equal to the pure time preference rate plus the product of the growth rate of consumption and the individual's (absolute) elasticity of the marginal utility of consumption. The growth rate affects the difference between consumption in the present and future, and ε_p reflects an aversion to inequality between periods (not impatience to consume in the present), and the combination of these involves an addition to pure time preference.

The above applies to an individual person; hence the p subscript is used. However, a substantial literature is based on the concept of a 'representative individual'. In this case, optimal plans are unambiguously based on the preferences of this representative individual and there are no difficulties over the aggregation of preferences. In fact, macroeconomic models using a so-called representative individual are strictly speaking constructed in terms of just one individual: there is no consideration of aggregation requirements.[4] In some growth models, the representative individual is assumed to be infinitely lived. In order to prevent the individual simply accumulating huge debts, a condition is imposed such that the rate of interest and the individual's

---

[4]From the demand analysis literature, it is known that quasi-homothetic (Gorman) preferences are required for aggregates to be interpreted as arising from the preferences of a representative individual. In this case demands are linear, with a common slope, although intercepts may differ to allow for, say, demographic factors.

discount rate are equal. In turn, this means that ε_p and ρ cannot be set independently, given g.

3.2.2   Social Evaluations

In practical social evaluations or cost–benefit evaluations involving multi-period contexts, it is often inappropriate to think of a single individual. Evaluations may be based on a social welfare function, as in the single-period case. A choice of welfare metric for each period must be made. In the following discussion this is taken to be aggregate consumption, which in the case of a fixed population size translates simply to consumption per person.

Hence, where the Cs now represent aggregates, the welfare function can be written as:

$$W_T = \sum_{t=1}^{T} \left(\frac{1}{1 + \rho_m} \right)^{t-1} W\left(C_t \right) \tag{3.15}$$

In this case, $W\left(C_t \right)$ represents the contribution of period t's aggregate consumption to the evaluation function, and ρ_m represents the pure time preference rate of the hypothetical judge. The corresponding ubiquitous iso-elastic function is thus:

$$W\left(C_t \right) = \frac{C_t^{1-\varepsilon_m}}{1 - \varepsilon_m} \tag{3.16}$$

In this context the discount rate is commonly referred to as the 'social time preference rate', r_m, and is given, where g_m is the aggregate growth rate of consumption, by:

$$r_m = \rho_m + \varepsilon_m g_m \tag{3.17}$$

Although equations (3.14) and (3.17) have the same basic form, there are no grounds for taking values appropriate to one and substituting in the other. Again, it must be stressed that the term ε_m represents the value judgements of a judge or policy maker. It may be possible to obtain empirical estimates of ε_p using data on saving behaviour over time for a sample of individuals; on the approach used, with a review of alternative estimates, see Pearce and Ulph

(1998). However, there are no grounds whatsoever for imposing $\varepsilon_m = \varepsilon_p$; the former involves a value judgement and there is no logical connection between the two rates.

When considering the appropriate values for ε_m in this context, quite different considerations apply compared with the case of single-period distributional judgements involving inequality aversion, ε_s, discussed earlier. The term ε_m is, in the multi-period framework, more accurately interpreted in terms of an aversion on the part of the judge towards variability – inequality between periods rather than inequality between persons. Yet unfortunately these terms are often conflated in the literature, where discussion proceeds as if ε_m, ε_p, ε_{LES} and ε_s were measuring the same thing.

Although the emphasis of this chapter is on the elasticity of marginal valuation, a further warning is worth sounding in the multi-period context. This is because an additional value judgement is needed for evaluations of the welfare function: this concerns the pure time preference rate of the hypothetical judge, ρ_m. Instead of examining the implications of adopting alternative value judgements by looking at a range of values – the legitimate role of the professional economist – it is not uncommon to find authors using standard rhetorical devices to impose their own value judgements. Thus dogmatic statements along the lines that 'positive pure time preference is morally indefensible' can often be found. However, it is worth remembering that zero pure time preference carries the implication that the judge would be prepared to impose starvation on the current generation in order to produce a tiny benefit for a distant generation.

3.3 Taxation and Equal Absolute Sacrifice

The previous sections of this chapter have criticised attempts to use empirical estimates, based on samples of households' observed consumption behaviour, as the basis of an argument over values which 'should' be imposed in social

evaluations. The present section turns to a quite different, but also illegitimate, approach involving attempts to estimate the implicit value judgements
revealed by tax and transfer policies. Some authors, such as Stern (1977),
Cowell and Gardiner (1999) and Evans (2005), have suggested that estimates
provide a guide to ε values which should be applied in policy evaluations.

There are two steps to such an approach. The first step attempts to infer,
from tax policy decisions, value judgements which are not otherwise made
explicit. Such an attempt can be defended – provided of course that the
model used to make inferences is plausible. For example, such estimates may
be useful in checking whether there is in fact any correspondence between
policies and basic value judgements of policy makers. Given the complexities
involved in tax policy design, it may be useful to know if a particular structure
is associated with implicit judgements that may actually be very different
from those held (though seldom made explicit). This is the view taken by van
de Ven and Creedy (2005) when examining adult equivalence scales implicit
in tax and transfer systems.

The second step is the wholly illegitimate one of suggesting that estimates
of implicit value judgements 'should' be used in making social evaluations.
This criticism applies even in the most unlikely case where implicit views can
be identified precisely.

This section considers the first 'positive' step taken by the authors mentioned above, and suggests that the model used is inadequate. The approach is based on the assumption that income tax policy makers aim to
achieve equal absolute sacrifice. It assumes that incomes are exogenously
given, rather than arising from endogenous labour supply behaviour (subject
to endowments and education which give rise to individual productivities).
Suppose x represents income and the tax function is $T(x)$. Equal absolute
sacrifice requires, for all x, that the absolute difference between pre-tax and

post-tax utility is the same for all individuals. Hence:

$$U(x) - U(x - T(x)) = k \tag{3.18}$$

where $U(.)$ represents a utility function which is considered to be the same for all individuals. The parameter k depends on the amount of revenue per person. The combination of equal absolute sacrifice with the iso-elastic function, $U(x) = x^{1-\varepsilon_\tau}/(1-\varepsilon_\tau)$ for $\varepsilon_\tau \neq 1$, gives, from (3.18):[5]

$$\frac{x^{1-\varepsilon_\tau}}{1-\varepsilon_\tau} - \frac{(x - T(x))^{1-\varepsilon_\tau}}{1-\varepsilon_\tau} = k \tag{3.19}$$

Differentiation and simplification gives, as in Evans (2005, p.207), the result that:

$$\log(1 - T'(x)) = \varepsilon_\tau \log\left(1 - \frac{T(x)}{x}\right) \tag{3.20}$$

where $T'(x)$ and $T(x)/x$ are marginal and average tax rates. This expression has been used to carry out ordinary least squares regressions using income tax schedules, so that ε_τ and its standard error are obtained as a regression coefficient. There is some difference of opinion over whether to include a constant in the regression: compare Cowell and Gardiner (1999) and Evans (2005), who also use different income measures. Alternatively, (3.20) can be rearranged to get $\varepsilon_\tau = \log(1 - MTR)/\log(1 - ATR)$, and 'estimates' of ε_τ are obtained and compared using simply the marginal and average tax rates at different income levels.

The first point to stress regarding this approach is that it automatically produces a value of ε_τ in excess of unity for a progressive tax system, for which the marginal tax rate exceeds the average tax rate. This feature was first discussed by Edgeworth (1897) and formally shown by Samuelson (1947). The values of ε_τ obtained in this way are thus severely constrained by the specification of the objective of equal absolute sacrifice. Furthermore, those

---

[5]Young (1987) actually showed that the iso-elastic form is required if an indexation requirement is imposed on the tax structure in addition to equal sacrifice. But of course fiscal drag is a common, indeed almost universal, feature of income tax structures.

using the approach to 'estimate' ε ignore the objections raised by Edgeworth and others concerning the various interpretations of sacrifice theories.[6]

For $\varepsilon_\tau > 1$, equation (3.19) can be rearranged as:[7]

$$T\left(x\right) = x - \left\{x^{1-\varepsilon_\tau} - k\left(1 - \varepsilon_\tau\right)\right\}^{1/(1-\varepsilon_\tau)} \tag{3.21}$$

Examples of marginal and average rate schedules based on this function are shown in Figure 3.2. The coefficient k is determined by the amount of revenue raised by the tax. Suppose that x follows a lognormal distribution with mean and variance of logarithms of $\mu = 10$ and $\sigma^2 = 0.5$ respectively. These values imply an arithmetic mean income of \$28,282. Suppose it is required to raise revenue per person of \$10,000 and that $\varepsilon_\tau = 1.5$. Using a numerical iterative search procedure, it is found that this requires $k = 0.0025$. This is based on a simulated population obtained from 5000 random draws from the assumed income distribution.

Of course, in practice tax functions are multi-step functions with ranges where the marginal rate is constant. In structures like that in the UK, there is a 'standard rate' which applies over a wide range of taxable income, so the above function obviously has difficulty capturing this range.[8] The imposition of $\varepsilon > 1$ is also highly restrictive (as with the use of the linear expenditure system mentioned above). Furthermore, the model applies only to positive taxes. It can thus relate at best to a small component of a much broader set of taxes and transfers.

---

[6]This does not apply to those, such as Richter (1983) and Young (1987) who were interested only in deriving the implications of various axioms.

[7]In stating this result, Young (1987, p. 212) rewrote $-k\left(1 - \varepsilon\right)$ as $\lambda^{1-\varepsilon}$, so that the tax function campares with a constant elasticity of substitution form.

[8]If equal absolute sacrifice is combined with a welfare function displaying constant absolute inequality aversion, α, such that $W = 1 - \exp\left(-\alpha x\right)$, a tax function of the form $T\left(x\right) = x + \frac{1}{\alpha}\log\left\{k + e^{-\alpha x}\right\}$ arise. This can be made to display rate schedules similar to those illustrated above. Dalton (1954, pp. 68-70) discussed several examples using alternative utility functions and sacrifice principles, and showed that if equal absolute sacrifice produces progression, equal proportional sacrifice produces a more progressive tax structure. In an early study, Preinreich (1948) considered the form of the utility schedule consistent with the US tax legislation, without imposing a specific functional form over the whole income range. He assumed equal proportional sacrifice.

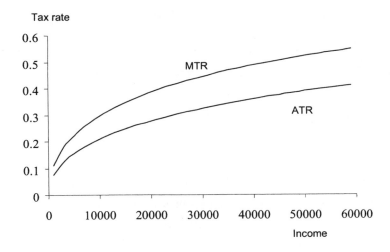

Figure 3.2: Marginal and Average Tax Rates: Equal Absolute Sacrifice

Hence some scepticism must be attached to interpretations of estimates obtained using this model as implicit value judgements. It seems most likely that the approach has been chosen largely – or indeed only – for its simplicity. On the other hand, the optimal tax framework has demonstrated the considerable complexity involved in the link between value judgements and the tax structure and, importantly, that progression can arise with values of $\varepsilon < 1$. But of course even if the estimation of implicit preferences were considered plausible, they cannot qualify as value judgements which should be imposed. There is no alternative to accepting that value judgements are required and the best attitude of professional economists is to report a range of results based on alternative value judgements. In reporting results, readers need to appreciate precisely what is implied about value judgements by different values of ε, since it is not immediately obvious whether, for example, a value of $\varepsilon = 0.5$ indicates a high or low aversion to inequality. This is considered in the following section.

3.4   Interpreting Orders of Magnitude

In examining the implications of alternative value judgements, using an iso-elastic weighting function with different values of ε, it is important to appreciate the precise nature of the comparisons being made. When the link between this type of social welfare function and a measure of inequality was introduced by Atkinson (1970), he recognised the difficulty of forming views about the orders of magnitude of ε using the welfare function $W = \sum_{h=1}^{H} \frac{y_h^{1-\varepsilon}}{1-\varepsilon}$. In order to help interpretation, he used the idea of a 'leaky bucket' experiment, which considers the extent to which a judge is prepared to tolerate some loss in making a transfer from one person to another.[9]

Consider two individuals, so that from the welfare function, setting the total differential equal to zero gives:

$$-\frac{dy_1}{dy_2}\bigg|_W = \left(\frac{y_1}{y_2}\right)^{\varepsilon} \tag{3.22}$$

The welfare function is thus homothetic, as the slopes of social indifference curves are the same along any ray drawn through the origin. Consider two individuals and, using discrete changes, suppose a dollar is taken from the richest, such that $\Delta y_2 = -1$. The amount to be given to the other individual to keep social welfare unchanged is thus:

$$\Delta y_1 = \left(\frac{y_1}{y_2}\right)^{\varepsilon} \tag{3.23}$$

For example, if $y_2 = 2y_1$ and $\varepsilon = 1.5$, it is necessary to give person 1 only 35 cents; a leak of 65 cents from the original dollar taken from person 2 is tolerated. If $\varepsilon = 1$, a leak of 50 cents is tolerated.

This type of experiment, and thus the sensitivity of the tolerance for a leaking bucket, is well-known in the literature on inequality measurement. But in other contexts in which the same kind of iso-elastic function is used,

---

[9]Okun (1975) examined a slightly different kind of leaky bucket experiment involving transfers between groups of indivduals.

relatively large values of ε are often adopted without, it seems, consideration of such implications; however, it is discussed by Pearce and Ulph (1998, pp. 280-281). For example, in the intertemporal literature, a value of $\varepsilon = 2$ is often used. Supose that total income (or consumption) in the first period is 100 and this grows at a rate of 0.02 per period. In period 10 it is thus 119.5, and a judge with $\varepsilon = 2$ would be prepared to take a dollar from period 10, and give only \$0.70 to period 1. By period 20 total income would be 145.7, and the same judge would reduce period 20's income by \$1 while adding only \$0.47 to the first period. The social time preference rate is thereby increased significantly above the pure time preference rate.

The leaky bucket experiment therefore provides a useful illustration of the implications, in terms of value judgements, of adopting particular values of ε in any policy evaluation.

3.5 Conclusions

This chapter has been concerned with the use of social welfare functions in evaluating actual or potential changes resulting from policies or other factors affecting a well-defined group of individuals. In particular, it has considered suggestions regarding the welfare weights to be used in comparing the gains and losses of different individuals (or other appropriate units of analysis), and a social time preference rate for use in cost–benefit evaluation. While these variables essentially reflect value judgements, some authors have argued that they can be estimated either from consumers' behaviour or from the judgements implicit in tax policy. It was instead suggested here that results are highly sensitive to the context and model specification assumed.

More importantly, the argument that an estimated elasticity of marginal utility or social time preference rate *should* be used in policy evaluations fails to recognise that fundamental value judgements are involved. The various estimates and models may be of interest, but they cannot be used by economists to *impose* value judgements. The main contribution economists can make is to examine the implications of adopting a range of alternative value judgements.

This argument is of course not new. Indeed it was stated most forcefully and eloquently by Robbins (1935) in his important book on the *Nature and Significance of Economic Science*. He argued, 'propositions involving the verb "aught" are different in kind from propositions involving the verb "is". And it is difficult to see what possible good can be served by not keeping them separate, or failing to recognise their essential difference' (1935, p. 149). It seems worthwhile to repeat these warnings of Robbins, along with his view that:

> All this is not to say that economist may not assume as postulates different judgments of value, and then on the assumption that these are valid enquire what judgment is to be passed upon particular proposals for action. On the contrary, as we shall see, it is just in the light that it casts upon the significance and consistency of different ultimate valuations that the utility of economics consists. (1935, p. 149)

Chapter 4

Sustainable Preferences

This chapter examines the implications of adopting alternative value judgements when evaluating consumption streams over a very long period. In
particular the use of a social welfare function with a positive and constant
pure time preference rate is compared with value judgements reflecting 'sustainable preferences', following Chichilnisky (1997), Heal (1998) and Li and
Lofgren (2000). This involves the use of a social welfare function for which
neither the present nor the future is favoured over the other (Chichilnisky,
1997, p. 468). It contrasts with a 'standard approach' in which either the
present or the future dominates, depending on whether the time preference
rate of the judge is positive or zero.

The alternative forms of social welfare function are used to examine,
within the framework of a simple growth model, the resulting optimal time
path of consumption. The context involves a policy designed to reduce some
form of damage, arising in the long term, by devoting current and future
resources to abatement.[1] The abatement policy imposes costs on current and
future generations in order to reduce damages that are expected to increase
over a long time horizon. Generic abatement and damage functions are
used, so no attempt is made to model the damage-generating process from

---

[1] The related issues of uncertainty and irreversibility surrounding the long-term effects
of phenomena such as climate change and population ageing are ignored here, thereby
avoiding questions about option values; for discussion of these see Arrow and Fisher (1974).

any particular phenomenon such as climate change or population ageing. Rather emphasis is on trying to understand the nature of and implications of adopting alternative value judgements. This is important in view of the extensive and heated debates in a range of contexts involving long-term plans. The arguments suggest that the standard form of social welfare function used to evaluate consumption streams reflects value judgements with which not everyone would agree.

Section 4.1 briefly discusses the general notion of sustainability adopted in the growth model applied later in this chapter. Section 4.2 briefly presents the 'standard model' and discusses the familiar ethical dilemma arising from discounting. Koopmans (1960) pointed out that time preference is required so that the infinite future does not completely dominate the present. Here the dilemma becomes clear: discounting solves this problem but means that the distant future is disregarded in favour of the present. Section 4.3 describes the value judgements described by Chichilnisky as involving 'sustainable preferences', along with the variant of Li and Lofgren (2000), whose slightly different approach results in a similar optimal path towards an identical stationary solution as the time horizon becomes infinitely large. Section 4.5 describes the growth model, along with the specification of damages and abatement functions, used to examine alternative preferences. Section 4.6 presents numerical results of applying alternative value judgements for different values of key parameters, and Section 4.7 concludes.

4.1   The Concept of Sustainability

If sustainability is to be made operational it must be defined and it must be measured. As Solow (1992, p. 163) said about sustainability, 'talk without measurement is cheap'. The Brundtland Commission (United Nations, 1987) defined sustainable development as development that, 'meets the needs of the present without compromising the ability of future generations to meet their own needs'.

Some critics have suggested that the Brundland definition is too vague to be of use as a practical guide to planning; see Stavins *et al.* (2003). For example, a society living forever at a minimum subsistence level of consumption would satisfy the Brundtland requirement, but it would obviously be wasteful in terms of foregone opportunities to use resources to improve well-being. However, others argue that the notion of sustainable development is inevitably vague, but not necessarily meaningless (Solow, 2005). One definition, suggested by Solow (1992), that is both imprecise but meaningful defines sustainable development as an obligation to leave behind a generalised capacity to create well-being. This implies an obligation to give future generations the capacity to be as well off as the present by preserving the existing capacity for material development. That is, future generations are not owed any particular thing – rather they are owed a capacity to enjoy a level of well-being at least equal to that of the present. As Aghion and Howitt (1998) put it, 'sustainability doesn't require that any particular species of owl or any particular species of fish or any particular tract of forest be preserved'. The implication is that all forms of capital, reproducible capital and natural capital for example, are substitutable to some extent in generating well-being.

This is the general interpretation of sustainability implicitly adopted in this chapter. The growth model developed and applied here has one generalised consumption good and one generalised form of capital. Hence damages to one form of capital which results in a loss of consumption can be compensated by building up other forms of capital which can replace the lost consumption. However, this general interpretation is not sufficient to define a unique sustainable path of consumption over time and therefore among generations. For example, with technical progress many paths of consumption would be sustainable in the sense that future generations are at least as well off as current generations; but some paths would see future generations better off than they would be under other paths. There is therefore a need to go further than Solow's definition of sustainability in order to define a unique consumption path. This requires an explicit valuation of future well-being that imposes, as Chichilnisky (1997) puts it, neither a 'dictatorship of the present' nor a 'dictatorship of the future'. Before considering such value judgements in detail, the following section discusses the standard form of welfare function that is extensively used in cost–benefit studies.

4.2   A Standard Welfare Function and Time Preference

Consider a time stream of consumption per capita, C_t, over the period $t = 1, ..., T$, where T represents a long time horizon. For simplicity, assume zero population growth and homogeneous consumption needs of the population.[2] A standard approach is to examine the implications of adopting an additive Paretian social welfare function, representing the value judgements of an independent judge, of the form:

$$V = \sum_{t=1}^{T} (1 + \rho)^{1-t} W(C_t) \tag{4.1}$$

Here $W(C)$ is a weighting function representing the weight attached by the judge to consumption and ρ is the constant pure rate of time preference.[3] Alternative value judgements can be specified by the selection of different forms of W (in particular with different degrees of concavity) and values of ρ. In the vast majority of studies, the implications of allowing W to take the isoelastic form $W(C_t) = C_t^{1-\beta} / (1 - \beta)$ are considered. Hence β is the

---

[2]If consumption needs differ with respect to age then C requires further clarification. In particular, it matters whether the social welfare function is expressed in terms of average consumption per equivalent person, or in terms of the ratio of average consumption to the average equivalent size; see Creedy and Guest (2008b).

[3]This is often referred to as a 'utility discount rate', from the different context of individual lifetime optimisation. Here, W is not a utility function.

constant 'elasticity of marginal valuation', which can be interpreted in terms of a constant relative aversion to variability over time. Maximisation of V subject to a wealth constraint gives rise to the familiar Euler equation for optimal consumption growth at t:

$$g_t = \frac{1}{\beta}(r_t - \rho) \tag{4.2}$$

where g_t is the growth rate of consumption and r_t represents the rate of interest (and the marginal product of capital, net of depreciation, in a closed economy model). Rearranging this gives the 'Ramsey equation', $r_t = \rho + \beta g$, so that along the optimal path, the judge equates the marginal product of capital (the return from saving), r_t , with the marginal cost of saving, represented by $\rho + \beta g$ which is often called the consumption discount rate. There is no necessary relationship between ρ and β on ethical grounds, but in a small open economy the two are related by the condition that $\rho = r_t - \beta g_t$ where r_t, β and g_t are all given. This condition ensures that consumption growth cannot deviate from output growth permanently as that would imply either permanently accumulating or decumulating foreign assets.

A number of authors have argued that a pure time preference rate of zero should be imposed. This clearly involves an attempt, using various rhetorical devices, to impose their own value judgements. Famous examples include Ramsey (1928, p. 543) and Pigou (1932, p. 25); see also Padilla (2002) and Caplin and Leahy (2000). However, Ramsey (1928) realised that without discounting, infinite utility streams would be non-convergent and therefore could not be ordered. His solution was to measure utility over time as a cumulative sum of the distance from a 'bliss' level of utility, but the main problem with this approach is the arbitrariness of the level of bliss.

One way of achieving a partial ordering of infinite utility streams without discounting is the overtaking criterion; see von Weizacker (1965). This says that utility stream A is preferred to utility stream B if, after some finite time period, T, the cumulative utility of stream A remains greater than stream

B for all time $t > T$. However this is only a partial ordering of utility streams because one stream may oscillate above and below another stream indefinitely – it may never permanently overtake. Also, rather than replacing the need for discounting, the overtaking criterion comes close to Koopmans' axiomatic defence of discounting, because it implies that, for example, utility stream A:$\{0,1,0,0,\ldots\}$ is preferred to stream B:$\{0,0,1,0,0,\ldots\}$. Stream B is stream A lagged one period. Hence stream A overtakes stream B in period 1 but is identical thereafter. Thus the preference for the overtaking stream reflects a time preference, as noted by Heal (1998).

The failure to rank all utility streams also applies to the Rawlsian criterion, which ranks the maxi-min utility stream above all others but fails to rank the others among each other. Similarly, an objective function that ranks the satisfaction of basic needs above all other outcomes fails to rank other outcomes.

The standard welfare function discussed above imposes a constant time preference rate. However, a number of authors have suggested using a rate which declines over time, that is, a hyperbolic time preference function (Laibson, 1996). Indeed, a feature of sustainable preferences discussed in the following section is that they imply a form of hyperbolic preferences. Both constant and hyperbolic time preference functions imply discount factors, $(1 + \rho_t)^{1-t}$, that decline at a decreasing rate; that is, the second derivative with respect to time is positive.

However, within this framework it is also possible to consider value judgements such that the time preference function is logistic. This implies that the judge's concern, refected in the discount factor, at time 0 for the well-being of individuals living in time $t > 0$ declines relatively slowly as t is increased, but then begins to decline at an increasing rate. Hence the judge cares almost as much about generations in the near future as the present generation, but at some point this concern begins to diminish more rapidly. This decline could not accelerate forever as the discount factor cannot be negative, so it would have to tail off after some point, with a point of inflexion. A logistic time preference rate function describes such intertemporal preferences. Their implications for the optimal consumption path are briefly reported below.

4.3 Sustainable Preferences

This section describes alternative social welfare function specifications which embody sustainable preferences and thus place a positive value on very long-run outcomes. Subsections 4.3.1 and 4.3.2 examine in turn the value judgements specified by Chichilnisky (1997) and Li and Lofgren (2000).

4.3.1 A Chichilnisky Social Welfare Function

Chichilnisky (1997) proposed an approach which assigns declining weights over time and then some extra weight to the last period. The judge's evaluation function thus consists of a weighted average of two terms: the sum of discounted values where the pure rate of time preference declines over time and the (undiscounted) value in the final period, T, which the judge chooses to be far into the future. Hence the social welfare function is of the form:

$$V = \theta \sum_{t=1}^{T} (1 + \rho_t)^{1-t} W(C_t) + (1 - \theta) W(C_T) \qquad (4.3)$$

where $\rho_t < 0$ and $0 < \theta < 1$. Chichilnisky's objective function differs from (4.3) in that in her model the weighting function, which she calls utility, U, rather than W is derived from both consumption, c, and a flow of services from the stock of natural capital, s. This implies an optimal combination of c and s at any time t. However, dropping s from the utility function, as we do here, doesn't affect the notion of sustainable preferences, the key ingredients of which are a declining discount rate applied to $U()$ and the second additive term in (4.3).

In explaining the choice of a declining, or hyperbolic discount rate in the first term in (4.3), represented by $\rho_t < 0$, Chichilnisky (p.468) refers to experimental evidence that the relative weight that people give to two subsequent periods in the future is inversely related to the distance of the two periods from today. This evidence suggest that it is worth examining the implications of a judge adopting such value judgements. It does not of course support the argument that evaluations should take this form (there is no legitimate route from 'is' to 'ought').

Chichilnisky (1997) proved that a hyperbolic discount rate in (4.3) is a necessary condition for an optimal path to exist in the limit as T approaches infinity. A constant discount rate would not yield a solution. Adding the second term in (4.3),$(1 - \theta) W (C_T)$, gives explicit recognition to consumption in the very long run, at time T. Taking a weighted average of the two terms implies a trade-off between the present and the future, yet neither need dominate completely.

These preferences are subject to the standard criticism of time inconsistency that applies to hyperbolic preferences since these are reflected in the first term in (4.3). But this criticism is weak when the objective is a socially optimal consumption path. From a social choice perspective, Heal (1998) argued that over time, new generations arrive and older ones drop out of the choice process, so there is no reason why the preferences of generations who have dropped out should be imposed on new generations in the name of time consistency.

Heal (1998) shows that as $T \to \infty$, the effect on the optimal path of the term $(1 - \theta) W (C_T)$ drops out. In other words in the limit the optimal path converges to the stationary solution from maximising (4.3) without the second additive term. This limiting solution is what Chichilnisky and Heal call the 'green golden rule' which is the analogue to the Phelps golden rule in a Ramsey model. The green golden rule applies where natural capital generates a flow of services that yield utility directly in addition to the utility derived from a general consumption good. In the Ramsey model utility is derived only from the general consumption good.

4.3.2 A Modified Li and Lofgren Social Welfare Function

This subsection describes the social welfare function reflecting sustainable preferences introduced by Li and Lofgren (2000), with minor differences. The differences are that the model here is in discrete time, replaces the conservationist in Li and Lofgren with a more generic person who may be thought of as a conservationist in the context of climate change, and damage abatement, A, replaces the environmental capital stock. It is assumed that society is composed of two representative individuals who have utility functions specified over T years, where T is large and spans multiple future life spans on the basis that the individuals care about their offspring. Following Barro (1974), all generations are effectively linked if parents care about their offspring, in which case they plan their consumption as though they will live forever. One individual discounts the future at a constant rate and the other does not discount. Individual 1 who is the discounter has a utility function, V_1:

$$V_1 = \sum_{t=1}^{T} (1+\rho)^{1-t} U\left(C_{1,t}, A_t\right) \tag{4.4}$$

In this case ρ represents the pure rate of time preference of the individual, and U is the utility at time t derived from consumption of $C_{1,t}$ and damage abatement, A_t (discussed further below). Damage abatement is a public good and therefore both representative individuals receive the same level of A_t.

Individual 2 has a utility function, V_2, of the form:

$$V_2 = \sum_{t=1}^{T} U\left(C_{2,t}, A_t\right) \tag{4.5}$$

The judge's evaluation, or social welfare, function is assumed to be a weighted average of the utilities of the two individuals:

$$V = \alpha V_1 + (1-\alpha) V_2 \tag{4.6}$$

where $0 \leq \alpha \leq 1$. This approach is therefore different from the approach
in Section 4.1 where the judge applied a weighting function to per capita
consumption that reflected the judge's preferences rather than the preferences of individuals in the society. That approach implied that no matter
how individuals in society may actually discount the future in their private
consumption decisions and whatever the degree of concavity of their utility
functions (the elasticity of marginal utility), the welfare function embodies
only value judgements of the judge. Here, in (4.4), the pure time preference
rate reflects the properties of individual 1, rather than those of the judge.
However, the judge's preferences are not irrelevant – they are embodied in the
relative preferences for each individual's welfare as reflected in the parameter
α in (4.6). It would be possible to rewrite the model such that individuals
1 and 2 are representing types, so that α measures the population share of
type 1 individuals. If this latter interpretation is taken, the welfare function
is in fact equivalent to a 'classical utilitarian' evaluation function, that is, a
simple sum of individuals' utilities. However, this would require aggregate
consumption, in the specification of the following subsection, to be expressed
as a weighted sum rather than a simple sum of the two consumption values.

The following section investigates the effect on the path of optimal consumption of α using a growth model including damage and abatement functions. It is shown that the social welfare function (4.6) implies a hyperbolic
effective social rate of time preference and that the rate of decline of the effective social rate of time preference depends on the consumption shares of the
two individuals which in turn depends on the judge's preference parameter,
α.

4.4 Logistic preferences

A characteristic of both hyperbolic and constant preferences is that they
imply utility weights which decline at a decreasing rate; that is, the second

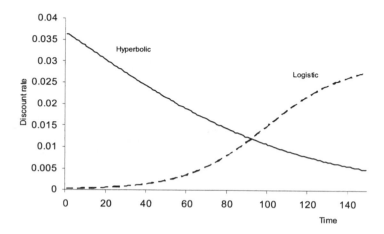

Figure 4.1: Hyperbolic and Logistic Time Preference Rate Functions

derivative with respect to time is positive. There are infinitely many possible time paths of utility weights. One such alternative path, briefly considered here, is represented by a logistic time preference function. This is a plausible characterisation of individuals' actual preferences. For example, a grand-mother may care almost as much about the well-being of her grandchildren as she does about her own children. But her concern for the well-being of more distant descendents may begin to decline at an increasing rate, imply-ing a positive second derivative in the utility weighting function. The rate of decline cannot accelerate forever but must tail off after some point. A logistic discount rate function would describe such intertemporal preferences which increase at an increasing rate initially and then at a decreasing rate, approaching a constant.

Figures 4.1 and 4.2 compare the time preference functions and utility weight functions, respectively, for the case of logistic preferences and the case of sustainable preferences, with $\alpha = 0.5$.

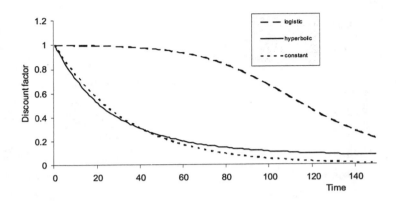

Figure 4.2: Alternative Discount Factors

4.5   Economy with Damage and Abatement Functions

This section presents a model in which there are damages in the form of future costs which can be to some extent avoided by a costly abatement policy. The model is used in the next section to examine the implications of adopting the modified Li and Lofgren evaluation function.

4.5.1   Structure of the Model

Consider a closed economy which incurs in period t a cost, A_t, of abating a potential future cost. This may be thought of as a pollution abatement cost or a cost of policies designed to reduce problems associated with, say, population ageing. The precise context is not important here as the aim is simply to investigate the way in which evaluation using a form of sustainable preferences affects policy judgements.

The judge maximises (4.6) subject to the closed economy accounting constraint:

$$Y_t = C_t + I_t + A_t \tag{4.7}$$

where Y_t is output, C_t is aggregate consumption equal to, $C_{1,t} + C_{2,t}$, and I_t is investment. Abatement is a policy variable and is assumed to be a constant proportion, ε, of GDP lagged one period. Hence $A_t = \varepsilon Y_{t-1}$. Investment is given by:

$$I_t = K_t - (1 - \delta) K_{t-1} \qquad (4.8)$$

where K_t is the capital stock and δ is a constant rate of depreciation. The final capital stock at time T is subject to the constraint that $K_T = K^*$. Output is a function of the capital stock and damages, D_t, net of abatement. Population growth is assumed to be zero, so labour inputs do not need to be included explicitly here and:

$$Y_t = \frac{K_t^\gamma}{(1 + D_t)} \qquad (4.9)$$

The damages function is given by the logistic form:

$$D_t = \frac{\mu C_{t-1}^\omega - A_t z}{1 + e^{-x(t-0.5T)}} \qquad (4.10)$$

The parameter μ is a damage scaling factor and ω is the elasticity of damages with respect to (lagged) total consumption. The parameter, z, is an abatement effectiveness term, measuring how much a given damage abatement expenditure, A_t, actually reduces damages. Abatement expenditure reduces damages both directly, through the term $A_t z$, and indirectly by diverting resources from consumption, thereby reducing C_t. Environmental damages are obviously positively related to consumption but this is probably not true of 'damages' from population ageing.

The damage function in (4.10) generates a pattern of damages which increases slowly for an initial period then accelerates for an intermediate period before slowing down to approach an asymptote in the long run. This is consistent with typical modelling approaches such as Stern (2007, p.665) which assumed that damages cease to increase after the year 2200 implying that the problem is contained after this time. The length and acceleration of damages in (4.10) can be varied through the parameter x. However there is no attempt here to model the underlying process generating damages as a function of variables other than time, such as temperature change or demographic change. This process simply assumed to be captured in a stylised way by a logistic function. Nordhaus (1994), for example, models damages as a function of temperature changes.

Damage abatement policies with respect to climate change and population ageing impose costs on current and future generations in order to reduce damages that are expected to increase over time. In the case of climate change, the policy is a mechanism to reduce greenhouse gases (such as a carbon tax or tradable pollution permits). In the case of population ageing the mechanisms include measures to smooth the fiscal costs of ageing and tax incentives to boost labour force participation. Again, these mechanisms are not modelled in detail here.

The utility function $U(C_t, A_t)$ is assumed to be additively separable in C_t and A_t on the assumption that people's valuation of another unit of abatement is independent of the level of consumption and vice versa. Each separable part in the utility function is assumed to take the isoelastic form. Hence $U\left(C_{1,t}, A_t\right) = \frac{C_{1,t}^{1-\beta}}{1-\beta} + \Phi\frac{A_t^{1-\beta}}{1-\beta}$ and $U\left(C_{2,t}, A_t\right) = \frac{C_{2,t}^{1-\beta}}{1-\beta} + \Phi\frac{A_t^{1-\beta}}{1-\beta}$ where Φ is a parameter reflecting relative preferences for abatement. In this context the parameter β reflects the elasticity of marginal utility of consumption of the individuals themselves (in contrast with the elasticity of marginal valuation of the independent judge in the standard approach discussed in Section 4.2). Since A_t is a common resource, both individuals consume the same amount at any time: A_t. The two individuals are assumed to have the same parameters in their utility functions and therefore the only distinguishing feature in their utility functions is the pure rate of time preference, which is zero for individual 2.

The optimal plan chosen by the independent judge, which maximises V

subject to the constraints give above, is obtained by forming the following Lagrangian:

$$L = \alpha \sum_{t=1}^{T} U_1\left(C_{1,t}, A_t\right)(1+\rho)^{1-t} + (1-\alpha)\sum_{t=1}^{T} U_2\left(C_{2,t}, A_t\right)$$

$$+ \sum_{t=1}^{T} \lambda_t \left(Y_t - \left(C_{1,t} + C_{2,t}\right) - [K_t - (1-\delta)K_{t-1}] - A_t\right)$$

$$+ \phi\left(K_T - K^*\right) \tag{4.11}$$

It is therefore necessary to derive the Euler equation describing the growth rate of aggregate consumption for each time period. This is obtained in the following subsection.

4.5.2 The Euler Equation

From the Lagrangian in equation (4.11), the following first-order conditions are derived for $t = 1, .., T-1$:

$$\frac{\partial L}{\partial C_{1,t}} = \alpha \frac{\partial U_1}{\partial C_{1,t}}(1+\rho)^{1-t} - \lambda_t\left(1 - \frac{\partial Y_t}{\partial D_t}\frac{\partial D_t}{\partial C_{1,t}}\right) = 0 \tag{4.12}$$

$$\frac{\partial L}{\partial C_{2,t}} = (1-\alpha)\frac{\partial U_2}{\partial C_{2,t}} - \lambda_t\left(1 - \frac{\partial Y_t}{\partial D_t}\frac{\partial D_t}{\partial C_{2,t}}\right) = 0 \tag{4.13}$$

where $\frac{\partial D_t}{\partial C_{1,t}} = \frac{\partial D_t}{\partial C_{2,t}}$ and:

$$\frac{\partial L}{\partial K_t} = \lambda_t\left(Y'(K_t) - 1\right) + \lambda_{t+1}(1-\delta) = 0 \tag{4.14}$$

and for $t = T$:

$$\frac{\partial L}{\partial K_t} = \lambda_T\left(Y'(K_T) - 1\right) + \phi = 0 \tag{4.15}$$

The Euler equation can be obtained in the following three stages. First, from (4.12), and using the functional forms given above:

$$\frac{\partial L/\partial C_{1,t}}{\partial L/\partial C_{1,t+1}} = \frac{\alpha\left(C_{1,t}^{-\beta}\right)(1+\rho)^{1-t}}{\alpha\left(C_{1,t+1}^{-\beta}\right)(1+\rho)^{-t}} = \frac{\lambda_t}{\lambda_{t+1}}\left(\frac{1-\Omega_t}{1-\Omega_{t+1}}\right)$$

$$= \left(\frac{C_{1,t+1}}{C_{1,t}}\right)^{\beta}(1+\rho) = \frac{\lambda_t}{\lambda_{t+1}}\left(\frac{1-\Omega_t}{1-\Omega_{t+1}}\right) \tag{4.16}$$

where:

$$\Omega_t = \frac{\partial Y_t}{\partial D_t}\frac{\partial D_t}{\partial C_{1,t}} = \frac{\partial Y_t}{\partial D_t}\frac{\partial D_t}{\partial C_{2,t}}$$

$$= \left(\frac{-K^\gamma}{(1+D_t)^2}\right)\left(\frac{\mu\omega C_{t-1}^{\omega-1}}{1+e^{-x(t-0.5T)}}\right) \qquad (4.17)$$

From (4.14) it can be seen that:

$$\frac{\lambda_t}{\lambda_{t+1}} = \frac{1-\delta}{1-Y'(K)} \qquad (4.18)$$

and substituting into (4.16) and rearranging gives:

$$\frac{C_{1,t+1}}{C_{1,t}} = \left[\left(\frac{1-\delta}{(1-Y'(K_t))(1+\rho)}\right)\left(\frac{1-\Omega_t}{1-\Omega_{t+1}}\right)\right]^{1/\beta} \qquad (4.19)$$

Taking natural logarithms, using a dot to indicate a first difference and using the approximation for small values that , $\log(1+x) \approx x$ gives:

$$\frac{\dot{C}_{1,t}}{C_{1,t}} = \frac{1}{\beta}[Y'(K_t) - \delta - \rho + \dot{\Omega}_t] \qquad (4.20)$$

This result gives the Euler equation for person 1's consumption path. Except for the last term which depends on the damage and production functions, this takes the familiar form as given in equation (4.2), letting r_t in (4.2) equal $Y'(K_t) - \delta$. However, it is necessary to derive the Euler equation for total consumption, so the next stage involves obtaining a relationship between the growth rates of consumption for the two individuals. Given that $\lambda_t\left(1 - \frac{\partial Y_t}{\partial D_t}\frac{\partial D_t}{\partial C_{k,t}}\right)$ is the same for both k, then from the first-order condition:

$$\alpha\left(\frac{dU_1}{dC_{1,t}}\right)(1+\rho)^{1-t} = (1-\alpha)\left(\frac{dU_1}{dC_{2,t}}\right) \qquad (4.21)$$

Therefore, substituting for marginal utilities and rearranging gives:

$$C_{2,t} = \left[\left(\frac{1-\alpha}{\alpha}\right)(1+\rho)^{t-1}\right]^{1/\beta} C_{1,t} \qquad (4.22)$$

For periods t and $t+1$, this gives:

$$\frac{C_{2,t+1}}{C_{2,t}} = (1+\rho)^{1/\beta} \left(\frac{C_{1,t+1}}{C_{1,t}}\right) \tag{4.23}$$

Again, taking logarithms and applying approximations:

$$\frac{\dot{C}_{2,t}}{C_{2,t}} = \frac{\rho}{\beta} + \frac{\dot{C}_{1,t}}{C_{1,t}} \tag{4.24}$$

Thus the optimal growth rate of person 2's consumption is equal to that of person 1, plus the ratio of 1's pure time preference rate to the common elasticity of marginal utility of consumption. Clearly, a higher value of the latter implies a higher aversion to variability of consumption over time, so the difference in the optimal growth rate for person 2 is correspondingly lower.

The third and final stage involves combining the above results to obtain the aggregate Euler equation. By definition:

$$\frac{\dot{C}_t}{C_t} = \frac{\dot{C}_{1,t}}{C_{1,t}} \frac{C_{1,t}}{C_t} + \frac{\dot{C}_{2,t}}{C_{2,t}} \frac{C_{2,t}}{C_t} \tag{4.25}$$

Substituting for $\frac{\dot{C}_{2,t}}{C_{2,t}}$ from (4.24) into (4.25) yields:

$$\frac{\dot{C}_t}{C_t} = \frac{\dot{C}_{1,t}}{C_{1,t}} \frac{C_{1,t}}{C_t} + \left(\frac{\rho}{\beta} + \frac{\dot{C}_{1,t}}{C_{1,t}}\right) \frac{C_{2,t}}{C_t} = \frac{\dot{C}_{1,t}}{C_{1,t}} + \frac{\rho}{\beta} \frac{C_{2,t}}{C_t} \tag{4.26}$$

Finally, substituting for $\frac{\dot{C}_{1,t}}{C_{1,t}}$ from (4.20) into (4.26) yields:

$$\frac{\dot{C}_t}{C_t} = \frac{1}{\beta} \left[Y'(K) - \delta - \rho\left(1 - \frac{C_{2,t}}{C_t}\right) + \dot{\Omega}_t\right] \tag{4.27}$$

Examination of (4.27) and comparison with (4.2), shows that, although the social welfare function does not contain an explicit pure time preference rate of the judge, it actually implies an effective time preference rate in each period of $\rho\left(1 - C_{2,t}/C_t\right)$. It therefore depends on the ratio of person 2's consumption to total consumption in that period. Furthermore, as $C_{2,t}$ grows faster than $C_{1,t}$ it can be seen that $\lim_{t\to\infty} C_{2,t}/C_t \to 1$, so that ultimately the individual who does not discount dominates completely. Hence the judge's implied pure time preference rate is hyperbolic, with an asymptote of zero.

4.5.3   A Solution Procedure

The values of C, K and Y are solved as follows. An initial steady state is assumed with C, K and Y constant and $D_0 = 0$. The initial capital stock, K_0, and initial output, Y_0, are determined from the production function, (4.9), given an assumed initial value of (K_0/Y_0). Initial consumption, C_0, is given by $Y_0 - I_0$ where $I_0 = \delta K_0$. The steady state is then shocked by allowing D_t to follow the damages function given above. The new steady state is found by a shooting algorithm in which an arbitrary initial level of consumption is chosen and variables solved forward using the above Euler equation for consumption and the equations for investment, output and capital stock. Repeated initial values of consumption are chosen until the target level of capital stock, $K_T = K_0$, is achieved.

4.6   Implications of Alternative Value Judgements

An explicit policy of damage abatement, $\varepsilon > 0$, is one way of protecting future consumption from the costs of damages. Another (not mutually exclusive) way is for the social judge to apply alternative value judgements, reflected in the parameter α in the intertemporal social welfare function that represents sustainable social preferences. Cases where $0 \le \alpha \le 1$ represent sustainable preferences as defined here, and the case where $\alpha = 1$ represents the standard approach in which the social rate of time preference is constant.[4] This section applies the growth model presented in the previous section to consider the implications for C_t of such alternative value judgements, compared with the implications of an explicit damage abatement policy. Both methods of protecting future consumption – damage abatement and sustainable preferences – shift consumption forward in time. However, in the latter

---

[4]Furthermore, the utility functions in the Li and Lofgren approach are considered to be weighting functions of the judge in the standard model.

Table 4.1: Benchmark Parameter Values

Scaling factor for damages	μ	0.25
Elasticity of damages with respect to consumption	ω	0.20
Rate of increase in damages	x	0.08
Damage abatement expenditure as a ratio of GDP	ε	0.01
Abatement effectiveness	z	5.0
Time horizon	T	200
Capital elasticity of output	γ	0.25
Initial capital to output ratio	$(K/Y)_0$	3.0
Depreciation rate	δ	0.05
Elasticity of marginal valuation	β	2.0
Time preference rate	ρ	0.035

case the cost of damages on consumption is compensated by creating a higher
stock of capital.

4.6.1   Calibration of the Model

The benchmark parameter values are given in Table 4.1. The first two parameters in the table, μ and ω, determine the scale of damages and their
responsiveness to consumption. The parameter, x, is the logistic function
parameter determining the underlying response of damages over time. Next
are the damage abatement expenditure, ε, and damage effectiveness, z, parameters. The parameters are chosen such that the damage function before
and after abatement is consistent with the magnitude and pattern of climate
change damages projected in Stern (2007).

The remaining parameters relate to production function and preferences.
The values of these parameters are typical values used in such models. The
solution is found by searching numerically for a new value of consumption
at the time that the damages shock is revealed ($t = 1$) that ensures that the
terminal condition is met.

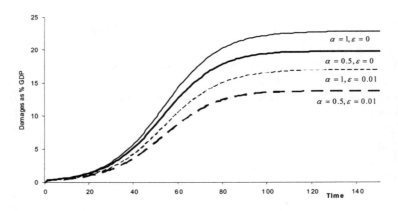

Figure 4.3: Damages as Percentage of GDP

4.6.2   Numerical Results

Figure 4.3 shows four illustrative series of damages as a percentage of GDP.
The series represent damages with and without abatement for each of two
values, $\alpha = 1$ and $\alpha = 0.5$. The damages ratio depends on α because damages
depend on the path of aggregate consumption which depends on α, and
also because GDP depends on α through its effect on capital accumulation.
Lower α implies greater capital accumulation and therefore higher GDP.
Gross damages (that is, without abatement) rise from zero to 20 per cent
of GDP after 100 years for $\alpha = 1$ and to 23 per cent for $\alpha = 0$. Damage
abatement reduces net damages by about 5 per cent of GDP. These levels
of gross damages are consistent with the projected damages from climate
change in Stern (2007) of 5 to 20 per cent, and also similar to the projected
costs to GDP per capita of population ageing in OECD countries – a cost of
between 10 and 15 per cent is commonly projected for OECD countries; see
for example Martins *et al.* (2005).

Figure 4.4 plots consumption per capita under alternative models of preferences: the standard model in which $\alpha = 1$; the sustainable preferences
model (for $\alpha = 0.2$, $\alpha = 0.5$, and $\alpha = 0.9$); and logistic preferences for the

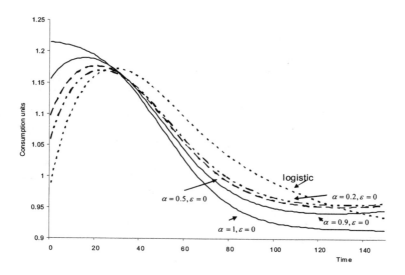

Figure 4.4: Consumption with Alternative Welfare Functions: Damages with Zero Abatement

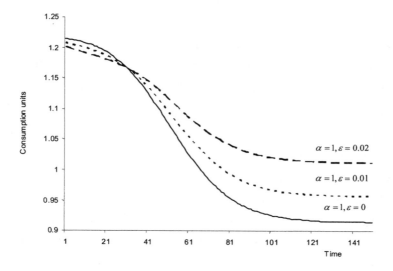

Figure 4.5: Consumption with Damage Abatement Policy: Constant Discount Rate

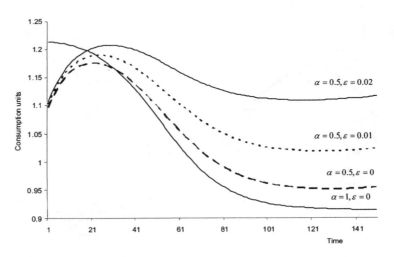

Figure 4.6: Consumption with Damage Abatement: Sustainable Preferences

functional form illustrated in Figure 4.1. There is no damage abatement in Figure 4.4 – abatement is introduced in Figure 4.5. In all cases in Figure 4.4 consumption is ultimately lower as a result of the damages shock. 'Lower consumption' means lower than the level before the damages shock. If allowances were made for labour productivity growth, consumption may still be higher in absolute terms notwithstanding damages. Compared with conventional preferences ($\alpha = 1$), consumption under sustainable preferences ($\alpha < 1$) is initially lower, but ultimately higher. This is because the social rate of time preference in the sustainable preference model, $\rho \left(1 - C_{2,t}/C_t\right)$ is less than ρ, which is in turn due to the effect on social welfare of the utility of the individual who has a zero rate of pure time preference. A lower social rate of time preference implies a lower desire to substitute present consumption for future consumption. The result is a flatter consumption path. Consumption remains higher in the long run because a higher capital stock is created by sacrificing consumption in the early years.

The higher consumption under sustainable preferences implies higher

damages, since damages are a function of consumption (4.10), but the resulting negative feedback effect on consumption is outweighed by the positive
effect on consumption of the higher capital stock created by sacrificing consumption earlier on. Sustainable preferences therefore protect consumption
in the long run compared with the outcome under standard value judgements.

Comparing the three cases of sustainable preferences in Figure 4.4 ($\alpha =$
0.2, $\alpha = 0.5$, and $\alpha = 0.9$), the lower the value of α the greater the fall in
current consumption and the higher the level of consumption in the long run.
This is because a lower value of α implies a higher relative weight given to
person who does not discount the future. Yet even a small regard for that
person's welfare (for example, $\alpha = 0.9$) implies an appreciable reduction in
consumption. The time stream of consumption under sustainable preferences
is also different in that it does not decline monotonically. It follows a hump
shape which is more accentuated the lower is the value of α. This can be
traced to the behaviour of three terms in the Euler equation, $Y'(K)$, $\frac{C_{2,t}}{C_t}$,
and $\dot{\Omega}_t$, all of which depend on α.

Figure 4.4 includes a logistic path of consumption, derived from a logistic
time preference function discussed above. This generates an even larger
initial reduction in consumption than in the sustainable preferences model,
because the concern for the well-being of close descendants is highest for this
preference specification. The implications of the logistic preference function
are not discussed further.

Figure 4.5 introduces damage abatement at two levels: $\varepsilon = 0.01$ and $\varepsilon =$
0.02, and shows that damage abatement protects consumption in the long run
in the same way as sustainable preferences, as discussed in Figure 4.4, that
is, by shifting consumption from present generations to future generations.
However, this is achieved by damage reduction directly through abatement,
rather than through capital creation. The sacrifice in initial consumption
is lower, to achieve a given increase in future consumption. This is partly
because abatement expenditure has a dual effect on damages. There is a

direct reduction, through the term $A_t z$ in the damage function (4.10), and an indirect reduction by diverting resources away from consumption which lowers damages through the term μC_{t-1}^{ω} in (4.10).

Figure 4.6 shows the combined effect of damage abatement and sustainable preferences on consumption. Given sustainable preferences (denoted in this case by $\alpha = 0.5$), no further loss of current consumption is incurred by introducing damage abatement, yet the gain to future generations is greater. This is evident from a comparison of the three series in Figure 4.6 for $\alpha = 0.5$. Among these three cases, greater damage abatement does not reduce current consumption but significantly increases future consumption. Certainly current consumption is lower in all three cases than under conventional preferences (denoted by the $\alpha = 1$ series), but there is no further loss of current consumption by introducing damage abatement. This is different from the case of the standard welfare function, shown in Figure 4.5, where a higher damage abatement implies a greater loss of consumption.

The numerical examples shown in Figure 4.6 therefore suggest that the terms of the intergenerational trade-off implied by damage abatement policy are different under sustainable preferences compared with the standard welfare function. The suggestion is that the cost to current generations is relatively smaller under sustainable preferences.

The terms of the intergenerational trade-off under both social welfare functions depend on the parameters in Table 4.1, in particular, the abatement effectiveness parameter, z. The base case value of 5 was chosen in order to generate a reduction of damages of 25 percent, from about 20 per cent of GDP to about 15 per cent of GDP, after 100 years. As a sensitivity check, the abatement effectiveness parameter is halved to 2.5. In this case, under conventional preferences, damage abatement results in a cost to current generations that is larger and lasts longer than for $z = 5$. However, for sustainable preferences, and assuming $\alpha = 0.5$, damage abatement leaves current generations no worse off, which is the same result reported for the

$z = 5$ case. This supports the suggestion that damage abatement does not penalise current generations under sustainable preferences as much as under the standard welfare function.

However, it is worth emphasising that the consumption paths resulting from all of these computations are the outcomes of optimal adjustments to consumption by an independent judge over a very long period of time. This framework is both a strength and a weakness. The strength is that the parsimony of the model allows the effects of ethical judgements and fundamental economic forces to be explored in a transparent way. It is worth investigating in a simple model how the optimal path responds to alternative assumptions about damages, damage abatement and ethical judgements about intergenerational equity. The weakness is that the model abstracts from many observed behavioural factors and exogenous forces, and it ignores distortions in markets that create deviations between the outcomes of a planned economy and a decentralised economy. These weaknesses restrict but do not disable the model as a tool for investigating the effects on consumption streams of alternative value in the context of damage abatement.

4.7 Conclusions

This chapter investigated, using numerical examples based on a simple growth model, the effect on optimal consumption streams of sustainable preferences in the context of damage abatement. Sustainable preferences address the dilemma that arises in applying the standard social welfare function, with positive time preference, in dealing with damages arising from phenomena having very long-run consequences such as climate change, nuclear waste disposal and population ageing. The perceived problem with discounting is that it discriminates against future generations. But the problem with not discounting is that it discriminates against present generations. Sustainable preferences balance the interests of present and future generations by implying a declining, or hyperbolic, discount rate with respect to time.

The results indicate that sustainable preferences protect long-run consumption in the face of long-run damages, by shifting consumption from the
present to the future. Even a small deviation from the standard welfare function (a value of α only slightly below 1) produces a 'humped' optimal profile
of consumption over time, compared with a continuously decreasing profile
with the standard social welfare function). A similar shift in consumption
arises from a policy of damage abatement. However, the terms of the intergenerational trade-off implied by a policy of damage abatement are different
under sustainable preferences compared with the standard approach. The
examples suggest that damage abatement does not penalise current generations as much, if at all, under sustainable preferences as it does under the
standard approach.

The basic position adopted here is that the appropriate role of economists
is not to impose their own value judgements but to investigate the implications of adopting alternative value judgements and to clarify precisely what
is involved in specifying social welfare functions. Within the context of the
'standard' approach to evaluating consumption streams, the range of value
judgements is restricted (to variations in the elasticity of marginal valuation and the time preference rate) and dominance either by the present or a
distant future generation is implied. The social welfare function implied by
sustainable preferences therefore appears to offer a useful additional alternative when considering sensitivity analyses.

Chapter 5

Representative Agent and Social Planner

This chapter examines the optimal path of aggregate consumption in the context of population ageing, where older age groups are considered to have relatively greater 'needs', resulting for example from additional health costs. These differences give rise to the concept of the 'equivalent number of persons', as distinct from the population size. Many models in this context employ the concept of a hypothetical representative agent who is assumed to be infinitely lived and who has the characteristics (that is, the 'needs') of an average person in the population in each year. The present chapter compares the representative agent approach with an alternative in which the optimal aggregate consumption stream is determined by a social planner who is considered to maximise a social welfare, or evaluation, function defined over the same time horizon. The value judgements of the social planner are made explicit in the form of the welfare function.

Using an individualistic and additive welfare function, total consumption per equivalent person contributes to social welfare in each period. In this preliminary investigation, individuals are considered to differ only by age and hence the planner is not concerned with inequality. One important issue relates to the choice of consumption unit in weighting the consumption per equivalent person in each period. Two cases are examined here – the use of individuals and of equivalent persons. Each of these cases has sensible, but possibly inconsistent, welfare rationales.

The analysis is motivated by the extensive debate regarding the implications of population ageing, and the potential for tax smoothing to achieve an optimal time path of aggregate consumption. The idea that governments should smooth the tax burden over time was first advanced by Barro (1979) who showed that, in a deterministic setting, a flat path of the tax rate over time would minimise the distortions to behaviour arising from taxation. A key insight is that the tax rate must not distort intertemporal consumption choices and must therefore tax consumption at the same rate through time in the long run (Chamley, 1986).[1] Therefore the path of the ratio of optimal income tax to GDP depends on the optimal path of consumption. Consumption smoothing implies a varying ratio of consumption to income and therefore a varying path of the optimal income tax to GDP ratio. In addition, because the optimal consumption path implies an optimal saving path, the analysis in the present chapter has implications for policies designed to affect optimal saving such as superannuation policy and the fiscal balance. It is shown that these policy implications depend on value judgements in the evaluation of social welfare.[2]

The dominant framework for macroeconomic modelling is based on the behaviour of representative agents because the outcomes can be traced to microeconomic foundations. These agents can have either infinite lives, single period lives leading over time to a dynasty of individuals, or finite multi-period lives which imply a number of overlapping generations at a point in time. The origin of this framework was provided by Ramsey (1928) who assumed an infinitely lived individual. It is widely used in modelling economic

---

[1]In the short run this rule is complicated by the optimal tax rate on the income from capital, which is 100 percent initially, falling to zero in the long run.

[2]These policy implications have not been acknowledged in Australian Government-commissioned analyses of the effects of population ageing. See the Intergeneration Report, Australian Government (2002) and Productivity Commission (2005).

growth and macroeconomic aggregates. Seminal expositions of a range of these models include, for example, Barro and Sala-i-Martin (1995) and Obstfeld and Rogoff (1996). All large scale multi-sector, multi-region models (computable general equilibrium models) used to model national and world economies are based on the behaviour of representative agents. Examples include the OECD's MINILINK model, the IMF's MULTIMOD model and the European Commission's QUEST model. For applications of these models to population ageing see: Werner and Veld (2002) for the QUEST model; Turner *et al.* (1998) for the MINILINK model; and Faruqee and Muhleisen (2001) for the MULTIMOD model. A common feature of these models is that the agents optimise intertemporally and this feature is the focus of attention here.

However, the representative agent framework has been subject to a number of strong criticisms; see, for example, Kirman (1992). Also, it has limitations in social welfare analysis of public policies such as fiscal policy where it is useful to know the socially optimal outcome. This is because the representative agent model generates Pareto optimal aggregate outcomes only under strict assumptions; see, for example, Lewbel (1989). For this reason it is sometimes assumed that the economy is run by a benevolent social planner or decision-maker.

This chapter contributes to the literature by identifying a source of difference between the representative agent and social planner paradigms in the particular context of population ageing. The difference turns out to depend on whether the social planner is concerned with individuals or equivalent persons in evaluating social welfare.

The basic framework of analysis, involving a difference between the number of people and the equivalent population size, is described in section 5.1. The optimal consumption path of a representative agent is examined in section 5.2. Section 5.3 turns to the optimal path determined by a social planner, where particular attention is given to the choice of the unit of analysis.

Some comparisons are made in section 5.5, followed by numerical examples in section 5.6.

5.1 The Basic Framework

This section outlines the basic framework of analysis, involving population growth arising from differential growth rates across age groups. The number of individuals aged i in year t is denoted $N_{i,t}$, so the total population in year t is $N_t = \sum_i N_{i,t}$. Individuals of different ages are assumed to have different 'basic needs', reflected in an equivalence size, s_i. This is similar in some ways to the type of adult equivalence scale used in the measurement of poverty and inequality. A higher value of s_i implies a lower capacity to derive utility from a given dollar amount of consumption. The scale is normalised such that it is unity at age i^*, so that $s_{i*} = 1$. The population size can therefore be adjusted to 'equivalent person' units. The equivalent size at time t, P_t, is thus:

$$P_t = \sum_i s_i N_{i,t} \qquad (5.1)$$

The average equivalent size per person at time t is given by:

$$
\begin{aligned}
s_t &= \sum_i s_i \left(\frac{N_{i,t}}{N_t} \right) \\
&= \frac{P_t}{N_t} \qquad (5.2)
\end{aligned}
$$

Over time, the population age structure is assumed to change in an exogenous manner, resulting in population growth at the proportional rate, n_t, where:

$$n_t = \frac{1}{N_t} \frac{dN_t}{dt} = \sum_i \left(\frac{N_{i,t}}{N_t} \right) \left(\frac{dN_{i,t}}{dt} \frac{1}{N_{i,t}} \right) \qquad (5.3)$$

and is a weighted sum of the proportional change in each age group. Similarly, the proportional change in the equivalent population size is given by:

$$p_t = \sum_i \left(\frac{P_{i,t}}{P_t} \right) \left(\frac{dN_{i,t}}{dt} \frac{1}{N_{i,t}} \right) \qquad (5.4)$$

Letting $n_{i,t} = \left(\frac{dN_{i,t}}{dt} \frac{1}{N_{i,t}} \right)$, then:

$$p_t - n_t = \sum_i n_{i,t} \left(\frac{N_{i,t}}{N_t} \right) \left(\frac{s_i}{s_t} - 1 \right) \tag{5.5}$$

and the difference between the growth rates is a weighted average over all age groups of the growth in each age group, with weights depending on the proportional difference between the equivalence scale for that age and the average equivalence size of the population.

Suppose the only changes taking place over time are the exogenous population changes affecting total population and its age composition, and average income changes which result from labour productivity growth at the fixed rate, g. Individuals alive at any time have been assumed to differ only in their ages; members of the same cohort have common income and consumption levels. The question considered here concerns the optimal aggregate consumption path associated with the productivity and population changes. Clearly, this must depend crucially on the way in which the objective function is specified.

5.2 The Representative Agent

Over time, the average age of the population, and hence its average 'equivalent size', changes. Consider a 'representative agent', who in each period is regarded as having the average age of the population and hence an equivalent size equal to the average equivalent size of the population. This artificial representative person is assumed to maximise a utility function, specified over an infinite horizon, which has as arguments the level of consumption in each period, c_t, expressed as a ratio of (average) equivalent size in each period. The term c_t is therefore not an average, but the consumption of the representative agent who has the average needs of the population. This differs from an alternative approach, which may be to define $c_{i,t}$ as the consumption of each person aged i at time t, where all individuals of the same age have the same consumption level. Average consumption at t is thus $\frac{1}{N_t}\sum_i N_{i,t}c_{i,t}$. The representative agent does not, in the approach adopted in the text above, attempt to maximize utility defined in terms of the ratio of average consumption to average equivalent population size.

The representative agent's optimisation problem is to select the time path of consumption, c_t. While individuals have finite lifetimes, the representative agent has the age and thus needs of an average person in each period and is assumed to maximise a utility function of the following isoelastic form:

$$U = \sum_{i=1}^{\infty} \left[\frac{c_t}{s_t}\right]^{1-\beta} \frac{(1+\theta)^{1-t}}{1-\beta} \tag{5.6}$$

where θ is the pure time preference rate and β is the representative agent's elasticity of marginal utility of consumption. The parameter β may be said to reflect the representative agent's (relative) aversion to consumption variability over time. The interpretation of this is discussed further below. The function, (5.6), is maximised subject to the intertemporal budget constraint, assuming no initial assets, given by:

$$\sum_{i=1}^{\infty} c_t(1+r)^{1-t} = \sum_{i=1}^{\infty} y_t(1+r)^{1-t} \tag{5.7}$$

where r is the constant interest rate.

The marginal rate of substitution between consumption in periods t and $t+1$, the ratio of marginal utilities, is:

$$\frac{\partial U/\partial c_t}{\partial U/\partial c_{t+1}} = \left(\frac{s_t}{s_{t+1}}\right)^{\beta-1} \left(\frac{c_{t+1}}{c_t}\right)(1+\theta) \tag{5.8}$$

Hence, substituting into the first-order condition for optimal consumption, $\frac{\partial U/\partial c_t}{\partial U/\partial c_{t+1}} = (1+r)$, gives:

$$\frac{c_{t+1}}{c_t} = \left(\frac{1+r}{1+\theta}\right)^{\frac{1}{\beta}} \left(\frac{s_{t+1}}{s_t}\right)^{\frac{\beta-1}{\beta}} \tag{5.9}$$

Taking logarithms of both sides and approximating, yields:

$$\frac{\dot{c}}{c} = \frac{1}{\beta}\left[r - \theta + (\beta-1)(\frac{\dot{s}}{s})\right] \tag{5.10}$$

Finally, assuming constant labour productivity growth, g, the growth rate of consumption per equivalent persons, deflated by productivity, is given by:

$$\frac{\dot{c}}{c} = \frac{1}{\beta}[r - \theta + (\beta - 1)(p - n)] - g \tag{5.11}$$

since $s = P/N$ and $\dot{s}/s = p - n$.

5.3 The Social Planner

This section considers the optimal consumption path determined by a social planner whose aim is to maximise an additive social welfare function defined over an infinite horizon. As it has been assumed that individuals alive at any time differ only in their ages, the social planner has no concern for within-period inequalities. Section 5.3.1 discusses the basic form of the welfare function, and examines the precise conditions under which welfare can be regarded as a function of the ratio of aggregate consumption to aggregate equivalent population size in each period. The question then remains of the choice of how to weight this term. This involves the choice of an appropriate unit of analysis – that is, whether the unit should be the individual or the equivalent person. This issue has been examined in the context of inequality and poverty measurement, where it has been shown that the choice depends on possibly conflicting value judgements. These issues are discussed in section 5.4. Subsections 5.4.1 and 5.4.2 examine in turn the implications of using the two units.

5.3.1 The Social Welfare Function

Suppose that the planner is concerned with per capita consumption per equivalent person in each period. The term entering the welfare function in each period is thus:

$$E\left(\frac{c}{s}\right)_t = \frac{1}{N_t}\sum_i N_{i,t}\left(\frac{c_{i,t}}{s_{i,t}}\right) \tag{5.12}$$

This may be compared with the ratio of average consumption, $\bar{c}_t$, to the average equivalent size of the population, s_t , which is given by:

$$\frac{\bar{c}_t}{s_t} = \frac{\frac{1}{N_t}\sum_i N_{i,t}c_{i,t}}{\frac{1}{N_t}\sum_i N_{i,t}s_{i,t}}$$

$$= \frac{C_t}{P_t} \tag{5.13}$$

where C_t is aggregate consumption at time t. Comparison of these two expressions shows that:

$$E\left(\frac{c}{s}\right)_t - \frac{\bar{c}_t}{s_t} = \frac{1}{N_t}\sum_i N_{i,t}\left(\frac{c_{i,t}}{s_{i,t}}\right)\left(1 - \frac{s_{i,t}}{s_t}\right) \tag{5.14}$$

In general the ratio of averages and the average of ratios are not equal. Complications arising from this are therefore examined in the following subsection.

5.3.2 Consumption per Adult Equivalent

This subsection examines the social welfare function expressed in terms of average consumption per equivalent person, and the relationship between a welfare function in terms of the ratio of average consumption to the average equivalent size. In terms of the average ratio of consumption to equivalent size, welfare is:

$$V = \sum_{t=1}^{\infty} N_t\left[E\left(\frac{c_{i,t}}{s_{i,t}}\right)\right]^{1-\beta}\frac{(1+\theta)^{1-t}}{1-\beta} \tag{5.15}$$

Writing $c_{i,t} = c_i\left(\bar{c}_t\right)$ and differentiating the above with respect to average consumption gives:

$$\frac{\partial V}{\partial \bar{c}_t} = N_t\left(\frac{1}{\bar{c}_t}\right)E\left(\frac{c}{s}\right)_t^{-\beta}(1+\theta)^{1-t}E_w\left(\frac{c}{s}\right)_t \tag{5.16}$$

The last term in this expression is a weighted average of c/s, with weights depending on the elasticity of consumption in each age group with respect to average consumption. Thus:

$$E_w\left(\frac{c}{s}\right) = \frac{1}{N_t}\sum_i N_{i,t}\left(\frac{\partial c_{i,t}}{c_{i,t}}\frac{\bar{c}_t}{\partial \bar{c}_t}\right)\left(\frac{c_{i,t}}{s_{i,t}}\right) \tag{5.17}$$

This approach is too cumbersome, and it is therefore necessary to consider the relationship between $E(c/s)$ and $E(c)/E(s)$ in more detail. For this purpose it is more convenient to work in terms of distributions.

Suppose $c_{i,t}$ and $s_{i,t}$ are jointly lognormally distributed with means and variances of logarithms denoted by μ, σ^2 with appropriate subscripts, and with a correlation of ρ. Then, dropping the t subscripts, and using the lognormal property that in general $E(x) = \exp(\mu_x + 0.5\sigma_x^2)$:

$$\frac{E(c)}{E(s)} = \exp\{\mu_c - \mu_s + 0.5(\sigma_c^2 - \sigma_s^2)\} \tag{5.18}$$

However, c/s is distributed lognormally as:

$$\Lambda(\mu_c - \mu_s, \sigma_c^2 + \sigma_s^2 - 2\rho\sigma_c\sigma_s) \tag{5.19}$$

Hence:

$$E\left(\frac{c}{s}\right) = \exp\{\mu_c - \mu_s + 0.5(\sigma_c^2 + \sigma_s^2 - 2\rho\sigma_c\sigma_s)\} \tag{5.20}$$

Dividing and rearranging gives the result that:

$$\frac{E(c)/E(s)}{E(c/s)} = \exp\{\sigma_s(\rho\sigma_c - \sigma_s)\} \tag{5.21}$$

For this ratio to equal unity, the term in brackets on the right hand side must be zero, so that:

$$\rho\frac{\sigma_c}{\sigma_s} = 1 \tag{5.22}$$

And since $\rho = \sigma_{cs}/(\sigma_c\sigma_s)$ and $\gamma = \sigma_{cs}/\sigma_s^2$ where γ is the regression coefficient in a linear regression of the log of c on the log of s, the condition applies only if the regression coefficient is unity. This condition is in fact equivalent, except for the addition of a random error term, to the assumption that the ratio c/s is the same for all age groups, since there is a unit elasticity of c with respect to s. This assumption is clearly very strong.

However, there is an alternative case, under which the two terms (the ratio of averages and the average of ratios) are not equal, but if the two variables are independent, so that $\rho = 0$, the ratio of averages is a proportion of the average of ratios, with the constant of proportionality being equal to $\exp(-\sigma_s^2)$. It is not unreasonable to suppose that this term is constant over time.

Thus, there are essentially two situations under which the social welfare function may be regarded simply as containing the term C_t/P_t for each period. The first is the case where individuals are considered to attempt to smooth needs-weighted consumption, $c_{i,t}/s_{i,t}$. If this term is constant, except for some purely random variation over the (finite) lifetime, it may be supposed that $c_{i,t}/s_{i,t}$ is the same for all ages, i (except for a random error term). While the difference in the needs of individuals over the life cycle means that the $c_{i,t}$ vary with i, the consumption per equivalent person may be assumed to be constant. In this case the difference above is zero, and the social welfare function can be expressed in terms of C_t/P_t for each period, since:

$$\frac{C}{P} = \frac{N_t \bar{c}_t}{\sum_i N_i \left(\frac{s_i}{c_i}\right) c_i} = \frac{N_t \bar{c}_t}{\left(\frac{s}{c}\right) \sum_i N_i c_i} = \frac{N_t \bar{c}_t}{\left(\frac{s}{c}\right) N_t \bar{c}} = \frac{c}{s} \tag{5.23}$$

The second context is where $s_{i,t}$ and $c_{i,t}$ are uncorrelated, in which case the two terms – the ratio of average consumption to average equivalent size and the average of the consumption per equivalent person – are proportional, with the constant of proportionality remaining constant over time. Again, the social welfare function can be expressed in terms of C_t/P_t for each period.

5.4 Alternative Consumption Units

As discussed in the previous section, the social welfare function is regarded as a function of consumption per equivalent person in each period. One approach is to treat the individual as the basic unit of analysis, so that the consumption per equivalent person is regarded as being assigned to each of the N_t individuals in the population. The value judgement inherent in this approach is that every person 'counts for one' irrespective of the demographic structure of the time period. This approach consequently has the property of anonymity. In the context of inequality and welfare measurement, this value judgement was called the 'compensation principle' by Shorrocks (2004) and the 'Pareto indifference principle' by Decoster and Ooghe (2003).

However, the use of the individual as the unit of analysis can give rise to a result that may at first seem paradoxical. The equivalence scale implies that a population consisting of a larger proportion of younger individuals is regarded as being 'more efficient' at generating welfare. Hence, a transfer of consumption from a period of low consumption (with many older people having high basic needs) to a richer period (with relatively few older people) may actually raise social welfare. Hence the use of individuals does not necessarily satisfy the 'principle of transfers', as shown by Glewwe (1991, p.213) and Decoster and Ooghe (2003).

An alternative approach to defining a unit of analysis is to use the 'adult equivalent person'. In the context of distributional analyses, this was proposed by Ebert (1997). The approach assigns to each of the P_t equivalent persons the consumption per equivalent person. It means that the measurement of consumption and the unit of analysis are treated consistently. Individuals no longer 'count as one' but have a weight depending on the demographic structure of the population to which they belong. An important feature of this approach is that it cannot give rise to the paradoxical situation described above.

Consequently, the choice between individuals and adult equivalents as the basic unit of analysis involves a choice between two incompatible value judgements. They can in principle lead to different conclusions about the effects of transferring consumption between time periods, which has implications for the path of optimal saving and the optimal income tax burden.

5.4.1 Individuals as Units of Analysis

Suppose that the social planner takes the individual as the basic unit of analysis. This implies that N_t is used as the weight attached to each period's contribution of consumption per equivalent person to social welfare function. If it is further assumed that the welfare function involves a similar isoelastic form to that of the representative agent, the welfare function takes the form:

$$V = \sum_{t=1}^{\infty} N_t \left[\frac{C_t}{P_t}\right]^{1-\beta} \frac{(1+\theta)^{1-t}}{1-\beta} \tag{5.24}$$

Here the parameters β and θ refer to the value judgements of the social planner, rather than the utility function of a hypothetical representative individual. This social welfare, or evaluation, function is maximised subject to the following resource constraint for the economy, again assuming no initial assets:

$$\sum_{t=1}^{\infty} C_t(1+r)^{1-t} = \sum_{t=1}^{\infty} Y_t (1+r)^{1-t} \tag{5.25}$$

where is Y_t aggregate income in period t.

The marginal rate of substitution between aggregate consumption in two periods is therefore given by:

$$\frac{\partial V/\partial C_t}{\partial V/\partial C_{t+1}} = \left(\frac{N_t}{N_{t+1}}\right) \left(\frac{P_t}{P_{t+1}}\right)^{\beta-1} \left(\frac{C_{t+1}}{C_t}\right)^{\beta} (1+\theta) \tag{5.26}$$

The first-order condition for maximising social welfare is given by $\frac{\partial V/\partial C_t}{\partial V/\partial C_{t+1}} = (1+r)$, so that:

$$\frac{C_{t+1}}{C_t} = \left(\frac{1+r}{1+\theta}\right)^{\frac{1}{\beta}} \left(\frac{N_{t+1}}{N_t}\right)^{\frac{1}{\beta}} \left(\frac{P_{t+1}}{P_t}\right)^{\frac{\beta-1}{\beta}} \tag{5.27}$$

Using $C_t = \bar{c}_t N_t$ this condition can be written in terms of changes in average consumption as follows:

$$\frac{\bar{c}_{t+1}}{\bar{c}_t} = \left(\frac{1+r}{1+\theta}\right)^{\frac{1}{\beta}} \left(\frac{N_{t+1}}{N_t}\right)^{\frac{1}{\beta}-1} \left(\frac{P_{t+1}}{P_t}\right)^{-\left(\frac{1}{\beta}-1\right)} \tag{5.28}$$

Taking logarithms and allowing for productivity growth gives:

$$\frac{\dot{c}}{c} = \frac{1}{\beta}\left[r - \theta + (\beta - 1)(p - n)\right] - g \tag{5.29}$$

This equation is the same as the result regarding the representative agent, except that the former is expressed in terms of the consumption in each period of a hypothetical infinitely-lived individual who in each period has needs determined by the average equivalent size of individuals. The optimal consumption path is the same for both cases – where the social planner's value judgements regarding β and θ are the same as the assumed preferences of the representative agent.

In the above approach, the social welfare function has been expressed in terms of consumption (per equivalent person) in each period, where the social planner is assumed to be averse to variability over time. This aversion is reflected in the parameter β, which applies in addition to the pure time preference of the planner, measured by θ. An alternative approach might express the social welfare function in terms of total utility in each period, given an additional assumption that all individuals have the same preferences. For example, suppose individuals have a common iso-elastic utility function, with parameter β_0, and the planner's aversion to variability is given by β_1. The above social welfare function then becomes:

$$V = \sum_{t=1}^{\infty} N_t \left(\frac{1}{1 - \beta_0}\left[\frac{C_t}{P_t}\right]^{1-\beta_0}\right)^{1-\beta_1} \frac{(1+\theta)^{1-t}}{1 - \beta_1} \tag{5.30}$$

However, it is found that the Euler equation governing the growth of average consumption is the same as that given above in equation (5.29), where β is replaced using:

$$\beta = \beta_1 + \beta_0\left(1 - \beta_1\right) \tag{5.31}$$

Hence comparisons can be made simply by reinterpreting the parameter β .

5.4.2   Equivalent Persons as Units

Assume that the social planner regards equivalent persons, rather than individuals, as the appropriate unit of analysis. The weight in each period is thus P_t, rather than N_t. The social welfare function becomes:

$$V = \sum_{t=1}^{\infty} p_t \left[\frac{C_t}{P_t}\right]^{1-\beta} \frac{(1+\theta)^{1-t}}{1-\beta} \tag{5.32}$$

The first order condition for aggregate consumption is given by:

$$\frac{C_{t+1}}{C_t} = \left(\frac{1+r}{1+\theta}\right)^{\frac{1}{\beta}} \left(\frac{P_{t+1}}{P_t}\right) \tag{5.33}$$

Converting to average consumption and allowing for productivity growth gives:

$$\frac{\dot{c}}{c} = \frac{1}{\beta}(r-\theta) + (p-n) - g \tag{5.34}$$

This Euler equation differs from that in the previous case where the individual is regarded as the appropriate unit of analysis. The difference between the two growth rates of consumption, $\left.\frac{\dot{c}}{c}\right|_N - \left.\frac{\dot{c}}{c}\right|_P$, is given by:

$$\left.\frac{\dot{c}}{c}\right|_N - \left.\frac{\dot{c}}{c}\right|_P = \frac{1}{\beta}(n-p) \tag{5.35}$$

Hence the relative growth rates of consumption depend on the growth rate of the population compared with its equivalent size. For example, if population ageing makes $n < p$, the growth rate of average consumption is lower if the individual is regarded as the unit, compared with the case where the equivalent person is the unit. This means that relatively more consumption is moved into earlier periods, when the population is younger and more efficient at converting consumption into welfare. Each individual 'counts as one', so more weight is given to these periods than when the unit is the number of equivalent persons.

5.5 Some Comparisons

The previous sections have derived alternative Euler equations governing the optimal consumption path of the economy. The form of the Euler equation for an infinitely lived representative agent, having in each period the average equivalent size of the population, was found to be the same as that for a social planner who regards the individual as the unit of analysis, or weight, in the social welfare function. The only difference is that the representative agent Euler equation is in terms of the consumption of the agent in each period, and that for the social planner is in terms of per capita consumption. However, if the equivalent person is regarded as the appropriate unit of analysis, the social planner's optimal consumption path differs from the other two cases. As discussed in the previous section, the choice of these consumption units, or population aggregates, is a normative issue, involving possibly conflicting value judgements.

The Euler equations differ in the way that the term $(p - n)$ affects the optimal consumption path. The term $(p - n)$ reflects the changing consumption demands, and therefore capacity for generating utility, implied by an ageing population. As the population ages, P rises relative to N and therefore $(p - n) > 0$, reflecting increasing consumption demands and declining capacity to generate utility.

To the representative agent and the social planner using the individual as the unit of analysis, $(p - n) > 0$ implies an additional subjective discounting factor. If a dollar of consumption is postponed one period it will reduce welfare because the demands on a dollar of consumption are higher. This creates a desire to shift consumption towards the present. On the other hand there is an offsetting desire to shift consumption towards the future which arises from the desire to smooth C/P. The desire to smooth consumption is stronger the larger is the value of β. These two opposite forces on intertemporal consumption are reflected in the term $(\beta - 1)(p - n)$ in the Euler equation. Hence the net rate of subjective discounting is $\theta - (\beta - 1)(p - n)$, which is compared with the interest rate, r, to determine whether consumption is tilted toward the future or the present.

To see this effect on consumption tilting, differentiate (5.29) with respect to the term $(p - n)$:

$$\frac{\partial}{\partial (p - n)} \left(\frac{\dot{c}}{c} \right) = \frac{\beta - 1}{\beta} = 1 - \phi \qquad (5.36)$$

where $\phi = 1/\beta$ is the intertemporal elasticity of substitution. This equation implies that the increasing average consumption demands implied by an ageing population tilts consumption towards the present if $\phi > 1$, towards the future if $\phi < 1$, and neither way if $\phi = 1$.

For the social planner adopting equivalent persons as units, the term $(p - n)$ implies no additional discounting motive because in deriving social welfare the planner is summing over P rather than over N. In other words, the growth of P relative to N has no relevance for the evaluation of social welfare. It has relevance only in determining the optimal growth of per capita consumption.

5.6   Numerical Examples

This section considers whether the difference between the two approaches – using individuals or equivalent persons as units – is important. Numerical examples are given, and sensitivity analyses are reported for alternative values of β and projections of $p - n$ using Australian data for the period 2004–2050. Subsection 5.6.1 examines population growth and the associated changes in the equivalent population size, using a flexible specification for the variation in s_i with age. The sensitivity of the optimal consumption stream to variations in the parameters describing the value judgements of the social planner is examined in subsection 5.6.2.

5.6.1 Population Projections

The population projections are taken from the Australian Bureau of Statistics (Catalogue 3222.0) series for total persons (as no distinction is made in the model between males and females). These data provide the series for N and therefore n.

In calibrating the age-specific consumption weights, s_i, which are used to calculate the series for P and hence p, it is desirable to specify these in terms of a parametric function relating the scales to age. This allows for sensitivity analyses to be carried out. The following semi-logarithmic functional form:

$$s_i = a + \frac{1}{b} \log(i) \qquad (5.37)$$

is sufficiently flexible and allows the scale to increase systematically with age. Initial, or 'baseline', parameter values were estimated using values of s_i which were calculated as a weighted average of private and social consumption weights. In the context of the social planner, these weights may perhaps be regarded as being determined by value judgements concerning, for example, the allocation of health resources to the aged. The private weights were calculated from Household Expenditure Survey data for 2003–4 (Australian Bureau of Statistics, Catalogue 6530.0, Table 19). Expenditure per equivalent adult was calculated by dividing household expenditure for each age category by the number of equivalent adults in the household. The latter were calculated using the parametric equivalence scales suggested by Cutler and Katz (1992) and used by, for example, Banks and Johnson (1994), Jenkins and Cowell (1994). This takes the form:

$$m = (N_a + \theta N_c)^\alpha \qquad (5.38)$$

where m is the number of equivalent adults in the household, N_a and N_c are the number of adults and children respectively. The parameter θ is a weight between zero and 1 reflecting the lower consumption needs of children, and

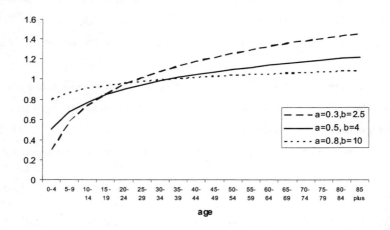

Figure 5.1: Consumption Weights, s_i, by Age

α is a parameter reflecting economies of scale in household budgets. The following examples use values of θ and α of 0.5 and 0.75 respectively; these are in the middle of the range reported by Creedy and Sleeman (2005), estimated using a wide range of scales suggested in the literature.

The social expenditure weights were calculated using data on age-specific health, education and aged care consumption for 2004 used by Productivity Commission (2005). Both the private and social consumption weights are assumed here to be constant over the projection period. The total consumption weights, s_i, were calculated by adding the private and social consumption weights, which are themselves weighted by the shares of private and social consumption in total consumption. The baseline values of a and b respectively were found to be 0.5 and 4.0. Figure 5.1 shows the profiles obtained using several parameter combinations.

The corresponding series for $p-n$ are plotted in Figure 5.2. The difference

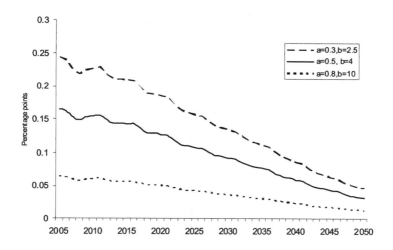

Figure 5.2: Series For $p - n$

in these growth rates tends to decline over time because the changes in the population age shares diminish over time. For example, in the initial years from 2005 there is a relatively large shift in the population from young to old age groups which tends to produce a large gap between p and n. As the age distribution stabilises, the gap between p and n diminishes.

5.6.2 Optimal Consumption Paths

Simulating the path of optimal consumption growth, $\dot{c}/c$, requires, in addition to the population series for n and p, values of the parameters r, β, θ and g. In all the following computations, the values of r and g are fixed at 4 per cent and 1.75 per cent respectively. Projections in Productivity Commission (2005) use a base case value of 1.75 per cent for g, and 4 per cent is a typical value for the real interest rate in long run macroeconomic models.

Three values of β are examined: 0.5, 1.5 and 2.5, which covers a wide range of plausible values for this parameter. It is useful to consider the precise nature of the comparisons being made. When Atkinson (1970) introduced his inequality measure based on the welfare function, $W = \sum_i \frac{y_i^{1-\epsilon}}{1-\epsilon}$, he recognised the difficulty of forming views about the orders of magnitude of ϵ. In order to help interpretation, he used the idea of a 'leaky bucket' experiment, which considers the extent to which a judge is prepared to tolerate some loss in making a transfer from one person to another. Consider two individuals, so that from the welfare function, setting the total differential equal to zero gives:

$$-\left.\frac{dy_1}{dy_2}\right|_W = \left(\frac{y_1}{y_2}\right)^\varepsilon \tag{5.39}$$

The welfare function is thus homothetic, as the slopes of social indifference curves are the same along any ray drawn through the origin. Consider two individuals and, using discrete changes, suppose a dollar is taken from the richest, such that $\Delta y_2 = -1$. The amount to be given to the other individual to keep social welfare unchanged is thus:

$$\Delta y_1 = \left(\frac{y_1}{y_2}\right)^\varepsilon \tag{5.40}$$

For example, if $y_2 = 2y_1$ and $\varepsilon = 1.5$, it is necessary to give person 1 only 35 cents – a leak of 65 cents from the original dollar taken from person 2 is tolerated. If $\varepsilon = 1$, a leak of 50 cents is tolerated. In the present intertemporal context (with an unchanged population), suppose that total consumption in the first period is 100 and this grows at a rate of 0.02 per period. In period 10 it is thus 119.5, and a judge with $\beta = 2$ would be prepared to take a dollar from period 10, and give only \$0.70 to period 1. By period 20 total income would be 145.7, and the same judge would reduce period 20's income by \$1 while adding only \$0.47 to the first period.

The discount rate, ρ, is given by the Ramsey equation, $\rho = \theta + \beta g$. In the following calculations, values of θ are given by the condition that $\dot{c}/c = 0$ in a steady state. This condition is required in non-overlapping generations

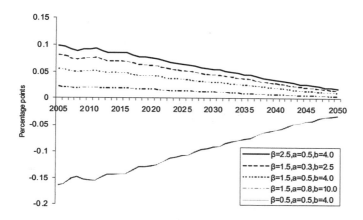

Figure 5.3: Optimal Consumption Growth for Social Planner: Individuals as Unit of Analysis

models, given a constant interest rate, in order to rule out inadmissible paths – in particular paths in which consumption goes to zero or infinity.[3] This implies that the discount rate is equal to r, so that $\theta = r - \beta g$. Hence θ is not set independently and is determined by the value of β adopted. The resulting series for $\dot{c}/c$ are given in Figures 5.3 and 5.4. Figure 5.3 applies to the case of the representative agent or the social planner using individuals as the unit of analysis. Figure 5.4 applies to the case of the social planner using equivalent persons as the unit of analysis.

The magnitudes of the differences between the paths in Figures 5.3 and 5.4 are indicated in Figures 5.5 and 5.6. Figure 5.5 shows $\left.\frac{\dot{c}}{c}\right|_N - \left.\frac{\dot{c}}{c}\right|_P = -\left(\frac{1}{\beta}\right)(p - n)$, which is the difference in optimal consumption growth, for

---

[3]In overlapping generations models this condition on θ is not required, because the cross-section profile of consumption in the economy is stable; see Obstfeld and Rogoff (1996, p. 136).

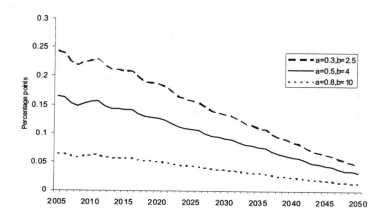

Figure 5.4: Optimal Consumption Growth For Social Planner: Equivalent Persons as Unit of Analysis

the various alternative combinations of parameters. Different growth rates imply different paths of consumption in levels. The paths of consumption in levels can be compared by solving for the initial value of consumption for the case where equivalent persons are used, $\dot{c}/c|_{P}$, that gives the same value of aggregate discounted consumption as in the case where the number of person is used, $\dot{c}/c|_{N}$. This is shown in Figure 5.6, where c^{N} and c^{P} refer to levels of consumption where individuals and equivalent persons, respectively, are the unit of analysis. The largest difference occurs for $\beta = 0.5$. In that case optimal consumption would be 4 percent higher in 2005 and 4 percent lower in 2050 if individuals are the unit of analysis rather than equivalent persons, for a given value of aggregate discounted consumption over the 46 year period. This is not trivial, nor arguably are the values around 1 and 2 percent for the other simulations.

Optimal consumption levels imply optimal saving levels which inform

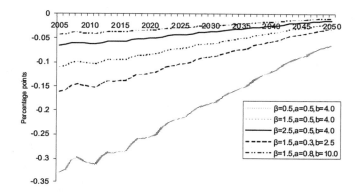

Figure 5.5: Difference Between Optimal Consumption Paths

policy decisions such as the appropriate fiscal balance and superannuation policy. If optimal consumption is higher for one social welfare function than another, then optimal saving is lower. In general, if $c^N = (1 + x) c^P$ and assuming income, y, is the same for both consumption paths,[4] then $\frac{s^N}{y} = \frac{s^P}{y} - x \left(1 - \frac{s^P}{y} \right)$. For example, if $\frac{s^P}{y} = 0.2$ and $x = 0.01$, a mid-range value in Figure 5.6, then $\frac{s^N}{y} == 0.192$. That is a difference of 0.8 percent in the optimal saving to income ratio which, again, is arguably not trivial.

5.7 Conclusions

This chapter has examined the optimal path of consumption over time in the context of population ageing. Emphasis was given to the difference between a framework involving a representative agent and one in which plans are made

---

[4]It differs slightly because different consumption paths imply different saving paths and hence different amounts of capital income.

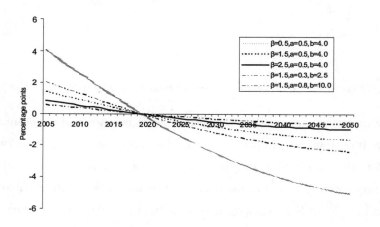

Figure 5.6: Percentage Difference in Consumption Levels for Given Present Value of Consumption Over the Period

by a social planner. The precise conditions under which consumption growth paths are the same under the representative agent and the social planner were established. This equivalence was found to hold only in the case where the social planner's value judgements are such that individuals are considered to be the appropriate unit of analysis. An alternative assumption, in which equivalent persons are regarded as the appropriate units, was found to give rise to a different optimal consumption path. Numerical examples demonstrated the relative orders of magnitude for a range of parameter values. The differences were found to be potentially important. The choice of appropriate consumption units – individuals or equivalent persons – is far from arbitrary since it involves possibly conflicting value judgements.

These value judgements, by influencing the optimal path of consumption in response to population ageing, have implications for policies designed to influence the optimal saving rate, such as superannuation policy and the fiscal balance. The numerical illustrations reported in this chapter suggest that the choice of social welfare function could imply a difference in optimal saving at a given time in the order of 1 percent of GDP, which is arguably not trivial. In addition, the optimal consumption path has implications for the optimal path of income taxes, on the principal that optimal income taxes should not distort intertemporal consumption choices.

Part III

Pensions and Taxation

Chapter 6

Pension Tax, Savings and Labour Supply

This chapter examines the labour supply and savings effects of a change in superannuation taxation. The labour supply effects of taxes on superannuation can take several forms because of the existence of three separate stages at which superannuation is taxed, including the contributions to a superannuation fund, the earnings obtained by the fund, and the income withdrawn from the fund after retirement. For example, a system is of the TTT variety if tax is imposed in all three stages; on the alternatives see, for example, Knox (1990), Piggott (1997), Doyle *et al.* (1999) and Whitehouse (1999). When compulsory superannuation was introduced in Australia, the TTT structure was adopted, making it the only OECD country with this form. The most common scheme in the OECD is EET, where contributions and fund earnings are exempt and only benefit income post retirement is subject to taxation. However, in the 2006 Australian Government Budget, benefits after retirement were made exempt from taxation, with the new rules taking effect on 1 July 2007; see Australian Government (2006a, b).

A complete analysis of the effects of changes in taxation, on individuals at various stages of the life cycle at the time of the change, requires a complex model of lifetime optimisation along with a method of dealing with the potential general equilibrium effects and the government's budget constraint.

The latter is relevant since the elimination of taxation on superannuation benefits obviously means that at least one other tax rate must be increased or other transfer payments or expenditures reduced. The effects on individuals at a given stage of their life cycle was analysed by Atkinson, Creedy and Knox (1996) using the LITES microsimulation model. Their focus in particular was on within-generation inequality implied by alternative retirement income strategies. But their model did not allow a general equilibrium analysis or an analysis of inequality between generations. Rather than to apply a complex general equilibrium analysis of life cycle effects, the modest aim of the present chapter is to provide a preliminary analysis using a highly simplified model of lifetime labour supply and consumption. Despite the simplicity of the model, it seems useful to consider the potential direction of changes in behaviour resulting from a superannuation tax change. In particular, the model can be used to investigate the extent to which the direction of some changes can be anticipated *a priori*, without the need for detailed empirical estimates. The model also has the potential to be extended and used as one component of a larger and more comprehensive model.

The model is set out in Section 6.1. The lifetime is modelled as consisting of three stages, the last of which is retirement. Hence it is not possible to use the model to examine questions relating to the age of retirement, which may be affected by an unanticipated change in policy. But the effects on pre-retirement labour supply and savings, other than the compulsory superannuation contribution, can be investigated. Section 6.2 then shows how the effects of tax policy changes on those in the middle stage of the life cycle can be examined. Some illustrative numerical examples are reported in Section 6.3 and brief conclusions are in Section 6.4.

6.1 The Lifetime Model

This section presents the basic model used to examine the effects on an individual's labour supply and consumption decisions of alternative tax structures. Suppose the lifetime is divided into three periods, with work in the first two periods and retirement in the final period. The exogenous wage rates in the two working periods are w_1 and w_2. There is a compulsory superannuation system, as in Australia, whereby individuals must contribute a proportion, x, of pre-tax earnings to a fund. These contributions are taxed at the fixed rate, t_c, while the fund's earnings are taxed at the rate, t_y. The benefits received by the fund at retirement are then taxed at the rate, t_b. This framework therefore corresponds to a simple TTT system.[1] Income tax is imposed at a constant proportional rate, t, on earnings and interest income arising from additional savings during the first two periods. The exogenously fixed rate of interest is equal to r. Subsection 6.1.1 examines the budget constraint facing the individual. Subsection 6.1.2 considers lifetime utility maximisation.

6.1.1 The Lifetime Budget Constraint

Consumption and leisure in each period are c_j and h_j, for $j = 1, ..., T$, with $T = 3$. The individual's time endowment in each period is 1, and the price of goods in each period is normalised at 1. During retirement, $h_3 = 1$. Private savings are treated as being made out of post-income tax income and accumulate at the post-tax interest rate. It is assumed that earnings, contributions and so on are made at the beginning of each period.

The two relevant after-tax interest rates are denoted by $r_y^* = r(1 - t_y)$ and $r^* = r(1 - t)$. As in standard labour supply models, the objective is to express the budget constraint in terms of the individual's 'full income'.

---

[1] See Kingston and Piggott (1993) for an analysis of equivalence relationships among the three tax rates t_c, t_y and t_b.

In this context, full income is the present value of income from all sources, if the individual devotes all the endowment of time to work during the first two periods of the life cycle. This is treated as if it were spent on goods and leisure, where the latter is priced at the net wage. It is useful to consider the relevant income flows, in particular those involving the superannuation fund. These flows are shown in Table 6.1. The first part of the table shows the accumulation of the fund, over two periods, arising from earnings obtained during the first period. The second part of Table 6.1 shows the contribution to the fund arising from earnings during the second period.

Table 6.1: Income Flows

	From period 1
Net earnings	$w_1 (1 - h_1) (1 - x) (1 - t) = Y_1$
Net contrib. to fund in 1	$x w_1 (1 - h_1) (1 - t_c) = B_1$
Net income of fund in 1	$r x w_1 (1 - h_1) (1 - t_c) (1 - t_y) = B_1 r_y^*$
Fund at end of 1	$B_1 \left(1 + r_y^*\right)$
Net income of fund in 2	$B_1 \left(1 + r_y^*\right) r_y^*$
Fund at end of 2	$B_1 \left(1 + r_y^*\right)^2$
	From period 2
Net earnings	$w_2 (1 - h_2) (1 - x) (1 - t) = Y_2$
Net contrib. to fund in 2	$x w_2 (1 - h_2) (1 - t_c) = B_2$
Net income of fund in 2	$r x w_2 (1 - h_2) (1 - t_c) (1 - t_y) = B_2 r_y^*$
Fund at end of 2	$B_2 \left(1 + r_y^*\right)$

The lifetime budget constraint, assuming there are no inheritances or bequests, is thus expressed as:

$$\sum_{j=1}^{T} c_j \left(\frac{1}{1 + r^*}\right)^{j-1} = Y_1 + B_1 (1 - t_b) + \left(\frac{1}{1 + r^*}\right) \{Y_2 + B_2 (1 - t_b)\} \quad (6.1)$$

Hence:

$$\sum_{j=1}^{T} c_j \left(\frac{1}{1 + r^*}\right)^{j-1} = \sum_{j=1}^{T-1} \left(\frac{1}{1 + r^*}\right)^{j-1} (Y_j + B_j (1 - t_b))$$

$$= \sum_{j=1}^{T-1} \left(\frac{1}{1 + r^*}\right)^{j-1} w_j (1 - h_j) E_j \quad (6.2)$$

where the term E_j is given by:

$$E_j = (1 - t) - x \left[(1 - t) - \left(\frac{1 + r_y^*}{1 + r^*} \right)^{T-j} (1 - t_c)(1 - t_b) \right] \qquad (6.3)$$

The lifetime budget constraint can therefore be expressed as:

$$\sum_{j=1}^{T} c_j \left(\frac{1}{1 + r^*} \right)^{j-1} + \sum_{j=1}^{T-1} \left(\frac{1}{1 + r^*} \right)^{j-1} w_j E_j h_j = \sum_{j=1}^{T-1} \left(\frac{1}{1 + r^*} \right)^{j-1} w_j E_j \qquad (6.4)$$

The left-hand side of (6.4) represents the present value of consumption, including goods and leisure. Hence, the price of leisure, $p_{h,j}$, in period j is given by:

$$p_{h,j} = \left(\frac{1}{1 + r^*} \right)^{j-1} w_j E_j \qquad (6.5)$$

The right-hand side of (6.4) is full income, denoted M. It is a simple matter to add a government non-means-tested benefit of, say b, each period, whereby M becomes:

$$M = \sum_{j=1}^{T-1} \left(\frac{1}{1 + r^*} \right)^{j-1} w_j E_j + b \sum_{j=1}^{T} \left(\frac{1}{1 + r^*} \right)^{j-1} \qquad (6.6)$$

It is clear from the form of the budget constraint that a change in any tax rate has both an income and price effect. For example, an increase in the income tax rate, t, implies a reduction in full income which may typically be expected to have a negative effect on leisure and hence a positive effect on labour supply. However, the increase in t also reduces the price, that is the opportunity cost, of leisure, leading to an increase in the demand for leisure and hence a reduction in labour supply. The two effects therefore have opposing effects on labour supply. Further analysis requires the specification of lifetime utility.

6.1.2   Utility Maximisation

As in the standard discounted utility model, suppose the individual maximises a lifetime utility function of the form:

$$U = \sum_{j=1}^{T} \left(\frac{1}{1+\rho}\right)^{j-1} U\left(c_j, h_j\right) \tag{6.7}$$

where the pure time preference rate is equal to ρ. For convenience, within-period utility is assumed to follow the Cobb-Douglas form:

$$U\left(c_j, h_j\right) = c_j^\alpha h_j^{1-\alpha} \tag{6.8}$$

for $j = 1, 2$, so that $U\left(c_3, 1\right) = c_3^\alpha$. Taking the logarithmic transformation of $U\left(c_j, h_j\right)$ and substituting into (6.7), the sum of the coefficients on log-terms, Φ, is:

$$\Phi = 1 + \frac{1}{1+\rho} + \alpha \left(\frac{1}{1+\rho}\right)^2 \tag{6.9}$$

Using the standard Cobb-Douglas result that the optimal value for any variable is the ratio of the coefficient on that variable to the sum of coefficients, multiplied by the ratio of full income to the relevant price, consumption in each period is therefore given by:

$$c_j = \left(\frac{\alpha}{\Phi}\right) M \left(\frac{1+r^*}{1+\rho}\right)^{j-1} \tag{6.10}$$

for $j = 1, ..., T$. Similarly leisure in each period is given by:

$$h_j = \left(\frac{1-\alpha}{\Phi}\right) \frac{M}{w_j E_j} \left(\frac{1+r^*}{1+\rho}\right)^{j-1} \tag{6.11}$$

for $j = 1, 2$. It is assumed that parameters and variables are such that $h_1 < 1$ and $h_2 < 1$; otherwise the treatment of corner solutions involving non-participation in the labour market involve considerable complexities.

The effect on leisure demand in any period of a change in, say, the income tax rate, t, can be expressed by differentiating (6.11) with respect to t, so that:

$$\frac{\partial h_j}{\partial t} = \left(\frac{h_j}{M} \frac{\partial M}{\partial t} - \frac{h_j}{p_{h,j}} \frac{\partial p_{h,j}}{\partial t}\right) \tag{6.12}$$

Dividing both sides by h_j shows that the proportional change in leisure demand, in response to a change in the tax rate, is equal to the proportional change in full income minus the proportional change in the relative price of leisure.

Private voluntary savings, s_j, in period j (that is not including the compulsory superannuation contributions) are equal to net income minus consumption, so that:

$$s_j = Y_j + b - c_j \qquad (6.13)$$

Substitution for Y_j and c_j and differentiation shows that $\partial s_j / \partial t$ is a complex function of all the parameters in the model, but is negative.

6.2   A Policy Change

This section considers the effects of introducing a tax policy change. Suppose that the tax rate on superannuation benefits from the fund is changed to t_b', at the start of a period. If $t_b' = 0$, this corresponds to a movement from a TTT to a TTE system. For aggregate tax revenue neutrality, at least one other tax rate must also be changed. Suppose the rate on earnings from employment is adjusted to t'. Consequently, r^* is adjusted to r'^*. The following results can easily be modified for changes to other rates. For simplicity, any potential general equilibrium effects on wage rates and interest rates are ignored here.

From the point of view of those at the start of the life cycle when the policy comes into effect, there is no need to modify the results obtained above, since their plans are simply made using the new rates. For those entering retirement when the policy is announced, labour supply and consumption decisions in the previous two stages have already been made, so the only adjustment is to consumption during retirement. Such individuals experience an unequivocal gain. The more complex effect is on those starting the second period when tax rates change. This is examined in the following subsection.

6.2.1   Effects of Unanticipated Tax Changes

Consider the problem of deciding on consumption in periods 2 and 3, and labour supply in period 2, given that a choice was made in the first period based on different tax rates. First the new budget constraint for this two-period problem must be obtained.

The retirement fund at the start of period 3 arising from contributions from the first period's earnings, Q, is given by:

$$Q = B_1 \left(1 + r_y^*\right)^2 \tag{6.14}$$

In addition, the private savings made during period 1 produce accumulated private savings at the start of period 2 of:

$$S = \{Y_1 + b - c_1\} \left(1 + r^*\right) \tag{6.15}$$

The new budget constraint, ignoring transfer payments for the moment, is thus:

$$
\begin{aligned}
\sum_{j=2}^{T} c_j' \left(\frac{1}{1 + r'^*}\right)^{j-2} =\ & w_2 \left(1 - h_2'\right)\left(1 - x\right)\left(1 - t'\right) + S \\
& + \left(\frac{1}{1 + r'^*}\right)[Q\left(1 - t_b'\right) + \\
& \{xw_2 \left(1 - h_2'\right) \times \\
& \left(1 - t_c\right)\left(1 + r_y^*\right)\}\left(1 - t_b'\right)]
\end{aligned}
\tag{6.16}
$$

where, as with the tax rates, a prime attached to a variable indicates that it is a new value resulting from revised plans following the unanticipated tax change. The right-hand side of (6.16) consists of earnings in period 2, net of income tax (at the new rate) and mandatory superannuation contributions, along with (the present value at period 2 of) accumulated superannuation contributions (arising from those already made in period 1 as well as new contributions in period 2). The constraint thus becomes:

$$\sum_{j=2}^{T} c_j' \left(\frac{1}{1 + r'^*}\right)^{j-2} = \left(\frac{1}{1 + r'^*}\right) Q\left(1 - t_b'\right) + S + w_2 \left(1 - h_2'\right) E_2' \tag{6.17}$$

where the new value of E_2, E_2', is given by:

$$E_2' = (1 - t') - x \left[(1 - t') - \left(\frac{1 + r_y^*}{1 + r'^*} \right) (1 - t_c) (1 - t_b') \right] \tag{6.18}$$

and:

$$\sum_{j=2}^{T} c_j' \left(\frac{1}{1 + r'^*} \right)^{j-2} + w_2 E_2' h_2' = M' \tag{6.19}$$

where M' is full income for this revised problem and is given by:

$$M' = \left(\frac{1}{1 + r'^*} \right) Q (1 - t_b') + S + w_2 E_2' \tag{6.20}$$

This is finally augmented by the term $b \sum_{j=1}^{2} \left(\frac{1}{1+r'^*} \right)^{j-1}$, which must be added to allow for transfer payments during the second and third periods.

The problem at the start of the second period is thus to maximise:

$$U' = U(c_2', h_2') + \left(\frac{1}{1 + \rho} \right) U(c_3', 1) \tag{6.21}$$

The sum of coefficients on log-values in this two-period utility function is given by $\Omega = 1 + \alpha/(1 + \rho)$. Hence, consumption is given, for $j = 2, 3$, by:

$$c_j' = \left(\frac{\alpha}{\Omega} \right) \frac{M'}{\left(\frac{1}{1+r'^*} \right)^{j-2}} \tag{6.22}$$

The revised value of leisure in the second period becomes:

$$h_2' = \left(\frac{1 - \alpha}{\Omega} \right) \frac{M'}{w_2 E_2'} \tag{6.23}$$

These results can then be used to obtained the revised value of private savings in the second period, as the difference between net income and consumption.

6.2.2 The Government's Budget Constraint

The previous subsection has examined the revised plans of an individual at the start of period 2 when new values of t_b and t are introduced. It is a simple matter to revise the above expressions for changes in another tax rate, or indeed a combination of all other tax rates, in response to a change in t_b. The main point is that the government is subject to a budget constraint of some kind. It is also possible to envisage the government as being able to finance a reduction in revenue from one tax by borrowing, though this may be subject to a borrowing constraint and a specific time period over which the budget must be balanced. This would introduce substantial complexities. In tax modelling it is usual to impose revenue-neutral, or deficit-neutral changes.

In the present model, where there are labour supply responses to tax changes and more than one cohort is alive at any one time, the budget constraint, however specified in detail, would be highly nonlinear. Its construction also involves the precise specification of population heterogeneity, as aggregation over individuals is required, and this means that allowance must be made for some individuals being below the wage threshold above which $h < 1$ in each period. If low wage individuals may not participate in one or more of the first two periods, depending on wage rate dynamics, the analysis of labour supply actually becomes a complex programming problem.[2] Hence it is not possible to obtain expressions for the change in one tax rate consequent on a change in another tax rate or government transfer payment. However, further progress may be made in view of the fact that the direction of changes is often unambiguous, although the order of magnitude depends on many complex factors.

For example, consider the change in an individual's labour supply resulting from a change in t_b, accompanied by a change in t designed to achieve aggregate revenue neutrality. Suppose that net revenue from the tax and transfer system (over a specified period and population group) is denoted R. The revenue neutral change in t may thus be denoted $\frac{dt}{dt_b}\big|_R$. Clearly, if t_b is reduced, t must be increased by an appropriate amount to compensate for the lost revenue from taxing superannuation benefits, so that $\frac{dt}{dt_b}\big|_R < 0$. The

---

[2]For an algorithm and discoussion in the context of two periods, see Creedy (1996, chapter 12).

change in labour supply can be divided into two partial changes, along with the relationship between tax rates, as follows:

$$\frac{dh_2}{dt_b} = \frac{\partial h_2}{\partial t_b} + \left(\frac{\partial h_2}{\partial t}\right) \frac{dt}{dt_b}\bigg|_R \tag{6.24}$$

Given a clear idea of the sign of the tax change, along with an idea of the partial effects on labour supply of the separate taxes, it is therefore possible to examine whether or not an unambiguous change in labour supply is to be expected. As mentioned above, determination of the size of $\frac{dt}{dt_b}\big|_R$, dictated by the revenue-neutrality requirement, depends on a large number of factors, including the sizes of different cohorts existing at any time, the distribution of wage rates for each time and cohort, including the life cycle pattern of wage, the nature of preferences (and any differences among cohorts) and of course the extend of labour supply responses themselves. In the absence of a specification of these additional elements, the approach adopted below is to consider the relevant partial terms and to examine the extent to which the direction of any changes may be unambiguous.

6.3 Some Numerical Examples

This section examines, using numerical examples, the properties of the model considered in the previous section. Consider a single individual with $w_1 = w_2 = 100$, and with a time preference rate of $\rho = 0.14$. This high value is appropriate in view of the fact that the lifetime is compressed into just three periods, so that it is not an annual rate. Suppose also that the rate of interest is $r = 0.10$ and that the transfer payment in each period is equal to $b = 25$. To take a set of 'benchmark' tax rates, let $t = 0.3$ and $t_c = t_y = t_b = 0.10$. The compulsory superannuation contribution in the benchmark case is assumed to be $x = 0.10$. When lifetime plans are made subject to these rates, the fact that time preference exceeds the rate of interest means that optimal consumption falls over time: it takes the values $56.92, 53.43$ and 50.15 for periods 1, 2 and 3 respectively. Labour supply is 0.57 and 0.60 respectively in the first and second periods, while private savings in the first two periods are 4.03 and 9.13.

6.3.1   Complete Life-Cycle Plans

The effects of variations in each of the tax and contribution rates in isolation, where all other values are held constant at their benchmark values, are shown in Figures 6.1, 6.2 and 6.3. These diagrams show, for each period, the variations in savings, labour supply and the 'price of leisure', as the relevant tax or contribution rate increases. For example, the top left-hand segment of Figure 6.1 shows the variation in the individual's private savings (that is, excluding compulsory superannuation contributions) in periods 1 and 2 as the tax rate on superannuation benefits increases, with all other parameters fixed at their benchmark values. Private savings in period 1 are consistently below those of period 2, in view of the assumptions regarding time preference and the rate of interest. The diagrams show that a reduction in the tax rate on superannuation benefits reduces private savings while increasing labour supply in each period of the working life, as the price of leisure increases.

The changes shown in these figures are comparative static in nature: they indicate how each variable 'responds' to changes in a single tax or contribution rate, when the optimal plans of such an individual are made at the beginning of the life cycle with full knowledge of those rates. They can be used to give some idea of the effects on an individual at the start of the life cycle of a change in the tax structure, using the kind of relationship shown in equation (6.24). For example, an increase in t_b can, on its own, be seen to result in a reduction in labour supply in both periods. Also, the partial effect of a rise in t is to reduce labour supply in both periods. The government budget constraint implies that t and t_b must change in opposite directions, as $\left.\frac{dt}{dt_b}\right|_R < 0$; therefore a revenue neutral change in t_b does not

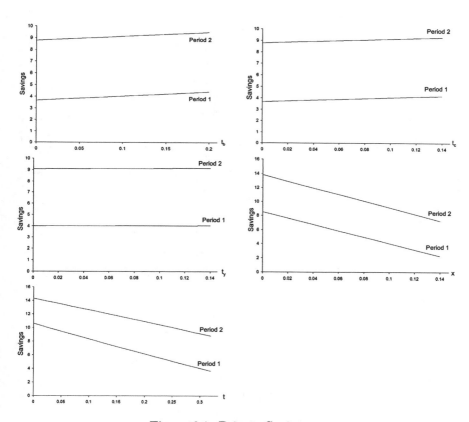

Figure 6.1: Private Savings

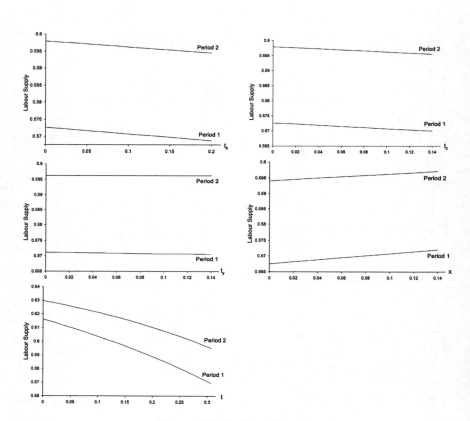

Figure 6.2: Labour Supply

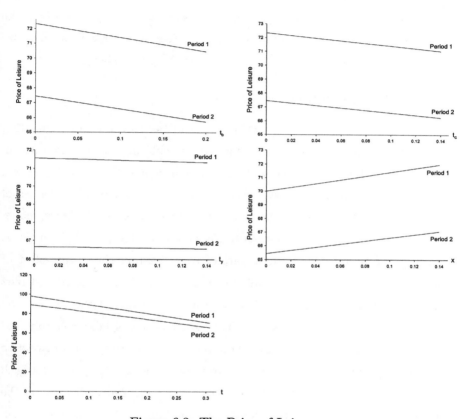

Figure 6.3: The Price of Leisure

give an unambiguous change in labour supply.

However, the effect on private savings is clear *a priori*, since a reduction in t_b on its own leads to a reduction in private savings, while the increase in t also leads to a reduction in private savings. Hence, irrespective of the size of the various effects, including the precise tax changes needed, it can be said that a revenue-neutral reduction in t_b reduces private savings for those at the beginning of the life cycle when the change takes place; that is, savings are lower than they otherwise would be, without the policy change.

6.3.2   Unanticipated Changes

Consider next the effects of a change in the tax rate on superannuation benefits, as it applies to an individual who is entering the second stage in the life cycle. Let $t_b' = 0$, representing a move from a TTT to a TTE system. Figures 6.4, 6.5 and 6.6 show, respectively, the revised period-2 values of labour supply, the price of leisure and private savings. Each figure shows, as a horizontal line, the pre-reform planned value for period 2, made at the start of period 1. The first part of each diagram shows the effect of combining $t_b' = 0$ with a new value of income tax, t, and the second part shows the effect of combining $t_b' = 0$ with a new value of the tax rate on superannuation contributions, t_c. The revised values of labour supply and savings in period 2 were found to show very little sensitivity with respect to changes in t_y, and are therefore not shown here. The starting point for each tax rate (that is the initial value of the relevant tax rate indicated on the horizontal axis) is the benchmark rate indicated above. For example the top part of Figure 6.4 indicates that the abolition of the tax on benefits from the superannuation fund during retirement produces, on its own, an increase in labour supply. But the resulting increase in t, required to achieve revenue neutrality, produces, as a partial effect, a reduction in labour supply. Hence the move to TTE can increase labour supply in period 2, compared with the

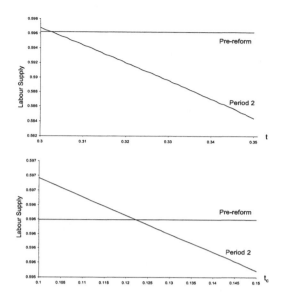

Figure 6.4: Labour Supply Following Change to TTE

pre-reform plan, only if it is accompanied by a very small increase in t. The effect on labour supply cannot therefore be predicted *a priori* – considerable information is needed merely to predict the direction of the change.

However, from Figure 6.6 it can be seen that private savings in period 2 unequivocally fall, compared with the pre-reform plans, as a result of the combined effect of the drop in t_b to zero combined with an increase in t: this is because both the drop in t_b and the increase in t have the same partial effects. When a policy shift from TTT to TTE is accompanied by an increase in t_c, required for revenue neutrality, the partial effects on saving plans do not move in the same direction. Nevertheless, it can be seen that a substantial increase in t_c would be required for savings in period 2 to increase relative to pre-reform plans.

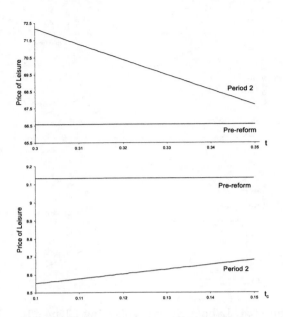

Figure 6.5: The Price of Leisure Following Change to TTE

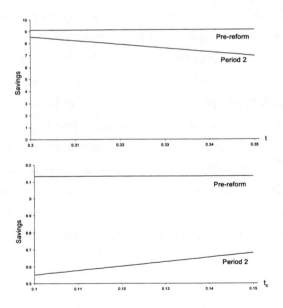

Figure 6.6: Private Savings Following Move to TTE

6.4 Conclusions

This chapter has provided a three-period analysis of anticipated and unanticipated changes in the taxation of superannuation. In particular it has analysed the effects on an individual's labour supply, consumption and private saving behaviour in the first two periods of the life cycle of tax changes. Particular attention was given to the case where the individual is in the middle stage of the life cycle when the tax change is made and therefore must, as a result of the unanticipated nature of the policy change, revise the plans previously made which influenced decisions taken in the first period. The model applies to a single individual, and therefore does not allow for any general equilibrium effects – for example on the wage rate in each period. The analysis has indicated that, even in the context of a highly simplified life cycle model with simple proportional taxes – indeed the basic structure of the model could hardly be simpler – determination of the effects of tax changes is highly complex.

It was nevertheless shown that the partial effects of tax changes, including a superannuation tax change, can be predicted both for those at the beginning and in the middle of the life cycle when the policy change occurs. Allowance was then made for the need to impose a revenue neutral change, and consideration was given to the direction of tax changes arising from the government's budget constraint. It was found that a move from a TTT to a TTE tax structure, requiring a combination of the elimination of the tax on superannuation benefits with an increase in one or more other taxes, has an unambiguous effect on individual private savings, irrespective of the stage in the life cycle when the policy change occurs – private savings fall. However, although the tax shift to TTE on its own increases labour supply, when combined with the income tax or contributions tax increase required for revenue neutrality, the overall effect on labour supply cannot be predicted *a priori*. It is suggested that the approach taken here provides a useful demonstration of the elements required of a much larger model which might be designed to handle aggregation and general equilibrium considerations.

Chapter 7

Private Pensions and Savings

Private pension tax structures can be broadly described in terms of the treatment during three separate stages. These concern the contributions to a pension fund from pre-tax income, the earnings obtained by the fund and the income withdrawn from the fund after retirement. The aim of this chapter is to examine unanticpicated shifts from a structure in which tax is imposed at each stage to alternative structures, using an overlapping generations general equilibrium model.

The model presented here is quite general in form and can be applied to a variety of countries. However, this chapter is motivated by the changes to the taxation of superannuation announced in the 2006 Australian Government Budget. Superannuation is the Australian term for private pensions and in this chapter the two terms are used synonymously. One important change was the decision to exempt from tax all superannuation benefits from taxed funds, whether taken in the form of a lump sum or annuity, for all people over 60 years of age and to apply from 1 July 2007. Australia was previously the only OECD country to tax superannuation at all three stages (see Horne, 2002). This policy change was unanticipated and therefore has the potential to significantly affect saving plans, especially for middle-aged workers, with resulting implications for intergenerational equity. There are also potential general equilibrium effects. Changes in tax rates can affect the relative price of leisure and present consumption relative to future consumption, thereby affecting labour supply and saving.

The budgetary implications for the government may be non-trivial given population ageing because the government has cut off a revenue stream that would otherwise have grown with the increasing proportion of households who are self-funded retirees. This is likely to be a bigger issue if superannuation contribution rates increase in response to the new tax incentives.[1] Importantly, the government faces a budget constraint, which implies that other taxes must ultimately rise, or spending must fall, in response to the superannuation tax concessions. These adjustments cause offsetting effects on labour supply, saving and equity.

It can be shown that under certain assumptions the various tax regimes are equivalent in the sense that a shift from one which taxes all stages (contributions, fund earnings and benefits), to one in which benefits are exempt, would have no effect on lifetime superannuation balances and therefore no behavioural effects for optimising agents; see the appendix to this chapter and, for a continuous time exposition, Kingston and Piggott (1993). However a critical assumption underlying this equivalence is neutrality with respect to superannuation revenue (in present value terms) which is unlikely to apply and could not be assumed by households to apply. This, and the fact that tax policy changes are almost always unanticipated by households, means that such changes have the potential to affect saving plans with resulting implications for intergenerational equity, macroeconomic variables and economic welfare. The initial effects are likely to be stronger than the long-term effects because the unanticipated nature of the policy causes relatively large

---

[1]Davidson and Guest (2007) calculated the potential fiscal costs of the tax exemption of superannuation benefits in the future given alternative assumptions about increasing contribution rates. The fiscal costs of the superannuation changes, while low at current contribution rates, could escalate substantially for modest increases in contribution rates. Their calculations were not based on optimising decisions and therefore did not attempt to model any general equilibrium effects, such as labour supply and saving responses, nor was there any consideration of intergenerational equity and social welfare.

adjustments immediately following the shock as middle aged households, in particular, adjust their behaviour over a short time frame.

The simulations ignore the many complexities of the regulations governing the taxation of superannuation which take into account a range of circumstances of taxpayers. Rather, the simulation model is based on the behaviour of a single representative household of each generation. This means that it cannot reveal effects on within-generation income inequality which could be substantial given the variation of superannuation balances of individuals within generations.[2]

Although the model determines the optimal labour–leisure choice of workers it does not consider the portfolio allocation problem in terms of the decision about the proportion of financial wealth to allocate between superannuation and other financial assets; the latter was analysed in a life-cycle model with endogenous leisure by, for example, Bodie, Merton and Samuelson (1992). Instead of endogenising the choice of portfolio mix the model assumes, in line with the Australian mandatory system, an exogenous and constant rate of superannuation contributions is initially assumed in the base case. Later, simulations are reported for increasing contribution rates over time. The retirement age is also exogenous. However, households optimally vary their labour force participation rates over their lifetime, given initial rates according to data. Kulish *et al.* (2006) examined a model of optimal retirement in response to population ageing in the Australian context, in order to consider the effects on the retirement age of changes in fertility and longevity, rather than to consider policy shocks as here.

The chapter proceeds as follows. Section 7.1 describes the simulation model. Section 7.2 describes the data and parameter values used to calibrate the model. Section 7.3 discusses the results.

---

[2]Atkinson, Creedy and Knox (1996) considered within-generation inequality in their analysis of alternative retirement income strategies using the LITES microsimulation model. But their model did not allow a general equilibrium analysis or an analysis of inequality between generations.

7.1   The Model

The simulation model is an open-economy, overlapping generations model with four sectors: firms, households, government and an overseas sector. These components are described in turn below.

7.1.1   Firms

A representative firm produces output of a single good according to a Cobb-Douglas production function. Output, Y, in period j is given by:

$$Y_j = A K_j^\alpha L_j^{1-\alpha} \qquad (7.1)$$

where K_j is the capital stock in period j and L_j is aggregate labour. The latter consists of the sum of the labour of all generations. Hence $L_j = \sum_{i=1}^{n} L_{i,j}$ where $L_{i,j}$ is the labour of generation i working in period j. The technology parameter, A, is constant, implying zero technical progress. The reason, as also given in Kulish *et al.* (2006), is that the leisure to consumption ratio would eventually decline to zero with continual productivity-induced rises in real wages; see Auerbach and Kotlikoff (1987) for a further discussion. It would be possible to introduce the parameter, A, into the utility function so that leisure grows at the same rate as consumption in the long run, but this is not pursued here.

The optimal capital stock, K_j, is determined by the first-order condition that the net marginal product of capital (net of depreciation, δ) is equal to the cost of capital, r, which is assumed to be constant implying the small open economy case. That is, $\frac{dY_j}{dK_j} - \delta = r$, which gives:

$$\frac{K_j}{L_j} = A \left(\frac{\alpha}{r + \delta} \right)^{1/(1-\alpha)} \qquad (7.2)$$

Investment, I_j, is given by:

$$I_j = K_j - K_{j-1} \left(1 - \delta \right) \qquad (7.3)$$

The price, $w_{L,j}$, of labour is equal to the marginal product of labour:

$$w_{L,j} = (1 - \alpha)A\left(\frac{K_j}{L_j}\right)^\alpha = \frac{Y_j}{L_j} - (r + \delta)\frac{K_j}{L_j} \qquad (7.4)$$

and it is a weighted average of the wages of all workers of age i in period j, $w_{L,i,j}$, which is achieved by calibration (see Section 7.2 below on data and parameters).

7.1.2 Households' Optimisation Problem

Firms produce a single good and households consume that good and leisure. A period of time is five years duration and a new generation of households is born each period; the use of five-year periods was chosen simply for computational convenience. Each household consists of one person who dies at age 90, implying that there are $h = 18$ overlapping generations of households alive at any time. The households supply labour for the $n = 11$ periods between the age of 15 and 70. Households pay tax on income from both capital and labour (discussed below). Future values of the demographic variables and the parameters are known with certainty, except for the policy shock which comes as a surprise at which time households must adjust their plans accordingly.

Households derive utility from consuming private goods, C, public goods, C_G (the price of which is normalised to one), and leisure, S. Following the approach in Foertsch (2004), C_G is exogenous and separable from both private consumption and leisure in generating utility. Therefore C_G does not affect the household's choice of private consumption or leisure. It is therefore ignored in the derivation of the household's optimisation problem. The assumption of separability between public and private consumption is a common assumption as noted in Foertsch (2004) because of lack of evidence about the substitutability between private and government consumption. The total resources available to the household from which to provide work effort are

normalised to 1; see the discussion of work intensity below. These resources
are time and a notional stock of 'effort'.

The composite index of consumption and leisure for a household of age i
is:

$$M_i = \left\{ \mu_i^{1/\Psi} C_i^{(\Psi-1)/\Psi} + (1 - \mu_i)^{1/\Psi} S_i^{(\Psi-1)/\Psi} \right\}^{\Psi/(\Psi-1)} \tag{7.5}$$

where Ψ is the elasticity of substitution between consumption and leisure.
The preference for consumption relative to leisure, captured by the parameter μ_i, is assumed to vary over the life cycle. It is assumed to rise up to
middle age and then fall. This pattern is designed to reflect the observed life
cycle pattern of consumption which tends to track the well-known observed
hump-shaped pattern of income to some degree, rising during the household's working life and falling after retirement. Hence μ_i follows an inverted
U-shape, given by the quadratic:

$$\mu_i = \xi_1 + \xi_2 i - \xi_3 i^2 \tag{7.6}$$

where ξ_1, ξ_2, ξ_3 and are parameters determined by calibration.

Each one-person household of age i in period j earns a wage, $w_{i,j}$. This is
less than the wage of each worker, $w_{L,i,j}$ in order to reflect a labour force participation rate of less than 1[3]. Hence $w_{i,j} = w_{L,i,j} L_{i,j}/N_{i,j}$. Superannuation
is deducted from earnings at an exogenous and constant rate of x per cent,
with the remainder of earnings subject to income tax at the rate, t_j. The
tax rates $t_{s,j}$, $t_{e,j}$ and $t_{b,j}$ are the tax rates on, respectively, superannuation
contributions, income on fund assets, $r_j B_{i,j}$, and end benefits, $B_{n,j}$, in period
j.

Households maximise the following lifetime utility function:

$$U = \sum_{i=1}^{h} \frac{M_i^{1-\beta}}{1 - \beta}(1 + \theta)^{1-i} + v(C_G) \tag{7.7}$$

---

[3]This is because the representative individuals must be workers, rather than non-
participants.

where θ is the pure time preference rate and β is the elasticity of marginal utility. The price of private consumption goods is normalised to 1 in each period, and the 'price of leisure' at age i in period j is denoted $p_{i,j}$. Utility is maximised subject to a lifetime budget constraint which takes the following form:

$$
\sum_{i=1}^{h} (C_i + S_i p_{i,j}) \left(\frac{1}{1 + r(1 - t_{y,j})} \right)^{i-1}
$$
$$
= \sum_{i=1}^{h} (p_{i,j} + f_{i,j}) \left(\frac{1}{1 + r(1 - t_{y,j})} \right)^{i-1} + Q \left(\frac{1}{1 + r(1 - t_{y,j})} \right)^{h-6}
$$
$$
- X \left(\frac{1}{1 + r(1 - t_{y,j})} \right)^{h} \tag{7.8}
$$

The left-hand side represents the present value of expenditure (on private consumption goods and leisure) and the right-hand side is the present value of lifetime income. The latter is defined to include transfer payments, $f_{i,j}$, received by households aged i in period j, an inheritance, Q, which is assumed to be received when the household is aged $h - 6 = 12$ and a bequest, X, made in period h. Households leave a bequest equal to 10 per cent of their total lifetime pre-tax income. The bequest is received by the generation 30 years younger, which is a simplification for the purpose of generating lifetime budgets because the demographic data used for the simulations reflects the actual patterns of age-specific fertility. For simplicity, total transfer payments paid by the government in a given period are allocated evenly across all households alive in that period, rather than being allocated to certain generations. Hence total transfers in period j are $f_j = N_j f_{i,j}$. The tax rate, $t_{y,j}$„ is the tax rate in period j applying to income from both labour and financial assets other than superannuation.

7.1.3   The Effective Price of Leisure

It can be shown, following the approach used in chapter 6, that the effective price of leisure in each period can be expressed as $p_{i,j} = E_{i,j} w_{i,j}$ where $E_{i,j}$ is the following function of the interest rate, tax rates and the superannuation contribution proportion, x:

$$E_{i,j} = (1 - t_{y,j}) - x\Psi \qquad (7.9)$$

where:

$$\Psi = (1 - t_{y,j}) - \left(\frac{1 + r(1 - t_e)}{1 + r(1 - t_{y,j})}\right)^{n-i+1} (1 - t_c)\{1 - t_b[(1 - \phi)]\} \qquad (7.10)$$

Here t_e is the constant tax rate on superannuation fund earnings, t_c is constant the tax rate on superannuation contributions which are not otherwise subject to income tax, t_b is the constant tax rate on superannuation benefits, ϕ is the proportion of benefits which is tax-free, and x is the mandatory superannuation contribution rate equal to the proportion of gross earnings contributed to the superannuation fund.

It is instructive to consider the implications for $E_{i,j}$ under alternative tax regimes. Under a TTE regime, for which $t_b = 0$:

$$E_{i,j} = (1 - t_{y,j}) - x\left\{(1 - t_{y,j}) - \left(\frac{1 + r(1 - t_e)}{1 + r(1 - t_{y,j})}\right)^{n-i+1}(1 - t_c)\right\} \qquad (7.11)$$

If, in addition, $t_e = t_c = t$, $E_{i,j}$ again reduces to the simple form $E_{i,j} = (1 - t_{y,j})$.

Under an ETT regime, for which $t_c = 0$:

$$E_{i,j} = (1 - t_{y,j}) - x\left\{(1 - t_{y,j}) - \left(\frac{1 + r(1 - t_e)}{1 + r(1 - t_{y,j})}\right)^{n-i+1}(1 - t_b[1 - \phi])\right\}$$
$$\qquad (7.12)$$

and again if , $t_e = t_b = t$, then $E_{i,j}$ reduces to $E_{i,j} = (1 - t_{y,j})$. Finally, if in the TTT regime all tax rates on superannuation are the same and equal to t_y, and there is no tax free threshold on benefits ($\phi = 0$), then it can be seen that:

$$E_{i,j} = (1 - t_{y,j})(1 - xt_{y,j}) \qquad (7.13)$$

in which case superannuation taxation reduces the relative price of leisure in the standard model by a factor $xt_{y,j}$, reflecting the size of the contribution, x, and the tax on superannuation at all stages, $t_{y,j}$.

7.1.4   Optimal Plans of Households

The household's superannuation fund balance at age i in period j is:

$$B_{i,j} = \begin{cases} B_{i-1,j-1}(1 + r(1 - t_e)) + (1 - t_c)xw_{i,j}L_{i,j} & i = 4, ..., 13 \\ B_{i-1,j-1}(1 + r(1 - t_e))(1 - t_b[1 - \phi]) & i = 14 \end{cases} \quad (7.14)$$

which assumes that workers retire at the age of 70 ($h - 4 = 14$), at which time superannuation is withdrawn and absorbed into other financial assets. This is a simplification and an alternative would be to allow funds to be retained in superannuation accounts during retirement and thereby attract the concessional tax rate, t_e. This is not modelled here because it would require a determination of the division of financial assets between superannuation and other assets in each period during retirement.

The balance of other financial assets at age i in period j is given by:

$$B_{F,i,j} = \begin{cases} B_{F,i-1,j-1}(1 + r(1 - t_{y,j})) \\ \quad + w_{i,j}L_{i,j}(1 - x)(1 - t_{y,j}) - C_{i,j} + f_{i,j} & \begin{matrix} i = 1, ..., 11, \\ 14, ..., 18 \end{matrix} \\ B_{F,i-1,j-1}(1 + r(1 - t_{y,j})) \\ \quad + w_{i,j}L_{i,j}(1 - x)(1 - t_{y,j}) - C_{i,j} + f_{i,j} + Q & i = 12 \\ \left(B_{F,i-1,j-1} + B_{i-1,j-1}\right)\left(1 + r\left(1 - t_{y,j}\right)\right) \\ \quad + w_{i,j}L_{i,j}\left(1 - x\right)\left(1 - t_{y,j}\right) - C_{i,j} + f_{i,j} & i = 15 \end{cases}$$

$$(7.15)$$

Given the (intertemporally) additive nature of the household's lifetime utility function, the optimisation problem can be solved in two stages. First, the profile of the consumption index, M, over the life cycle must be determined. The household's intertemporal problem is solved by maximising the utility function in (7.7) subject to the budget constraint (7.8). This yields the following relation between consumption of goods and leisure:

$$\frac{\mu_i S_{i,j}}{(1 - \mu_i)C_{i,j}} = p_{i,j}^{-\Psi} \quad (7.16)$$

Solving (7.16) for $S_{i,j}$ and substituting into (7.5), yields:

$$C_{i,j} = M_{i,j}\mu_i[\{\mu_i + (1 - \mu_i) p_{i,j}^{1-\Psi}\}^{\Psi/1-\Psi} \quad (7.17)$$

and repeating for $C_{i,j}$ yields:

$$S_{i,j} = M_{i,j}(1 - \mu_i)p_{i,j}^{\Psi}[\{\mu_i + (1 - \mu_i)\,p_{i,j}^{1-\Psi}\}^{\Psi/1-\Psi} \tag{7.18}$$

Defining $P_{i,j}$ as the minimum price that buys a unit of the consumption index, $M_{i,j}$ it is possible to write $P_{i,j}M_{i,j} = C_{i,j} + p_{i,j}S_{i,j}$ into which is substituted (7.17) and (7.18), yielding:

$$P_{i,j} = [\{\mu_i + (1 - \mu_i)\,p_{i,j}^{1-\Psi}\}^{1/1-\Psi} \tag{7.19}$$

Hence (7.17) and (7.18) can be simplified using (7.19) to give:

$$C_{i,j} = \mu_i \left(\frac{1}{P_{i,j}}\right)^{-\Psi} M_{i,j} \tag{7.20}$$

$$S_{i,j} = (1 - \mu_i)\left(\frac{p}{P}\right)_{i,j}^{-\Psi} M_{i,j} \tag{7.21}$$

To obtain the Euler equation, first use (7.20) and (7.21) to substitute for $C_{i,j}$ and $S_{i,j}$ in the budget constraint (7.8). Then maximise the utility function (7.7) with respect to $M_{i,j}$ subject to (7.8). This yields:

$$\frac{M_{i,j}}{M_{i-1,j-1}} = \left[\frac{1 + r(1 - t_{y,j})}{1 + \theta}\left(\frac{P_{i-1,j-1}}{P_{i,j}}\right)\right]^{1/\beta} \tag{7.22}$$

The solution to the optimisation problem can be obtained numerically as follows. Specify a trial value of $M_{i,j}$ for $i = 1$, then solve forward for $M_{i,j}$ for $i = 1, ..., h$ according to the Euler equation (7.22). For $i = 1, ..h$ calculate $C_{i,j}$ and $S_{i,j}$ according to (7.20) and (7.21). Then calculate $B_{F,h,j}$; if it does not equal the target bequest, then adjust $M_{i,j}$ for $i = 1$ and repeat the algorithm iteratively until the target bequest is met within a degree of tolerance. When the unanticipated superannuation change occurs, households will be at various stages of their lifetime plans – young households will be nearer to the start than older households. At this point they revise their plans for the remainder of their lifetimes given the new relative price of leisure, $p_{i,j}$ and any change in transfer payments, $f_{i,j}$ due to the need for the government to balance its budget.

The labour supply of households aged i in period j, $L_{i,j}$, is equal to $1 - S_{i,j}$, by appropriate normalising of the raw demographic data. The labour market is assumed to clear in each period. Competitive firms demand labour up to the point where the marginal product of labour is equal to the real wage, according to (7.4). Labour supply depends on the real wage via the demand for leisure of each household. The real wage adjusts instantaneously to equate labour demand to labour supply. Firms then adjust their demand for capital in response to the level of employment in order to maintain the desired capital–labour ratio, which is determined by (7.2).

7.1.5 Government

Government spending is denoted, G, and, other than transfer payments, is assumed for simplicity to be government consumption spending. Hence:

$$G_j = C_{G,j} + f_j \tag{7.23}$$

An assumption maintained throughout the simulations is that the government runs balanced budgets every period, so that:

$$G_j = T_j \tag{7.24}$$

where T_j denotes total tax revenue, given by

$$T_j = T_{W,j} + T_{K,j} + T_{S,j} \tag{7.25}$$

and where T_W is tax levied on wage income, T_K is tax levied on income from financial assets other than superannuation, T_S is tax levied on superannuation at the constant rates t_c, t_y and t_b as defined above. These can therefore be expressed as:

$$T_{W,j} = \sum_{i=1}^{h} w_{i,j} L_{i,j} (1 - x) t_{y,j} \tag{7.26}$$

$$T_{K,j} = \sum_{i=1}^{h} B_{F,i,j} r t_{y,j} \tag{7.27}$$

$$T_{S,j} = x t_c \sum_{i=1}^{h} w_{i,j} L_{i,j} + t_e r \sum_{i=1}^{h} B_{i,j} N_{i,j} + t_b (1 - \phi) B_{14,j} N_{14,j} \tag{7.28}$$

Substituting (7.27) into (7.25) gives an expression for $t_{y,j}$ of the form:

$$t_{y,j} = \frac{T_j - T_{s,j}}{\displaystyle\sum_{i=1}^{h} B_{i,j} r + \sum_{i=1}^{h} w_{i,j} L_{i,j} (1 - x)} \tag{7.29}$$

However, this expression is actually highly nonlinear in $t_{y,j}$ because several terms on the right-hand side are functions of this and other tax rates. Hence the budget constraint must be solved numerically, which is achieved through the iterative procedure of solving the life-cycle plans of households, as follows. Households are assumed to have perfect foresight and therefore know the future values of all variables that affect their plans, one of which is the tax rate, $t_{y,j}$. Their plans are solved iteratively starting with a trial vector of values of all future variables; each new plan uses the updated vector until the values stabilise.

The balanced budget condition implies that a reduction in taxation on superannuation must be budget neutral and therefore must be accompanied by either raising the tax rate applying to non-superannuation income, or reducing government spending. In the simulations it is assumed that the adjustment falls on government spending in the form of transfer payments, f_j. The alternative would be to adjust the tax rates applying to non-superannuation income. Therefore f_j is reduced to match any reduction in superannuation revenue. This implies a reduction in the household budget which therefore affects consumption of goods and leisure.

The small open economy paradigm is applied, implying that the interest rate is exogenous and equal to the world interest rate. There is only one good (other than leisure) implying no distinction between traded and non-traded goods which in turn implies a constant real exchange rate of one. Given these assumptions, the standard national accounting identity gives the evolution of foreign liabilities:

$$D_j = D_{j-1}(1+r) + \sum_{i=1}^{T} C_{i,j} + C_{G,j} + I_j - Y_j \tag{7.30}$$

7.1.6 Value Judgements

Any evaluation of the path of aggregate consumption over time requires value judgements about consumption in the future relative to present consumption to be made explicit. This is achieved by using a social welfare function, which is assumed to represent the veiws of an independent judge. First, it is assumed that the judge evaluates only the consumption that occurs in the present and the future, implying that there is no regard for past consumption even by generations still alive, on the grounds that past consumption cannot be influenced by current and future policy.

The social welfare function used to evaluate alternative time profiles is:

$$V = \sum_{j=1}^{H} N_j \left[\frac{M_j}{1 - \beta_s} \right]^{1-\beta_s} (1 + \theta_s)^{1-j} \tag{7.31}$$

where $M_j = \sum_{j=1}^{h} M_{i,j}$ is the aggregate value of the consumption index of all households alive in period j; $j = 1$ in 2005; H is arbitrarily far in the future. The parameter θ_s is the pure rate of time preference of the judge and β_s reflects the constant relative aversion to variability of the judge: it is the (absolute value of the) elasticity of marginal valuation. The form of the social welfare function also assumes that the judge takes the view that the appropriate unit of analysis is the individual, so that values are weighted by N_j in each period.

7.2   Calibration of the Model

This section describes the calibration of the model for Australia. Government spending as a share of GDP is set equal to 0.3 for the period up to 2005 after which it increases at the same rate as age-related spending as calculated by the Australian Government in Productivity Commission (2005). The categories of age-related government consumption spending are given in Productivity Commission (2005) and consist of health, aged care, carers and education; and the categories of f_j are age and service pensions, family tax benefits, disability support benefit, unemployment allowances and parenting payments. Age-related spending of the Australian Government is projected to increase by 5.7 per cent between 2004 and 2045 according to the Productivity Commission (2005).

The calibration is such that the size of superannuation tax revenues as a proportion of GDP in 2005 is equal to those reported for the year 2004 by the Institute of Actuaries of Australia (IAA) (2006). The IAA calculates the following superannuation tax revenues as percentages of GDP for 2004: contributions tax of 0.5 per cent, income tax on fund income of 0.2 per cent, and benefits tax of 0.05 per cent. For the contributions tax, the value of x is set at that giving the total of 0.5 per cent of GDP in 2005. This figure turns out to be 5 per cent which is less than the 9 per cent compulsory contribution rate currently applying in Australia. This is at least partly because the 5 per cent is assumed to apply to all labour income in the economy whereas in reality some self-employed and casual workers would not contribute to superannuation at 9 per cent (although some workers would contribute more than 9 per cent). The IAA points out that a small proportion of superannuation benefits attract the benefits tax, due to the tax-free proportion, and there are ways in which the tax can be avoided. A value of the tax-free proportion, ϕ, equal to 0.8 generates the IAA figure of 0.05 per cent of GDP for the benefits tax. The interest rate on superannuation fund income is assumed to be equal to the constant interest rate, r, which applies to all forms of saving and borrowing. This generates tax revenue from super fund income equal to 0.12 per cent of GDP which is less than the IAA figure of 0.2 per cent but close enough to avoid the complication of setting a return on super fund income higher than r.

It is also necessary to allow for the likely growing popularity of superannuation as a saving vehicle. In Australia, superannuation assets have been projected to more than double between 2005 and 2020 (IFSA, 2007), compared with an increase in GDP in the order of 60 per cent (at 3 per cent compound growth). Hence superannuation assets to GDP could nearly double over this period. There are several reasons for this growth. The Investment and Financial Services Association (IFSA) (2007) reports a study suggesting that 23 per cent of this growth can be attributed to the changes introduced in the 2006 Australian Government Budget. Other factors include: the cumulative effect of the 9 per cent compulsory contribution rate that has applied since July 2002; the growing awareness of the benefits of superannuation and its increasing flexibility; and an older workforce implying a higher average propensity for superannuation saving across the workforce.

Hence, an alternative set of simulations allow x to increase gradually over time from its base case rate of 5 per cent, increasing by 1 per cent every 5 year period after 2005 implying that, by 2050, 14 per cent of labour income is being contributed to superannuation. This is plausible given the growth in popularity of superannuation which will be accentuated in Australia by the incentives introduced in the 2006 Budget. However, this does not apply to the base case simulations, for which x is fixed at 5 per cent.

The demographic data consist of actual historical population levels, and projected future population levels, for each age group. These data are given in the following Australian Bureau of Statistics (ABS) Catalogues: historic population, Catalogue 320109.1; projected population, Catalogue 3222.0; labour force participation rates by age, Catalogue 6291.0; and wage rates by age,

Catalogue 6310.0. The data source for government expenditure is Productivity Commission (2005).

The wage of each worker by age in period j, $w_{L,i,j}$, is calibrated such that the weighted average of $w_{L,i,j}$ over all workers of age i in period j is equal to the price of labour, $w_{L,j}$; that is:

$$\sum_i w_{L,i,j} L_{i,j} = w_{L,j} L_j \qquad (7.32)$$

This is achieved by first normalising exogenous data on wages by age,$\bar{w}_{L,i,j}$, such that $\sum_i \bar{w}_{L,i,j} = 1$. The $\bar{w}_{L,i,j}$ are then weighted by:

$$\gamma_j = \frac{w_{L,j} L_j}{\sum_i \bar{w}_{L,i,j} L_{i,j}} \qquad (7.33)$$

giving:

$$w_{L,i,j} = \bar{w}_{L,i,j} \gamma_j \qquad (7.34)$$

Table 7.1 presents other parameter values. The interest rate of 4 per cent is a typical value of the world interest rate used in CGE simulations; the assumption is that Australia is a small open economy. Households' rate of time preference, θ, is set equal to $r(1 - 0.3)$ where 0.3 is the initial tax rate, since this is consistent with constant initial consumption.

The capital share parameter in the Cobb–Douglas production function is consistent with a capital to output ratio of 3.0, its approximate value for Australia in 2005. The initial tax to GDP ratio is set equal to 0.3 which is also the approximate actual value for Australia in 2005. The ratio of foreign liabilities to GDP, D/Y, in 2005 is calibrated so that it equals 0.6 (which is approximately the actual value) by finding the ratio of D/Y in 1920 that gives D/Y =0.6 in 2005, where 1920 is the year in which household aged 85 in 2005 was born. The values of the elasticities, β and Ψ, are set equal to common values used in related studies in the literature, see for example Foertsch (2004).

Table 7.1: Base Case Parameters and Initial Values

Parameter		Value
Interest rate	r	0.04
Rate of time preference of households	θ	0.028
Capital elasticity of output	α	0.27
Depreciation	δ	0.05
Initial capital to output ratio	$\frac{\bar{K}}{Y}$	3.0
Foreign liabilities to GDP ratio in 2003	D/Y	0.6
Elasticity of marginal utility	β	2.0
Elasticity of substitution between consumption and leisure	Ψ	0.8
Bequest as a proportion of a household's lifetime income		0.1
Initial tax rate on all non-superannuation income	t_y	0.3
Tax rate on contributions to superannuation funds	t_c	0.15
Tax rate on investment income of superannuation funds	t_e	0.15
Tax rate on superannuation benefits	t_b	0.15
Superannuation contributions as a proportion of wages	x	0.05
Quadratic parameters in function for μ_i	$\xi_1,$	-0.004
	$\xi_2,$	0.066
	ξ_3	0.338

A sensitivity analysis with respect to these parameter values indicated that the effects of the superannuation tax concessions were robust with respect to a reasonable range of values for each parameter. In all of the sensitivity simulations conducted, the effect of the tax concession on any endogenous variable in any given period was within 15 percent of the effect under the base case parameter value. For example, if the effect of a tax concession were to boost lifetime consumption for a particular generation by 0.5 percent, then no variation in a single parameter produced an effect outside plus or minus 15 per cent of 0.5 per cent, which is a range of 0.42 to 0.58 percent.

There is no assumption that the economy is in a steady state prior to the tax smoothing policy shock, nor that the economy converges to a steady state. Nevertheless, the overlapping generations feature of the model generates fairly well-behaved state variables. In particular, debt and the capital stock do not take extreme values at any point in the optimal path. In the case where taxation is imposed at all three stages, the three superannuation tax rates are set equal to 15 per cent. An exemption of income from any of the three taxes implies setting the relevant tax rate equal to zero from 2005 onwards.

7.3   Simulation Results

The aim of this section is to compare the various tax regimes for superannuation. It is convenient to introduce standard notation to describe the regimes. The letters T and E are used respectively to indicate whether the component is taxed or is exempt, so that, for example, a system is described as being of the TTT variety if tax is imposed in all three stages. Hence possible structures can be described as TTT, TTE, ETT and EET. These alternatives are compared here in terms of their implications for intergenerational equity, national living standards, labour supply, national saving and social welfare.

7.3.1   Consumption

Consider first the effect of alternative tax regimes on lifetime consumption of successive generations. Unless otherwise stated, 'consumption' refers to the value of the consumption index, M, and lifetime consumption is the sum of consumption over the household's life.[4] The effect of a change in tax regime on lifetime consumption depends on its effect on lifetime income, as reflected in the budget constraint, (7.8). The elimination of a superannuation tax implies an increase in the after-tax wage or relative price of leisure, $p_{i,j}$. This is offset by a decrease in transfer payments, $f_{i,j}$, according to the assumption that the government balances its budget in each period by offsetting any change in superannuation revenue by a dollar-for-dollar change in transfer

---

[4] An alternative would have been to consider the effects on goods consumption, C, only, thereby ignoring leisure. Inspection of the simulation results showed the effects on goods consumption, C, were not qualitatively different to the effects on the consumption index, M.

payments. However, the offset is not exact for several reasons. The main reason is that the tax change is unanticipated, the effect of which is discussed further below; and there are other minor factors at work meaning that even if the tax change were entirely anticipated there would still be small net effects on lifetime income which would differ among generations. In any given period the budgetary cost of the tax exemption, which is met by a reduction in transfer payments, is spread evenly across all households, whereas the boost in after-tax income accrues more to households at a higher income stage of their lifecycle. Also, the cost in lost transfer payments relative to the gain in after-tax labour income in a given period also depends on the support ratio.

Figure 7.1 plots the difference between lifetime consumption under three alternative tax regimes: TTE, ETT and EET, compared with the base case: TTT.

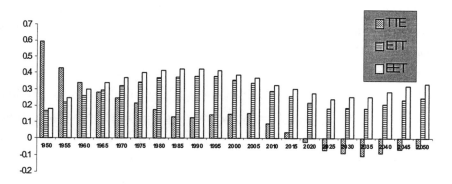

Figure 7.1: Percentage Change in Lifetime Consumption by Generation

Exempting benefits in the TTE system boosts the after-tax superannuation balances of older generations more than it does for younger generations because older generations have larger balances at the time the exemption is introduced and hence receive a relatively large windfall, yet they have not had to pay for the cost of this windfall through lower transfer payments during their lives. However, younger generations however pay for the tax exemption enjoyed by older generations before they in turn receive the tax exemption. Hence the net lifetime gain to older generations is greater than for younger generations. This is reflected in the declining size of the bars in Figure 7.1 for the TTE case.

Exempting super contributions (ETT) generates the opposite pattern on lifetime consumption of successive generations. It boosts the after-tax super-annuation balances of younger generations more than that of older genera-tions for the simple reason that younger generations have more years from which to benefit from higher after tax contributions than older generations. Hence, Figure 7.1 displays a rise in the size of the bars for successive genera-tions from the 1950 generation to generations born recently. For subsequent generations the ETT series follows a slight cyclical pattern. This can be explained by the cyclical pattern of the support ratio. The support ratio at a given time determines the superannuation contributions for all workers alive at that time. Hence when the support ratio is falling, the size of super contributions is falling and the benefit of a tax exemption on contributions is therefore smaller. This explains the relatively smaller gain for generations born around 2025 because the support ratio falls quite steeply at that time.

The EET case turns out to be little different from the ETT case in its effect on lifetime consumption (see Figure 7.1) and other variables of interest. This implies that exempting from tax superannuation fund income as well as contributions makes little difference. This can be verified by differentiating (7.11) with respect to each of the tax rates, which shows that the impact of t_e is smaller than for the other tax rates. For this reason results for the EET case are not reported beyond the result given in Figure 7.1.

Figure 7.2 shows the effect of the ETT and TTE regimes on average consumption per capita, or living standards, in each period from 2005 to 2050. In the initial few periods from 2005 the impact on living standards is greater in the TTE case than the ETT case. This is because of the large adjustment of older generations as described above. However, over time this relationship is reversed – the ETT effect becomes greater. In the long term, the effect of removing the benefits tax is relatively small because the tax free threshold on benefits implies that only 20 per cent of benefits are subject to tax, whereas 100 per cent of contributions are subject to tax. The absolute size of the effect on consumption per capita declines from 1.4 to 0.2 per cent in the TTE case and from 0.8 to 0.4 per cent in the ETT case.

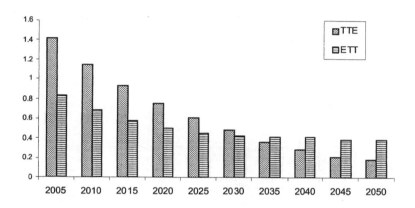

Figure 7.2: Percentage Boost to Living Standards

7.3.2 Labour Supply

The effect on labour supply depends on the difference between the income effect and the substitution effect. More precisely, the labour supply effect is measured by the elasticity of demand for leisure with respect to the tax rate which equals the difference between the elasticity of future full income with respect to the tax rate and the elasticity of the price of leisure with respect to the tax rate.

In the TTE case, the elasticity of future full income is relatively large for older generations because the reduction in benefits tax applies to all of

their past accrued benefits, and is therefore a relatively large proportion
of their remaining lifetime full income compared with the case for younger
generations. Hence the income effect for older generations is relatively strong
and outweighs the substitution effect resulting in a larger decline in labour
supply for older households; see Figure 7.3. A way of interpreting this is that
older households have, in hindsight, overworked during their lives in aiming
for their target bequest. They immediately adjust by buying more leisure
and hence reducing their labour supply. As the effect on the labour supply
of older generations falls, the aggregate effect on labour supply diminishes
over time, as shown in Figure 7.3.

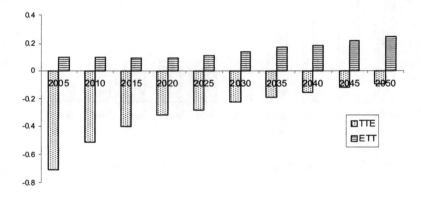

Figure 7.3: Percentage Change in Aggregate Labour Supply

7.3.3   National Savings

The effects on national savings are reported because the desire to boost savings is a motive not just for superannuation reform in Australia but more
generally for pension reform in OECD countries. The aim is to shift the fund-
ing of retirement incomes from the public to the private sector. This requires

an increase in private saving so that the present generation of workers can fund the retirement incomes of two generations of workers – themselves and the current generation of retirees who still rely heavily on the public pension. However, the effect on private saving would be diminished to the extent that workers shift savings from other saving vehicles to superannuation. It has been estimated with respect to Australia for example that compulsory allocations of saving into superannuation results in up to a 50 per cent leakage from other saving vehicles (Freebairn, 1998). The question of interest here is whether such a leakage occurs in response to tax concessions on superannuation.

The assumptions of the model call for a qualified response to this question. For instance the portfolio allocation problem is ignored – the superannuation contribution rate is exogenous and constant. Households' bequests are also fixed as a proportion of lifetime income. Furthermore, the government's budget is balanced by reducing transfer payments dollar for dollar with any tax concession on superannuation. Given these assumptions and drawing on the earlier discussion, a lower tax rate on superannuation raises the price of leisure which calls for a substitution of consumption for leisure thereby reducing saving. This can be seen from (7.21) after substituting $E_{i,j}$ into $p_{i,j}$ and $P_{i,j}$. The income effect is close to zero because every dollar of superannuation tax concession is offset by a dollar reduction in transfer payments in terms of the effect on the government's budget. This is reflected in the lifetime budget constraint, (7.8), by an increase in $p_{i,j}$ offset by a decrease in $f_{i,j}$. The net outcome of a neutral income effect and a negative substitution effect on saving is a lower saving rate. This is illustrated in Figure 7.4.

Under all tax regimes the saving rate falls over time as the standard consequence of population ageing in models such as this – the reason being that the proportion of households at the age with high income and high saving declines. The tax concessions do not alter this effect qualitatively, but they reduce saving in all periods – in the ETT case by a constant 0.4 per

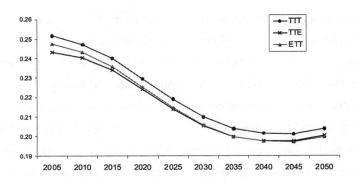

Figure 7.4: The National Saving Rate as Proportion of GDP

cent in all periods, and in the TTE case by 0.8 per cent initially and falling to 0.4 per cent by 2050.

7.3.4 Social Welfare

The measure of social welfare, V, is cardinal and therefore the effect on V can be calculated directly. The effect could in principle be sensitive to the choice of parameters β_s and θ_s. Hence results are reported for various combinations of values of these parameters. Except in the extreme case where $\beta_s = 10$, the effects on V are within 5 percent of the base case values.

The results are given in Table 7.2. Under the base case parameter values: $\beta_s = 2$ and $\theta_s = 3$ per cent, the effect of the TTE, ETT and EET regimes compared with the TTT regime is to increase social welfare by 0.38, 0.42 and 0.46 percent, respectively. The ranking by size of the effects is consistent with the results discussed above. One source of the welfare gain is the reduction in the distortionary effects of taxation since the elimination of a tax which distorts the price of leisure, $p_{i,j}$, is funded by a reduction transfer payments, $f_{i,j}$, which are in lump-sum form and therefore non-distortionary.

The welfare effect is also a result of the social evaluation of the intertemporal consumption effect of the change in taxation, which depends on the

Table 7.2: Effect on social welfare, V

θ_s	β_s	Percentage gain		
Per cent		TTE	ETT	EET
0.0	2.0	0.33	0.41	0.45
2.8	2.0	0.38	0.42	0.46
8.0	2.0	0.43	0.44	0.47
4.0	0.2	0.31	0.34	0.37
4.0	1.0	0.00	0.00	0.00
4.0	10.0	3.34	3.76	4.09

form and parameters of the social welfare function. In particular, consumption gains near to the present are 'worth' more than the same gains further in the future. This explains why the elimination of the benefits tax (TTE) yields a large welfare gain relative to the amount of tax revenue generated. It also explains why the welfare gains for smaller values of β_s tend to produce smaller welfare gains than for higher values of β_s, given that the annual gains in aggregate consumption tend to be greater in the short term following the shock. For example, the extremely high value of $\beta_s = 10.0$ produces a much greater welfare gain from the tax concessions because the relatively large gains in the short term are given much greater weight than the smaller gains in the long term.

7.3.5 Higher Superannuation Contribution Rates

For reasons discussed earlier, simulations were run where the superannuation contribution rate is gradually increased by 1 per cent every 5 year period after 2005 until 2050 by which time 14 per cent of labour income is being contributed to superannuation compared with the constant rate of 5 per cent in the previous simulations. Concern is not so much with the effect of higher contributions per se but the effect of the various tax exemptions, given higher contribution rates.

The higher contribution rate magnifies the effect of tax exemptions on

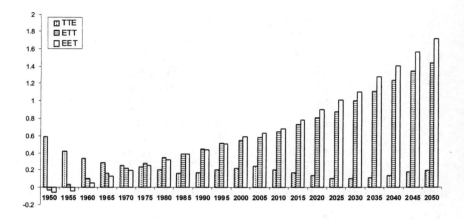

Figure 7.5: Percentage Change in Lifetime Consumption by Generation

lifetime consumption of successive generations, national living standards, aggregate labour supply and national saving. It generally does not alter the
patterns described for these variables, perhaps with one exception – the effect on lifetime consumption of successive generations, which is illustrated in
Figure 7.5. The difference in the pattern compared with that in Figure 7.1
is that because the contribution rate steadily increases, so does the lifetime
gain from exempting contributions from tax. By 2050 exempting contributions from tax would increase the lifetime consumption of the generation
born in 2050 by 1.7 per cent compared with 0.25 per cent in Figure 7.1.

The effect on national living standards is only slightly higher than for
the case of a constant 5 percent contribution rate which was illustrated in
Figure 7.2 – but the effect of the various tax exemptions on living standards
remains less than 1 per cent in any year. The boost to labour supply from
exempting contributions from taxation rises to 1 per cent by 2050 compared
with 0.2 per cent under a constant 5 percent contribution rate; see Figure
7.3. The effect in the case of the benefits tax exemption is slightly higher,
which means a smaller negative effect than that shown in Figure 7.3 – it

is zero by 2050. The national saving effect is virtually unchanged as is the effect on social welfare.

7.4 Conclusion

This chapter has shown that changes in the taxation of superannuation (the term for private pensions in this chapter) changes the lifetime consumption plans of households. The effect occurs through the after-tax wage which is the relative price of leisure and therefore affects the work–leisure choice. The income effect of the change in the after-tax wage is muted, in the model applied here, by offsetting reductions in government spending in order to balance the government's budget. The unanticipated nature of the effect causes a stronger response in the short-term because households make corrections to plans that have become inconsistent with their target bequest. The biggest short term adjustment occurs in the case of an unanticipated tax exemption on superannuation benefits because middle aged working households derive a windfall which causes relatively large adjustments to their labour supply and consumption.

The simulation results show that the intergenerational effects differ for a benefits tax exemption compared with a contributions tax exemption. The former confers a larger windfall on middle-aged households than on young or post-retirement households. The contribution tax exemption benefits younger households more than older households.

The positive outcome for social welfare of tax exemptions under all of the tax regimes modelled suggests that the reduction in taxation of superannuation is an unambiguous welfare improvement. However, as always simulation results reflect the assumptions of the model. Some of these assumptions have already been emphasised – the balanced budget assumption, the exogenous contribution rate, the exogenous bequest as a proportion of lifetime income. But also important is the representative agent assumption – that is, all households of a given generation are represented by a single household, so that there is no allowance for inequality within generations. This acts to qualify the results because changes in taxation and transfer payments do not in reality affect all households of a given generation equally. Accounting for within-generation equality would require a more complex microsimulation model.

Subject to these qualifications, the results have demonstrated the potential effects of superannuation tax exemptions on intergenerational equity, national accounting aggregates, and social welfare. Whether these effects are large enough to warrant further policy responses is a matter of judgement.

Appendix: Equivalence of TTT, TTE and ETT

This Appendix shows that the TTT, TTE and ETT models are equivalent under certain assumptions; see Kingston and Piggott (1993) for a continuous time exposition that also includes equivalence of EET. Let $xw_{i,j}$ be the pre-tax superannuation contribution in period i in year j; r_j be the return on the superannuation assets held in the fund in period j; $t_{s,j}$, $t_{e,j}$ and $t_{b,j}$ be the tax rates on superannuation contributions, investment income earned by superannuation funds, and end benefits respectively in period j; B_n the value of superannuation assets when withdrawn at the end of n number of periods of superannuation contributions. Assume that there are no tax-free thresholds, that contributions net of contributions tax are made at the start of each period and that the earnings tax is calculated on end of period values. The expression for B_n is:

$$B_n = \left(\sum_{i=1}^{n} xw_{i,j} \left(1 - t_{s,i}\right) \prod_{j=1}^{n} \left[1 + r_j \left(1 - t_{e,j}\right)\right] \right) \left(1 - t_{b,n}\right) \qquad (7.35)$$

If it is assumed that the tax rates on contributions and benefits are constant over time, then B_n becomes:

$$B_n = \left(\sum_{i=1}^{n} xw_{i,j} \prod_{j=1}^{n} \left[1 + r_j \left(1 - t_{e,j}\right)\right] \right) \left(1 - \left[t_c + t_b(1 - t_c)\right]\right) \quad (7.36)$$

$$= \left(\sum_{i=1}^{n} xw_{i,j} \prod_{j=1}^{n} \left[1 + r_j \left(1 - t_{e,j}\right)\right] \right) - T_{CB,j} \qquad (7.37)$$

where $T_{CB,J}$ is the sum of taxes paid on superannuation contributions and benefits over n periods. If a switch between the TTT, ETT and TTE regimes is both fully anticipated and neutral in its effect on $T_{CB,J}$ then B_n is unchanged, implying that the switch is Ricardian equivalent. In that case it would make no difference to forward-looking governments and investors whether tax is levied on the way into the fund or on the way out. However the assumptions of neutrality with respect to $T_{CB,J}$ and full anticipation of changes in tax policy are unrealistic. Hence an unanticipated shift from one regime to another can be expected to affect the lifecycle plans of households.

Part IV

Population Ageing

Chapter 8

Tax Smoothing and Population Ageing

The purpose of this chapter is to analyse the implications for intergenerational equity and social welfare of smoothing the fiscal costs of population ageing. This is done by simulating an overlapping generations computable general equilibrium (CGE) model, calibrated to the Australian economy, and using historical and projected demographic data along with projections of demographically sensitive government spending. The effects of tax smoothing on intergenerational equity are found by comparing the effects on lifetime utility of different generations; and the effects on social welfare are evaluated using a social welfare function.

The motivation for this exercise is the establishment in Australia of the Future Fund (FF). The FF was set up primarily to fully fund the Australian Government's superannuation liabilities, estimated in the 2005-2006 Budget papers to be around $91 billion. The Government plans to issue about $5billion of Commonwealth Government Securities each year by running budget surpluses. The surpluses will be deposited into the FF during the accumulation phase which is planned to occur up to at least 2020, after which funds can be withdrawn for the specific purpose of meeting the Australian Government's superannuation liabilities.

The FF is seen by the Government as a way of spreading the fiscal costs of population ageing over time, as implied in the Australian Government's 2005-2006 Budget Papers, Statement 7: '[the FF] will reduce calls on the budget in the future, at a time when significant intergenerational pressures are expected to emerge'. These 'pressures' are the spending implications of an ageing population. They consist mainly of health and aged care expenditures, and pensions, which are expected to account for an increase in spending of the Australian Government of 5.7 percent of GDP between 2005 and 2045 (Productivity Commission, 2005). Age-related spending by State Governments is expected to amount to additional 0.8 percent of GDP over the same period. The FF acts as a vehicle for pre-funding these expenses. This amounts to tax smoothing in the sense that current generations will bear a greater tax burden, and future generations a lower burden, than they would under continuously balanced budgets.

Guest (2006) compared the projections of the ageing-related government spending in Productivity Commission (2005) with projections using a general equilibrium model that allowed for various behavioural feedback effects in response to changes in tax rates. One aim was to see whether the behavioural feedback effects would make much difference to the spending projections. The model gave higher spending projections than those in Productivity Commission (2005) by an amount stabilising at 1 percent of GDP. The present chapter extends that study primarily by modelling intergenerational equity effects which requires an overlapping generations model, whereas the model in Guest (2006) was based on the behaviour of an infinitely lived household. The overlapping generations framework allows us to identify winners and losers from tax smoothing. The fact that some generations lose and some win as a result of tax smoothing implies the need for a social evaluation of tax smoothing. This is done using a social welfare function under a range of alternative value judgements regarding the choice of parameters.

There are other relevant studies. Cutler et al. (1990), a seminal study in the macroeconomics of population ageing for the U.S., found trivially small gains from tax smoothing of the costs of ageing. Floden (2003) argued that the findings of Cutler *et al.* (1990) apply to the U.S. only because tax rates there are relatively low. He found the efficiency gains to be non-trivial for a number of other OECD countries that have higher tax burdens. Both of these studies applied infinitely lived dynasty models and were therefore unable to say anything about intergenerational equity. Oksanen (2003), in a study for the European Commission, was concerned with intergenerational fairness of tax smoothing in response to population ageing, but applied a simple partial equilibrium analysis rather than a multi-sector CGE model. Oksanen concluded in favour of partial smoothing on intergenerational equity grounds. Davis and Fabling (2002) estimated the efficiency gains of smoothing the costs of ageing in New Zealand. They found gains a little larger than those in Cutler but smaller than those in Floden. However, theirs was also a partial analysis based on a calibrated deadweight loss function. The innovation in the present study is that it uses an overlapping generations CGE model to explicitly trace out the effects of tax smoothing on each age cohort and determines the effect on social welfare.

The chapter proceeds as follows. Section 8.1 focuses on the intergenerational equity effects of tax smoothing in simple terms using a diagrammatic approach. Section 8.2 describes the simulation model and Section 8.3 discusses the social welfare function including the role of social value judgements. The simulations and results are discussed in Section 8.4. A brief discussion of limitations of the model for the purpose of a social evaluation of tax smoothing via the Future Fund is in Section 8.5.

8.1 Effects of Tax Smoothing

The idea that governments should smooth the tax burden over time was first advanced by Barro (1979). He showed that, in a deterministic setting, a constant tax rate over time would minimise the distortions to behaviour arising from taxation. In doing so he assumed that the distortions would increase more than proportionally to increases in the tax rate, which had already been established analytically by Harberger (1964), cited in Browning (1987). An important distortion, or deadweight loss, arises from the substitution of leisure for work in response to taxation on labour. Also, taxes on income from capital distort consumption between time periods, favouring consumption today relative to consumption tomorrow (Lucas, 1990). A policy of tax smoothing would reduce the magnitude of these distortions and therefore lead to a more efficient allocation of resources.

8.1.1   Intergenerational Equity: An Illustrative Model

The basic intuition for the intergenerational welfare effects of tax smoothing can be illustrated using a simple stylised model. Assume single person households who live for four periods of equal duration. They attend full-time education in the first period during which they receive no income, they work in the second and third periods, and are retired in the fourth period. At any time therefore four overlapping generations exist: retired, middle-aged worker, young worker, and future worker (currently in full-time education). Assume a single tax rate applying to all income and that this tax rate is projected to rise over time, under a balanced budget policy, due to the fiscal pressure of population ageing. Now suppose that the government introduces an unanticipated policy to smooth the tax rate by switching from a balanced budget to a budget surplus for one period after which balanced budgets are resumed for all subsequent periods. In all of these subsequent periods government assets are higher than they would have been under balanced budgets, which allows the tax rate to be lower. Hence under tax smoothing the tax rate is higher for the initial period and lower for all subsequent periods.

In order to set up a simple two-period framework, suppose that following the policy shock the remaining lifetimes of all generations are divided into two periods. The two periods are of equal length for a given generation but will be shorter for older generations because they have less remaining lifetime to divide up. Households must decide how to allocate consumption over these two remaining periods of their lives. This becomes a standard two-period consumption allocation problem for each generation. Let W_1 be the level of wealth of each generation at the start of period 1 at which time the policy shock occurs; let Y_i be income earned at the start of period i $(i = 1, 2)$; let C_i be consumption during period i; let r be the constant interest rate, and let t_i be the flat rate of tax on both labour income and capital income in period i. Finally, assume that the household has a target bequest of zero. Then the household's discounted budget constraint over its remaining lifetime, divided into two periods, is:

$$C_1 + \frac{C_2}{1 + r(1 - t_2)} = W_1 + Y_1(1 - t_1) + Y_2\left(\frac{1 - t_2}{1 + r(1 - t_2)}\right) \quad (8.1)$$

Consider Figure 8.1, which depicts the choices facing the young worker in allocating consumption over the two periods of life remaining after the shock. Assume also that labour supply is exogenous in this simple model: however, it is endogenous in the formal simulation model. The young worker will be working in the first of these periods when the tax rate is lower as a result of tax smoothing and working for part of the second period when the tax rate is higher. The horizontal axis in Figure 8.1 measures consumption and income in period 1 and the vertical axis measures consumption and income in period 2. Two budget lines are drawn representing the lifetime budget constraint 8.1 for the tax smoothing case and the balanced budget case. The slope of the budget line is $-[1 + r(1 - t_2)]$. It is steeper in the tax smoothing case because t_2 is lower than it is under the alternative policy of continuous balanced budgets. The effect of tax smoothing on the intercepts depend on the values of W_1, Y_1, Y_2, t_1, t_2 and r. In Figure 8.1 the effect on the intercepts is such that the budget lines intersect, which is likely if $W_1 + Y_1$ is close to Y_2 – this is plausible for the young worker who has little wealth at the time of the shock. The intersection point of the budget lines occurs where the intertemporal consumption allocation is unaffected by the policy change.

There are two sets of indifference curves, U, in Figure 8.1 representing different rates of time preference. U_1 and U_2 are implied by a low rate of time preference, and U_3 and U_4 by a high rate of time preference. The optimal intertemporal consumption choice is the point at which the indifference curve is tangential to the budget line. The young worker is more likely to be better off the lower their rate of time preference. Intuitively, with a low rate of time preference they are prepared to sacrifice current consumption when tax rates are high (in Figure 8.1 they move from $C_1[bal]$ to $C_1[sm]$) in order to transfer capital income to the future when tax rates are low (moving from $C_2[bal]$ to $C_2[sm]$). The result is an increase in utility from U_1 to U_2. On the other hand, when the rate of time preference is high, such an intertemporal trade-off would be too costly in terms of lost utility in the present. In that case their optimal consumption choice implies lower utility (U_4 compared with U_3). Tax smoothing has less effect on lifetime utility for young workers than it does for middle-aged or future workers (discussed below) because young workers experience a higher tax rate for the early part of their working life but a lower tax rate later on.

Figure 8.2 depicts the case for the middle-aged worker for whom the remaining two periods of life following the shock consist of a period of work (period 1) and a period of retirement (period 2). Under tax smoothing they pay a higher tax rate on their labour income in period 1 and a lower tax rate on their retirement income in period 2. Tax concessions for retirees ensure that they pay very little tax in retirement and therefore the change in their effective tax rate, t_2, as a result of tax smoothing is very small. The result is that both intercepts are lower in Figure 8.2 and that middle-aged households are unambiguously worse-off under tax smoothing irrespective of their rate of time preference.

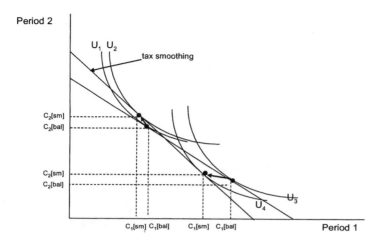

Figure 8.1: The Young Worker

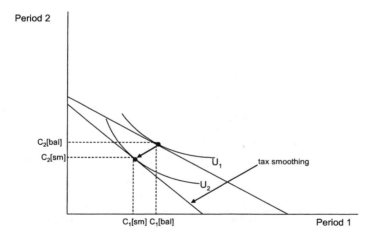

Figure 8.2: The Middle-Aged Worker

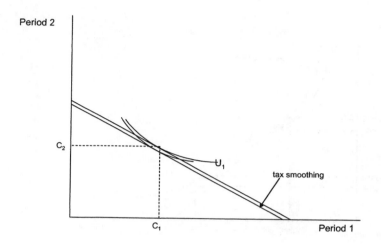

Figure 8.3: The Retired Worker

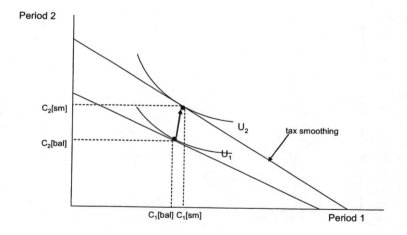

Figure 8.4: The Future Worker

The case for the retired person is illustrated in Figure 8.3. The difference between these people and the middle-aged workers is that they are retired at the time of the tax smoothing shock and, it is assumed, will be dead by the time the lower tax rate arrives. Hence although they face higher tax rates for the rest of their lives, their income is low and therefore their remaining lifetime incomes are little affected. This is reflected by the closeness of the budget lines in Figure 8.3.

Finally, Figure 8.4 represents the case for the future workers who have just commenced full-time education at the time of the shock and are therefore paying no tax. They are unambiguously better off under tax smoothing because by the time they enter the workforce in the next period the tax rate is lower than it would have been under balanced budgets. They therefore enjoy lower tax rates for the entire income-earning period of their lives, implying a budget line with steeper slope and shifted to the right.

This illustrative model provides the basic intuition for the intergenerational effects of tax smoothing. The CGE model, discussed and applied below, allows for more complexity and key behavioural feedback effects (such as the effect of the tax rate on labour supply); it also facilitates a social welfare evaluation of tax smoothing.

Before moving on to the simulation model, a brief comment on the taxation of capital income is warranted. Tax smoothing implies changes to taxes on capital income that will have efficiency and equity effects that are somewhat more complicated than those applying to taxes on labour income. In an intertemporal setting, Chamley (1986) shows that the long run optimal tax on capital is the outcome of a trade off between conflicting objectives. Because capital is fixed in the short run, the principal that taxes on fixed factors do not distort behaviour requires a positive optimal tax rate on capital. However, in the long run a positive tax rate on capital income distorts consumption between time periods. In order to avoid these complications it is sometimes assumed in intertemporal welfare analyses of taxation that the tax on capital income is zero; for example, see Davis and Fabling (2002). However, concern here is not with optimal taxation and it is simply assumed that the tax rate on capital income is the same as the tax rate on labour income. Firms pay the pre-tax cost of capital but households receive the after-tax return on capital, which creates a wedge consisting of foregone net gains from employing capital.

An open economy framework potentially complicates this analysis because the supply of savings can come from foreign households. But in fact this does not change the analysis much because in Australia, as in most countries, non-residents are liable for Australian tax on all assessible income earned in Australia. This includes income from capital in the form of interest, dividend and royalty income. The amount of tax payable depends on whether the recipient is a resident of a country that has a tax treaty with Australia. In the simulation model applied here it is implicitly assumed that foreign and domestic lenders are subject to the same rate of tax.

8.2   The Simulation Model

The simulation model is an open economy, overlapping generations model with four sectors: firms, households, government and an overseas sector.

8.2.1   Firms

A representative firm produces output of a single good according to a Cobb-Douglas production function. Output, Y, in period j is given by:

$$Y_j = A K_j^\alpha L_j^{1-\alpha} \tag{8.2}$$

where K_j is the capital stock and L_j is aggregate labour consisting of the sum of the labour of all generations: $L_j = \sum_{i=1}^n L_{i,j}$ where $L_{i,j}$ is the labour of generation i working in year j. The technology parameter, A, is constant, implying zero technical progress. The reason, as also given in Kulish *et al.*

(2006), is that the leisure to consumption ratio would eventually decline to zero with continual productivity-induced rises in real wages; see Auerbach and Kotlikoff (1987) for a further discussion. It would be possible to specify a non-standard utility function which could deal with this problem in the presence of technical progress, but this is not pursued here.

The optimal capital stock, K_j, is determined by the first order condition that the marginal product of capital (net of depreciation, δ) is equal to the cost of capital, r_j. That is, $\left(\frac{dY_j}{dK_j} - \delta\right) = r_j$, which gives:

$$\left(\frac{K}{L}\right)_j = \left(\frac{A\alpha}{r_j + \delta}\right)^{\frac{1}{1-\alpha}} \tag{8.3}$$

And investment, I_j, is given by:

$$I_j = K_j - K_{j-1}\left(1 - \delta\right) \tag{8.4}$$

Competitive firms equate the price of labour, w_j, to the marginal product of labour:

$$w_j = (1 - \alpha) A \left(\frac{K}{L}\right)_j^{\alpha} = \left(\frac{Y}{L}\right)_j - (r_j + \delta)\left(\frac{K}{L}\right)_j \tag{8.5}$$

As in the previous chapter, the wage of each worker is given by:

$$w_{L,i,j} = \bar{w}_{L,i,j}\gamma_j \tag{8.6}$$

where $\bar{w}_{L,i,j}$ is given by data and γ_j is a weight reflecting movements in the marginal product of labour $w_{L,j}$.

A variation in this chapter is that the interest rate is no longer constant but is a function of the level of foreign liabilities as a share of GDP, as follows:

$$r_j = \bar{r} + \varphi\left(\frac{D}{Y}\right)_j \tag{8.7}$$

This reflects extensive evidence that capital is not perfectly mobile internationally even for small open economies. For a discussion of the various explanations see Gordon and Bovenberg (1996).

8.2.2   Households

Each household consists of one person who dies at the age of 90 with certainty. A period of time is five years in duration and a new generation of households is born each period, implying that households live for $h = 18$ periods and that there are h overlapping generations of households alive at any time. The households supply labour between the age of 15 and 70; hence there are eleven generations of workers. Households pay the same single tax rate on income from both capital and labour. Future values of the demographic variables and the parameters are known with certainty, except for the tax smoothing shock which comes as a surprise at which time households must adjust their plans accordingly.

Households derive utility from consuming a composite index of private goods, C, and leisure, S. Households also derive utility from consuming public goods, G^C, which is exogenous and separable from both private consumption and leisure in generating utility, following the approach in Foertsch (2004). Therefore G^C does not affect the household's choice of private consumption or leisure and can therefore be ignored in solving the household's optimisation problem. The assumption of separability between public and private consumption is quite common, as noted in Foertsch (2004), because of lack of evidence about the substitutability between private and government consumption.

The composite index of consumption and leisure is:

$$M_{i,j} = \left[\mu_i^{1/\Psi} C_{i,j}^{\Psi-1/\Psi} + (1 - \mu_i)^{1/\Psi} S_{i,j}^{\Psi-1/\Psi} \right]^{\Psi/\Psi-1} \tag{8.8}$$

where $C_{i,j}$ and $S_{i,j}$ are the goods consumption and leisure, respectively, of generation i in period j. The preference for consumption relative to leisure, captured by the parameter μ_i, is assumed to vary over the lifecycle. In particular it is assumed to rise up to middle-age and then fall. Hence μ_i

follows a hump-shape which is given by the quadratic:

$$\mu_i = \xi_1 + \xi_2 i - \xi_3 i^2 \tag{8.9}$$

The hump-shape pattern on μ_i generates a hump-shape path of consumption relative to leisure over the life cycle. This pattern is designed to reflect the observed life cycle pattern of consumption which tends to track the hump-shaped pattern of income to some degree, rising during the household's working life and falling after retirement (see, for example, Deaton, 1999).

Households maximise the following intertemporal utility function:

$$U = \sum_{i=1}^{h} \frac{M_{i,j}^{1-\beta}}{1-\beta} (1+\theta)^{1-i} + v\left(G_j^C\right) \tag{8.10}$$

with respect to $C_{i,j}$ and $S_{i,j}$ after substituting for $M_{i,j}$, and subject to a lifetime budget constraint:

$$\sum_{i=1}^{h} (C_{i,j} + S_{i,j} p_{i,j})(1 + r_j(1 - t_j))^{1-i}$$

$$= \sum_{i=1}^{h} (p_{i,j} L_{i,j} + f_{i,j})(1 + r_j(1 - t_j))^{1-i} +$$

$$Q(1 + r_j(1 - t_j))^{1-(h-6)} - \bar{A}_{1-h,j}(1 + r(1 - t_j))^{1-h} \tag{8.11}$$

where the right-hand side is the present value of lifetime income. The latter includes transfer payments, $f_{i,j}$,[1] and inheritance, Q, which is received when the household is aged 60 years, less a target bequest, $\bar{A}_{1-h,j}$; t_j is the tax rate in year j applying to income from both labour and capital; and $p_{i,j} = w_{i,j}(1 - t_j)$ is the after-tax wage, and therefore relative price of leisure, facing a household of age i in year j. Households leave a bequest equal to 10 percent of their total lifetime pre-tax income. The bequest is received by the generation 30 years younger, which is a simplification for the purpose

---

[1]For simplicity, total transfer payments paid by the government in a given year are allocated evenly across all households alive in that year, rather than being allocated to certain generations. Hence $f_{i,j} = f_j/N_j$.

of generating lifetime budgets because the demographic data used for the simulations reflects the actual patterns of age-specific fertility.

The household's intratemporal problem is solved by maximising the utility function in (8.10) subject to the budget constraint (8.11). This yields the following relation between consumption of goods and leisure as a function of the relative price of leisure:

$$\frac{\mu_i S_{i,j}}{(1 - \mu_i) C_{i,j}} = p_{i,j}^{-\Psi} \tag{8.12}$$

Solving (8.12) for $S_{i,j}$ and substituting into (8.8), yields:

$$C_{i,j} = M_{i,j} \mu_i \left[\mu_i + (1 - \mu_i) p_{i,j}^{1-\Psi} \right]^{1/1-\Psi} \tag{8.13}$$

and repeating for $C_{i,j}$ gives:

$$S_{i,j} = M_{i,j} (1 - \mu_i) p_{i,j}^{1-\Psi} \left[\mu_i + (1 - \mu_i) p_{i,j}^{1-\Psi} \right]^{1/1-\Psi} \tag{8.14}$$

Defining $P_{i,j}$ as the minimum price that buys a unit of the consumption index, $M_{i,j}$, then $P_{i,j} M_{i,j} = C_{i,j} + p_{i,j} S_{i,j}$, and substituting (8.13) and (8.14):

$$P_{i,j} = \left[\mu_i + (1 - \mu_i) p_{i,j}^{1-\Psi} \right]^{1/1-\Psi} \tag{8.15}$$

Now (8.13) and (8.14) can be simplified to give:

$$C_{i,j} = \mu_i \left(\frac{1}{P_{i,j}} \right)^{-\Psi} M_{i,j} \tag{8.16}$$

$$S_{i,j} = (1 - \mu_i) \left(\frac{p}{P} \right)_{i,j}^{-\Psi} M_{i,j} \tag{8.17}$$

To obtain the Euler equation, first use (8.16) and (8.17) to substitute for $C_{i,j}$ and $S_{i,j}$ in the budget constraint (8.11). Then maximise the utility function (8.10) with respect to $M_{i,j}$ subject to (8.11). This yields:

$$\frac{M_{i,j}}{M_{i-1,j-1}} = \left[\frac{1 + r_j (1 - t_j)}{1 + \theta} \frac{P_{i-1,j-1}}{P_{i,j}} \right]^{1/\beta} \tag{8.18}$$

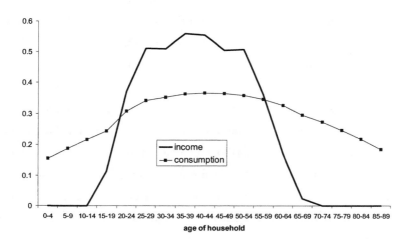

Figure 8.5: Household Post-Tax Labour Income and Consumption: Balanced Budget Case

Figure 8.5 shows household labour income (after tax) and consumption over the lifecycle. The slight hump in the consumption path is due to the assumed path of t discussed above. The balance of financial assets at age i in year j is given by:

$$A_{i,j} = A_{i-1,j-1}\left(1 + r_j\left(1 - t_j\right)\right) + \left(w\frac{L}{N}\right)_{i,j}\left(1 - t_j\right)$$
$$-C_{i,j} + f_{i,j} \quad \text{for } i = 1, ...11, 13, ..18 \tag{8.19}$$

$$A_{i,j} = A_{i-1,j-1}\left(1 + r_j\left(1 - t_j\right)\right) + \left(w\frac{L}{N}\right)_{i,j}\left(1 - t_j\right)$$
$$-C_{i,j} + f_{i,j} + Q \quad \text{for } i = 12 \tag{8.20}$$

The wage of a worker, $w_{i,j}$, is multiplied by $(L/N)_{i,j}$ to reflect the fact that there are $L_{i,j}$ workers but $N_{i,j}$ households of age i in year j.

The solution to the household's optimisation problem is obtained numerically as follows. Specify a trial value of $M_{i,j}$ for $i=1$, then solve forward for $M_{i,j}$ for $i = 1, ...h$ according to the Euler equation (8.18). For $i = 1, ...h$ calculate $C_{i,j}$ and $S_{i,j}$ according to (8.16) and (8.17). Then calculate $A_{h,j}$. If it does not equal the target bequest, adjust $\Pi_{i,j}$ for $i = 1$ and repeat the algorithm iteratively until the target bequest is met within a degree of tolerance.

The labour supply of households aged i in year j, $L_{i,j}$, is equal to $1 - S_{i,j}$ by appropriate normalising of the raw demographic data. The labour market is assumed to clear in each period. The target bequest is set exogenously as a proportion of the household's lifetime income. In the base case this proportion is 10 percent. See the previous chapter for further discussion.

The standard national accounting identity gives the evolution of foreign liabilities:

$$D_j = D_{j-1}\left(1 + r_j\right) + \sum_{i=1}^{h} C_{i,j} + G_j^C + I_j - Y_j \tag{8.21}$$

8.2.3   Government

Government spending, G_j, is an exogenously given share of GDP. It is set equal to 0.3 for the period up to 2005 after which it is assumed to increase according to the increase in age-related spending of the Australian Government as projected in Productivity Commission (2005). The projected increases in age-related spending of State governments from 2004–2045 is only 0.8 percent of GDP (compared with 5.7 percent for the Australian Government) and is ignored here to enable comparisons with the Future Fund which is drawn only from the Australian Government budget. All government spending other than transfer payments is assumed for simplicity to be government consumption spending. Hence:

$$G_j = G_j^C + f_j \tag{8.22}$$

The categories of age-related G_j^C spending are given in Productivity Commission (2005) and consist of health, aged care, carers and education; and

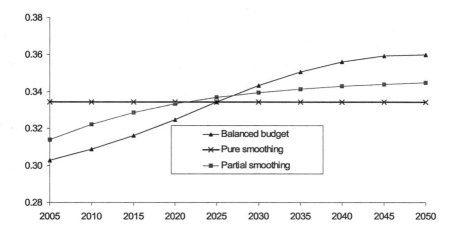

Figure 8.6: Fiscal Pressure From Population Ageing: Projected Path of Tax to GDP Ratio

the categories of G_j^C are age and service pensions, family tax benefits, disability support benefit, unemployment allowances and parenting payments. The resulting series for aggregate $(G/Y)_j$ is plotted in Figure 8.6 as the series labelled 'balanced budget' because under balanced budgets $(G/Y)_j$ is also the tax to GDP ratio, $(T/Y)_j$. As Figure 8.6 indicates, age-related spending of the Australian Government is projected to increase by 5.7 percent of GDP between 2003 and 2045 according to the Productivity Commission (2005).

The government faces the following dynamic budget constraint:

$$D_j^{gov} = D_{j-1}^{gov} \left(1 + r_j\right) + G_j - T_j \tag{8.23}$$

where D_j^{gov} is government debt (net) and T_j is total taxes.

8.3   Value Judgements

An evaluation of tax smoothing requires value judgements which can be made explicit by defining a social welfare function. It is assumed that the independent judge evaluates only the aggregate consumption of society in the present and the future. This implies that there is no regard for past consumption of generations still alive. This assumption can imply time inconsistent aggregate consumption paths as shown by Calvo and Obstfeld (1988) in the context of optimal fiscal policy implemented by a central planner. On the other hand Heal (1998) argues that time consistency is an unreasonable requirement in a social planning context over multiple generations. Also, by considering only aggregate consumption the social evaluation does not explicitly account for the lifetime utility of particular generations.

The social welfare function applied here is:

$$V = \sum_{j=1}^{H} N_j \left[\frac{M_j}{1 - \beta_s} \right]^{1-\beta_s} (1 + \theta_s)^{1-j} \tag{8.24}$$

where $M_j = \sum_{i=1}^{h} M_{i,j}$ is the aggregate value of the consumption index of all households alive in period j; $j = 1$ in 2005; H is an arbitrarily long time in the future; and V is a measure of discounted social welfare, which we will simply call social welfare.

Although the social evaluation in (8.24) is concerned only with aggregate consumption, it accounts for intergenerational equity indirectly through the parameters that weight future consumption. These parameters are β_s and θ_s, which are analogous in their role to the parameters β and θ in the household's utility function. The parameter θ_s is a social rate of pure time preference, which is the rate at which intra-period j social welfare is discounted in deriving our measure of social welfare. The parameter β_s measures the social degree of aversion to variability in consumption at any given point in time. Both parameters β_s and θ_s discount consumption occurring at different time periods. θ_s discounts a given level of future consumption according to the distance of that consumption in the future, whereas β_s discounts consumption at a given point in the future according to the size of that consumption.

Although they are analogous, the values of the social and private discount

Table 8.1: Base Case Parameters and Initial Values

Interest rate for a zero level of foreign liabilities	$\bar{r}$	0.03
Interest rate risk premium parameter	φ	0.02
Household's rate of time preferance	θ	0.03
Depreciation	δ	0.05
Capital elasticity of output	α	0.27
Initial capital to output ratio	$\bar{K}/\bar{Y}$	3.0
Initial tax rate on all income	t	0.3
Foreign liabilities to GDP ratio in 2003	D/Y	0.6
Elasticity of marginal utility w.r.t consumption index	β	2.0
Elasticity of substitution between consumption and leisure	Ψ	0.8
Bequest as a proportion of household's lifetime income		0.1

parameters need not be equal. For example, while it may be privately optimal for individuals to adopt a zero rate of pure time preference it may not be socially optimal, as an implication of the axioms in Koopmans (1960). In particular, if $\theta_s = 0$, the consumption of generations near to the present would have negligible weightings in social welfare when H is large. The result would be that the future swamps the present in social importance. It could justify crushing the present generation to yield an infinitely small increase in the utility of each generation in the future.

8.4 Empirical Application

8.4.1 Data and Parameters

The demographic data consist of actual historical population levels, and projected future population levels, for each age group. These data are given in the following Australian Bureau of Statistics (ABS) Catalogues: historic population, Catalogue 320109.1; projected population, Catalogue 3222.0; labour force participation rates by age, Catalogue 6291.0; and wage rates by age, Catalogue 6310.0. The data source for government expenditure is Productivity Commission (2005).

Table 8.1 gives the parameter values. The base case value of the interest rate parameter, γ, is 0.02, implying that an increase in the foreign liabilities to GDP ratio of 10 percent would imply an increase in the interest rate of 0.2 percent. The value of $\bar{r}$ is determined such that the interest rate in 2005 is equal to 4 percent given the value of D/Y in 2005. The latter value is set equal to its actual value of 0.6 by calibration – in particular, by finding the required ratio of D/Y in the period 1915–1919 which is the period when the household aged 86–90 in 2005 was born. The household's rate of time preference, θ, is equal to $r - \beta\varphi$ which is the rate that would, if both the tax rate and the parameter μ_t were constant, ensure that consumption grows at the long-run rate of growth of output.[2] The capital elasticity of output, α, is calibrated such that the initial capital to output ratio is equal to 3.0, the approximate actual value for Australia in 2005. The initial tax to GDP ratio is set equal to 0.3, the actual value for Australia in 2005. The values of the elasticities, β and Ψ, are set equal to 2 and 0.8, respectively, which are common values used in related studies in the literature; see, for example, Foertsch (2004).

There is no assumption that the economy is in a steady state prior to the tax smoothing policy shock, nor that the economy converges to a steady state. Nevertheless, the properties of the overlapping generations model lead to fairly well-behaved state variables. In particular, debt and the capital stock do not take extreme values at any point in the optimal path.

8.4.2   Simulations and Results

The three paths of the tax rate illustrated in Figure 8.6 consist of the continually balanced budget case and two tax smoothing scenarios: a pure smoothing scenario in which the tax rate is constant, and a partial smoothing case in which the tax rate rises more steeply than in the balanced budget case but

---

[2]However, this equation for θ is not a condition for a stable equilibrium in OLG models.

does not jump instantly to a constant rate as in the pure smoothing case. The partial smoothing scenario is an attempt to mimic the outcome of the Future Fund in which the income stream from the Fund allows the tax rate to be lower after 2020 than it would otherwise be. The partial smoothing scenario implies budget surpluses of around 1 percent of GDP for the next 20 years, after which the surpluses decline to zero by about 2040. The pure smoothing scenario is a somewhat hypothetical case in which the tax rate immediately jumps by 3 percent of GDP generating budget surpluses that decline from 3 percent to zero by about 2040. Such a sudden jump in the tax rate would be politically infeasible and is not implied by the Future Fund. Nevertheless, it is shown here as the limiting case.

The implications of these smoothing scenarios for government assets are shown in Figure 8.7. In the pure smoothing case the stock of government assets stabilises at a little over 70 percent of GDP by 2045; in the partial smoothing case the figure is around 30 percent by 2040 which is consistent with projections of the likely Future Fund balance.

A key aim of the analysis is to determine whether households of different generations are better off or worse off under tax smoothing, and by how much. The most appropriate indicator for this purpose is household lifetime utility (8.10) because it takes account of optimal adjustments between leisure and goods consumption, and between consumption in one period relative to another. The effect on lifetime utility is calculated and expressed in units of equivalent annual income. This facilitates the sensitivity analysis reported below since comparisons in units of utility are not valid when parameters in the utility function are changed. The change in equivalent annual income is found by an iterative procedure that adjusts annual income for a household by a constant percent in each period, in the balanced budget scenario, until the lifetime utility is the same value as that in the smoothing scenario. Figure 8.9 shows the equivalent percentage change in annual income, as a result of tax smoothing, for each generation currently alive and future generations

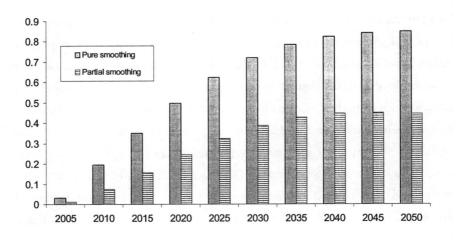

Figure 8.7: Net Government Assets as Proportion of GDP

born up to the year 2050.

All current and retired workers will be worse off under tax smoothing. The magnitudes range from 0.5 percent to 1.9 percent in the pure smoothing case, and from 0.2 to 1.0 percent in the partial smoothing case. The greatest losses apply to the generations born around 1965–70 because they will pay higher tax rates throughout the high income earning years of their lives than they would have under balanced budgets. Figure 8.1 shows that the youngest workers, aged around 15–20, are least affected by tax smoothing because the higher taxes paid initially are offset by lower taxes later on. Future workers – those generations born after 1990 – are better off under tax smoothing, with the greatest gains accruing to generations born after 2025 (3.8 percent and 2.2 percent in the pure and partial smoothing cases, respectively).

These results are consistent with the diagrammatic analysis presented in Section 8.1, where it was suggested that middle-aged workers would be worse off, young workers and retired workers would be less affected (retired workers would be a little worse off and young workers could be either a little worse or a little better off), and future workers would be unambiguously better off.

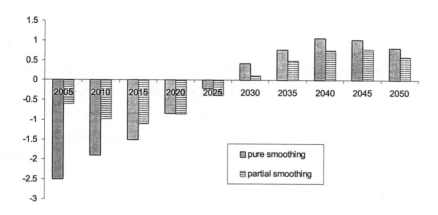

Figure 8.8: Percentage Change in Labour Supply From Tax Smoothing

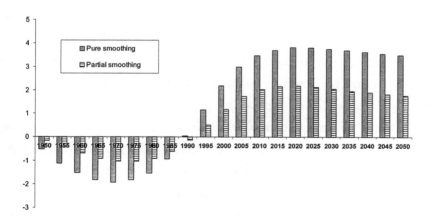

Figure 8.9:   Percentage Change in Equivalent Annual Income from Tax Smoothing for Representative Household Born in Year Indicated

Sensitivity to key parameters is discussed further below, but the essential outcome is that the results are qualitatively unaffected by a plausible range of parameter values.

The higher tax rate that applies for an initial period under tax smoothing causes a relatively sharp decrease in labour supply in the 2005 period, relative to the balanced budget case, which lessens over time and eventually becomes an increase in labour supply relative to the balanced budget case. This pattern can be explained as follows. The unanticipated shock causes an adjustment to lifecycle plans of all generations of workers. The adjustment occurs through both the income and substitution effect of higher taxes on their labour supply. For middle-aged households the income effect is unambiguously negative, as illustrated earlier for the simple model), which tends to lower demand for leisure and raise labour supply. But the substitution effect on leisure is positive, raising demand for leisure and lowering labour supply, and this effect slightly outweighs the negative income effect, resulting in a net decrease in labour supply for middle-aged households. For young households, the negative income effect on leisure is not as strong, because they benefit from lower taxes later, but the substitution effect is positive as for middle-aged households. Therefore younger households also reduce their labour supply. The result is a relatively large drop in labour supply following the shock. However, as time passes, the gap between the smooth tax rate and the balanced budget rate narrows and eventually the smoothed rate becomes the lower of the two. This implies that the substitution effect on leisure switches to negative, raising labour supply. Offsetting this is the income effect on leisure which for newer generations becomes increasingly positive as they experience the benefits of the lower smoothed tax rate for a larger proportion of their lifetimes. Hence the ultimate increase in labour supply is not as great as the initial decrease in labour supply; see Figure 8.8.

Having identified the generations of winners and losers from tax smoothing, consider the social welfare function (8.24) to make a net social evaluation

Table 8.2: Social Welfare Gains from Tax Smoothing in Units of Equivalent GDP per year

Social time pref rate (θ_s)	Aversion to inequality parameter (β)	Pure smoothing per cent	$ Per capita	Partial smoothing per cent	$ Per capita
0.0	2.0	2.0	900	1.0	450
3.0	2.0	1.8	810	0.9	405
6.0	2.0	1.7	765	0.8	360
4.0	0.2	1.6	720	0.7	315
4.0	1.0	1.7	765	0.8	360
4.0	10.0	1.8	788	0.9	405

of tax smoothing which jointly takes account of efficiency and equity effects of tax smoothing. Efficiency gains from tax smoothing arise from the reduction in distortions to both the labour–leisure choice arising from taxation of labour income and to the intertemporal consumption allocation arising from the taxation of capital income. Intergenerational equity is accounted for indirectly, as noted in the previous section, through the parameters in (8.24) that weight future consumption. No attempt was made to isolate the relative contribution to the gains in social welfare from the reduction in the two distortions and from the intergenerational equity effects.

The results are reported in Table 8.2 by expressing gains in social welfare in terms of equivalent annual gains in GDP per annum from tax smoothing. These were calculated by finding the annual increase in GDP under continual balanced budgets that would generate the same value of social welfare as in the tax smoothing scenario. Results are given for a range of values of the two key parameters in the social welfare function: the social discount rate, θ_s, and the parameter measuring the social aversion to inequality in consumption, β_s. The values chosen for θ_s range from zero to 8 percent; and the values chosen for β_s range from 0.2 to 10. The first point to note is that the gains are positive for all of the parameter combinations. This indicates net social gains from tax smoothing. For the hypothetical limiting case of pure tax smoothing the annual gains range from 0.8 to 2 percent of GDP. However, for practical purposes the pure smoothing case can be safely ignored, as argued above. The magnitudes for the partial smoothing case range from 0.7 to 1 percent of GDP in annual gains from tax smoothing. These amount to $315 and $450, respectively, per annum per person, based on a 2004-2005 GDP of $900 billion and a population of 20 million, or a per capita annual GDP of $45,000.

8.4.3 Sensitivity

A sensitivity analysis was conducted for some key parameters. The results are reported in Table 8.3. The rate of time preference was shown to be potentially important in the illustrative model of Section 8.1, at least for young workers. Table 8.3 reports results for a zero rate of time preference, compared with the base case value of 3 percent. The results partly support the intuition given in Section 8.1, in that young workers are better off the lower the rate of time preference, but the effect is still slightly negative even for a zero rate of time preference. A similar effect occurs with a higher rate of interest, because workers are induced by the higher return on saving to postpone consumption; see the row in Table 8.3 for value of of 4 per cent which is one per cent higher than the base case value of 3 per cent.

None of the alternative parameter values alters the direction of the effect of tax smoothing on lifetime utility that was found for the base case parameter values. The effect for all current generations of workers, and retired workers, remains negative and the effect for future workers remains positive, for all alternative parameter values. The range of values in Table 8.3 is small. For existing workers the range is well within 1 percentage point and for future workers the range is 1.6 percentage points.

The final column in Table 8.3 reports the effect of alternative parameter values on social welfare as defined by (8.24). In each case the values of the

Table 8.3: Percentage Effect of Partial Tax Smoothing on Lifetime Utility of Generation Measured in Equivalised Annual Values

		Birth cohort				Gain in V
		1935	1960	1985	2010	$\theta_s=0.03$
	Parameter					$\beta_s=2.0$
	Base case parameters	-0.12	-0.92	-0.63	2.04	0.80
θ	0 (base=0.03)	-0.13	-1.04	-0.74	2.21	0.70
$\bar{r}$	0.04 (base=0.03)	-0.20	-1.17	-0.46	3.64	1.00
γ	0 (base = 0.02)	-0.18	-1.23	-0.71	3.12	0.90
β	1.0 (base=2.0)	-0.26	-1.47	-0.88	3.22	0.95
Ψ	1.2 (base=0.8)	-0.29	-1.52	-0.74	3.06	0.45
Bequest	0 (base = 0.1)	-0.14	-1.40	-0.22	3.28	1.50

parameters in (8.24) have been held at their base case values – the sensitivity with respect to those parameters was reported in Table 8.2. Again, the direction of the effect is unaltered by the alternative parameters chosen for the sensitivity analysis. That is, the effect on social welfare remains positive, ranging from 0.45 per cent to 1.5 per cent in terms of equivalent annual gains in GDP. Converted to dollars per capita as reported for the base case, this range is equivalent to a range of $225 to $675, respectively, per year per person.

8.5 Conclusion

This chapter has analysed the welfare effects of tax smoothing, both in terms of the welfare of successive generations of representative households and in terms of social welfare. It was motivated by the decision of the Australian Government to establish the Future Fund into which budget surpluses will be deposited during an accumulation phase which is anticipated to continue until around 2020. The chapter was also motivated by a lack of evidence in the literature about the implications of tax smoothing for intergenerational equity taking account of general equilibrium effects.

The simulation analysis reveals differential generational effects of tax smoothing compared with continual balanced budgets. For all of the parameter values that were simulated, current generations of workers are worse off in terms of lifetime utility, but by magnitudes that may be considered small. The magnitudes in the partial smoothing simulation, which mimics the effect of the Future Fund, are about -0.2 per cent for retired workers, -1 per cent for middle-aged workers, and -0.6 per cent for young workers, where these numbers measure the effect on lifetime utility in terms of equivalent annual income. Future workers are better off and by larger magnitudes, in the range of 2 to 3 per cent in terms of equivalent annual income.

An evaluation of these gains and losses requires value judgements about appropriate discount weights and about the degree of aversion to inequality over time. These value judgements are embodied in the social welfare function. It turns out that tax smoothing increases social welfare under a range of values for the social welfare function parameters and other parameters in the model. The implication is that the lifetime utility gains to future generations outweigh the losses to current generations in terms of social welfare. The magnitudes of the increases in social welfare for the partial smoothing case are approximately 1 per cent, plus or minus 0.5 per cent, in terms of equivalent annual increases in GDP. A figure of 1 per cent converts to around $500 of additional GDP per person per annum.

A more complete social evaluation of the Future Fund would encompass political economy issues. An issue is the risk that the Fund may be raided for political purposes, or there may be political interference in the investments undertaken by the Fund. The extent to which this can be prevented through legislation is not clear *a priori*. A related political issue is the effect that a significant income stream generated by the Fund might have on discipline to control government spending. There are also the governance and management costs of the Fund to be considered. Future work could attempt to incorporate these political economy effects along with the conventional economic mechanisms captured in the CGE model applied here. Another avenue for future work would be to attempt to separate the social welfare gains arising from reductions in distortions to labour supply from those arising from reductions in distortions to intertemporal consumption: a separation of these effects was not considered in this chapter.

Chapter 9

Demographic Change in OECD Countries

The aim of this chapter is to assess the effect of population ageing on national living standards by taking account of emerging evidence of potential dividends from demographic change. The calculation of these potential dividends from demographic change is the main contribution here to recent evidence such as that reported in Martins *et al.* (2005), Guest and McDonald (2004) and, for Australia, Productivity Commission (2005). Also, the calculations are applied to all 30 OECD countries using the most recent demographic projections from the United Nations World Population Prospects 2004 Revision. The calculations are mechanical in that there are no behavioural feedback effects or explicit optimising behaviours. Hence this is not an exercise in the general equilibrium modelling of population ageing. In this sense the approach is similar to that in Productivity Commission (2005) for Australia, unlike many other studies that apply CGE models such as Martins *et al.* (2005) and Guest and McDonald (2004) and most recently for Australia, Kulish *et al.* (2006). An advantage of the mechanical approach is simplicity and transparency, but at the cost of ignoring behavioural feedback effects.

Section 9.1 describes the demographic transition and sets up a simple analytical framework for analysing the effects of demographic change on living standards. These effects are then discussed in Section 9.2 where the emphasis is on recent developments with respect to potential dividends from population ageing. Section 9.3 describes the data and reports the calculations for all 30 OECD countries.

9.1   The Demographic Transition and Prosperity

Population ageing is best thought of as a demographic transition that comes with economic development. The process comes in stages, starting with declining infant mortality and increases in adult life expectancy, followed later by declining fertility rates. Demographic projections show that almost all OECD countries are getting older, although countries are at different stages in this demographic transition. Two new OECD countries, Mexico and Turkey, for example, will experience a rise in the working age population share between 2006 and 2050. The first pair of columns in Table 9.1 give the working age population share for all 30 OECD countries. These data will be discussed in more detail below.

Simple demographic ratios do not in themselves suggest much about the effect of ageing on national prosperity. For that purpose it is appropriate to look directly at a measure of national prosperity which we will define here as national consumption per person, or living standards. This can be expressed in the following terms that will be helpful to anchor ideas. Let national income be the sum of labour income and capital income:

$$NI = wL + rW \tag{9.1}$$

and define national consumption as national income minus national saving:

$$
\begin{aligned}
C &= NI - S \\
&= wL + rW - S
\end{aligned}
\tag{9.2}
$$

where, NI is national income, C is national consumption, S is national saving, w is the wage rate, L is labour supply, r is the interest rate, and W is national wealth which is defined here as capital stock, K, plus net foreign assets, F. Therefore consumption per capita, or living standards, is:

$$\frac{C}{N} = \frac{L}{N}\left(w + r\frac{W}{L} - \frac{S}{L}\right) \qquad (9.3)$$

Defining saving as the change in wealth, saving per worker (S/L) is approximately equal to the change in wealth per worker plus the saving required to keep wealth per worker constant:[1]

$$\frac{S}{L} \simeq \Delta\frac{W}{L} + n\frac{W}{L} \qquad (9.4)$$

where n is the growth rate of new workers. Therefore:

$$\frac{C}{N} = \frac{L}{N}\left(w + (r-n)\frac{W}{L} - \Delta\frac{W}{L}\right) \qquad (9.5)$$

Equation (9.5) allows the effects of demographic change on living standards in an open economy setting to be decomposed. These effects are discussed in the next section and are captured in the calculations described in section 9.3.

9.2 Demographic Change and Living Standards

A decomposition of the effects of demographic change on living standards based on (9.3) is obtained as follows. Let $c = C/N$, assets $a = W/L$ and $\gamma = L/N$. Then (9.5) can be written, as in Elmendorf and Sheiner (2000, p. 8) where they assume a steady state in which $\Delta a = 0$, as:

$$c = \gamma\left(w + (r-n)a - \Delta a\right) \qquad (9.6)$$

---

[1]The approximation applies to discrete changes in time.

Express L in efficiency units as $A^{1/(1-\alpha)}L$ and substitute into (9.6):

$$c = \gamma \left(y \left(k \right) - nk + \left(r - n \right) f - \Delta a \right) \tag{9.7}$$

where lower case letters y, k and f denote, respectively, Y, K and F per worker in efficiency units. Totally differentiating (9.7) and ignoring second-order terms gives:

$$dc = d\gamma \left(\frac{c}{y} \right) - \gamma \left[dn \left(k + f \right) - dr \left(k + f \right) - \left\{ y' \left(k \right) - n \right\} dk - \left(r - n \right) df \right] \tag{9.8}$$

Dividing by c and noting that $a = k + f$:

$$\frac{dc}{c} = \frac{d\gamma}{\gamma} - \frac{\gamma}{c} \left[\left\{ y' \left(k \right) - n \right\} dk - \left(r - n \right) df - adr - adn \right] \tag{9.9}$$

This indicates several effects of population ageing. The dependency effect is $d\gamma/\gamma$; the open economy Solow effect is $-\left(\gamma/c \right) adn$; and the saving (wealth deepening) effect is $-\left(\gamma/c \right) \left[\left\{ y' \left(k \right) - n \right\} dk - \left(r - n \right) df - adr \right]$.

In the calculations reported here, it is assumed for simplicity that the interest rate, and therefore the capital–labour ratio, are constant in a steady state, in which case the saving effect becomes $\left(\gamma/c \right) \left[\left(r - n \right) df \right]$. Cutler *et al.* (1990, p. 17) also adopt this assumption in their closed economy version of (9.9), where the wealth–labour ratio is replaced by a constant steady state capital–labour ratio. However, in their model there are no foreign assets, because of the closed economy assumption, and therefore $df = 0$ and the saving effect is zero.

The remaining dividend reported here is called the imperfect substitutability dividend. It increases labour in efficiency units by increasing total factor productivity, A. In other words it is a source of technical progress. This is not directly captured in (9.9) because y, k, and f are measured in units of efficiency labour, $A^{1/(1-\alpha)}L$.

The support ratio in a given year is commonly calculated as:

$$\frac{L}{N} = \frac{\sum_{i=1}^{m} \alpha_i LFPR_i N_i}{\sum_i N_i} \tag{9.10}$$

where m is the number of age groups of workers, α_i is the productivity weight of workers of age i, $LFPR_i$ is the labour force participation rate of age group i and N_i is the population of age i.

9.2.1 Demographic Change and the Support Ratio

Population ageing lowers the support ratio by lowering the working age population share: $\sum_{i=1}^{m} N_i / \sum_i N_i$. However, there are a number of reasons to expect the decline in the support ratio to be mitigated by a rise in the LFPRs of older workers in the future.

Younger cohorts of the population are better educated than their predecessors, which means that when they are older, their LFPRs will be higher than that of current older cohorts, because better educated people participate at higher rates in the labour market due partly to their higher wage rates. Also, the demand for their labour will be higher due to their higher productivity. In Australia for example, Day and Dowrick (2004) provide evidence that the decline in fertility since the 1960s has been associated with a substantial increase in female LFPRs. They argue that this will continue – in particular with respect to older women, as the higher educational attainments of young women today will result in much higher LFPRs of older women in the future. The Productivity Commission (2005) projections for Australia take account of these cohort effects by assuming that future older workers participate at higher rates than current older workers, and more so for women. The result is that the aggregate L/N falls by 10 percent over the next 40 years, whereas the working age share of the population is projected to fall by 12 percent (their measure of L is hours worked).

In OECD countries considerable policy attention is being directed towards increasing LFPRs of older workers and ensuring that there is demand for their labour.[2] Policies are focusing on retirement incomes and welfare

---

[2]The OECD has published a series of country studies called *Ageing and Employment Policies*, covering about 20 countries, in which it explains the policy initiatives that have

reform, incentives for older workers to enter labour market training programmes, and various forms of careers and employment guidance for older workers. Of these, the changes to superannuation and pension arrangements have received the greatest attention. Steps are being taken to change cultural norms and attitudes in order to help to raise the LFPRs of older workers. Examples include anti-age discrimination legislation and government campaigns such as the 'Age Positive' campaign in the United Kingdom which promotes the benefits of employing a mix of older and younger workers, by distributing publications and offering awards for 'good practice'.[3] Re-engineering of workplaces, improvements in the health of older people, the growth of less physically demanding 'knowledge jobs', and flexible working arrangements are all factors that can potentially increase the LFPRs of older workers in the future.

There are feedback effects on LFPRs through changes in wage rates and tax rates associated with population ageing. A decline in labour supply relative to demand leads to higher wages which will tend to raise LFPRs. In addition, to the extent that population ageing lowers consumption per capita, both consumption of goods and leisure would be lower. Lower leisure in turn implies greater work effort, thereby boosting effective labour supply. Effects in the opposite direction, however, will occur through the negative effect of higher taxes on after-tax real wages; see Disney (1996) for discussion of this point.

Finally, working age populations themselves may turn out to be higher in coming decades than indicated by current projections, due to pro-fertility policies being adopted in many OECD countries. For a survey of these policies in 15 EU nations, see Gautheir (2000). Pro-fertility policies being adopted in many OECD countries vary from cash payments to new mothers, to policies designed to make simultaneous child-raising and participation in

---

been taken, and are planned to be taken, to boost the employment of older workers.

[3]Details can be found at agepositive@dwp.gsi.gov.uk

the labour market more attractive to women. The latter include parental leave and child care subsidies. International empirical evidence suggests that pro-fertility policies generally do boost fertility (Milligan, 2005; Moffit, 1997), although part of the measured effect may be a timing effect where mothers bring forward childbirth in their lifecycle rather than increasing the number of births over their lifetimes.

9.2.2 Ageing and Average Labour Productivity

The effect of population ageing on labour productivity is a critical relationship because labour productivity growth could potentially offset – indeed swamp – the economic burden implied by a falling support ratio.

The impact of labour productivity growth on living standards is shown by expressing the real wage rate, w, in (9.5) as a function of the capital to labour ratio as follows, assuming a constant returns to scale Cobb-Douglas production function and that labour is paid its marginal product:

$$
\begin{aligned}
w &= \frac{Y}{L} - r\frac{K}{L} \\
&= A\left(\frac{K}{L}\right)^{\alpha} - r\frac{K}{L}
\end{aligned}
\tag{9.11}
$$

where Y is output, A is a technology parameter, K is the capital stock (net of depreciation) and α is the elasticity of output with respect to capital. Average labour productivity is Y/L. Equation (9.11) indicates two sources of labour productivity growth: technical progress (growth in A) and increases in the capital-labour ratio. With respect to the former, the magnitude and direction of the effect of demographic change on technical progress remains an elusive question – unresolved in theory and empirically; see Birdsall *et al.* (2001) and Mason (2001, chapters 1 to 8). For this reason most studies take an agnostic view in assuming that the net effect of demographic change on technical progress is zero; see, for example, Martins *et al.* (2005) for the OECD and Productivity Commission (2005) for Australia.

The other source of labour productivity growth – increases in the K/L ratio – can be affected by demographic change in two ways. The first is a mechanical effect as capital takes time to adjust to changes in labour for any desired ratio. This implies a short-run rise in K/L in response to population ageing. The second effect is a change in the desired long-run ratio. The latter link is weaker the more open is the capital market to international capital flows, and therefore the more that a change in saving affects net foreign assets, F, per worker rather than capital per worker. The desired K/L ratio is determined by the cost of capital. The more open is the capital market the more the cost of capital reflects the international cost of capital rather than domestic saving and investment.

Two potentially important effects on Y/L can also occur through the age distribution of a given workforce size. One of these effects is well known, whereby middle-aged workers tend to be more productive than younger and older workers. The other effect has received less attention in the literature. Despite econometric evidence to the contrary, as in Card and Lemieux (2001), perfect substitutability of workers of different ages continues to be the typical assumption in macroeconomic modelling of demographic change. Examples of complementary, rather than perfectly substitutable, age-dependent skills are not hard to imagine: the physical strength, higher education levels and dynamism of young workers complementing older workers' experience, maturity of judgement, reliability, and people skills including their mentoring role. This would imply that even though 35 year olds may have the same marginal productivity as 65 year olds, as reflected in equal wage rates, employing either two 35 year olds or two 65 year olds would yield less output than employing one of each.

The notion of synergies or complementarities of workers by age gives rise to the possibility of an optimum age mix of a firm's workforce. It can be shown that, under standard neoclassical assumptions, the optimum age mix of a given workforce depends on two factors: the relative marginal productivity of workers by age and the degree of substitutability between workers by age (Lam, 1989). In the context of population ageing, the question arises as to whether an older workforce is closer to the optimum age mix of the workforce or further away from it. When moving closer to the optimum, there is a dividend in terms of aggregate labour productivity and therefore economic well being. This would be a free lunch in the sense that it would not cost any resources. On the other hand, when moving further away from the optimum, there is an efficiency loss in terms of lower labour productivity and therefore economic well-being. Evidence is emerging, based on simulations of calibrated macroeconomic models, to suggest that population ageing is likely to move the workforce age mix closer to the optimal mix, implying a dividend rather than an efficiency loss (Prskawetz and Fent, 2004; Guest, 2005). The calculations in Section 9.3 attempt to measure the size of this potential dividend for each OECD country. They should be interpreted, however, as subject to wide confidence intervals due to lack of evidence about the elasticity of substitution among workers of different ages.

Human capital is another channel through which demographic change can affect Y/L, although there is no attempt to measure this effect in the calculations reported in Section 9.3. Lower fertility rates may boost human capital creation because parents can afford to spend more on the education of each child, on average (Becker *et al.*, 1990). This negative relationship between fertility and human capital creation also operates in the other direction, because parents who have high levels of human capital face a high opportunity cost of having children which typically outweighs any positive income effect, thereby lowering fertility (Becker *et al.*, 1990). The bi-directional relationship between fertility and productivity is supported by recent empirical evidence for Australia (Guest and Swift, 2008) using data from 1950 to 2002. This further calls into question the merits of pro-fertility policies, discussed above, to the extent that they might reduce labour productivity. Note that any reduction in labour productivity from higher fertility would be permanent if the population becomes stable at a higher fertility rate.

Improvements in human capital due to lower fertility rates can be expected to increase labour productivity growth in the short run and probably in the long run.[4] The short-run effect occurs through an improvement in the quality of labour inputs used in current production. Longer-run feedback benefits can occur as knowledge begets knowledge – discoveries lead to further discoveries. In this sense productivity growth caused by human capital is endogenous; see, for example, Lucas (1988) and Romer (1990).

Finally, brief mention is made of the potential for demographic change to affect Y/L via changes in the sectoral composition of demand for goods and services. This can affect labour productivity because some industry sectors have a higher capital intensity than others; and because some sectors, such as the long-term aged care sector, have less potential for technical progress than other sectors such as manufacturing. In their OECD study, Martins *et al.* (2005) provide some evidence for their conclusion that ageing-induced changes in consumption shares are not large because they tend to offset each other across age groups and therefore will not produce major structural changes in the economy.

9.2.3   Ageing and Saving per Worker

There is strong evidence to support partial – not perfect – life cycle consumption smoothing implying a bell-shaped life cycle saving pattern; see Campbell and Mankiw (1989) and Martins *et al.* (2005). This means that aggregate saving per worker will change in response to changes in the age composition of the working age population. When the proportions of middle aged workers is rising aggregate saving per worker, S/L, rises. There is also econometric evidence for this effect; for example, in Kelley and Schmidt (1996) and Hig-

---

[4]There is a debate about whether improvements in human capital increase the long run rate of productivity growth. According to 'new growth theory' they do, but according to neoclassical theory productivity growth is higher only in the short run; see the discussion in Day and Dowrick (2004).

gins and Williamson (1997). The resulting wealth accumulation, or wealth deepening, manifests in some combination of higher per worker levels of the domestic capital stock, K/L, and higher net foreign assets ,F/L. As (9.5) indicates, these higher levels of wealth support higher living standards later on when the proportion of middle-aged workers begins to fall, the point at which most OECD countries find themselves now. The result is higher living standards in the long run than would have been possible without consumption smoothing. Mason and Lee (2004) describe this as the 'second demographic dividend'. Here it is described as a saving or wealth-deepening dividend and is measured for all OECD countries in a stylised way in the calculations below.

In addition, for any desired W/L ratio a fall in employment growth implies lower accumulation of domestic and foreign assets for wealth widening purposes which frees up resources for consumption. In terms of (9.5), n is lower which allows higher C/N for a given W/L. This is an open economy version of the Solow dividend (Elmendorf and Sheiner, 1999) and is also calculated below.

The effect of demographic change on C/N can also be mitigated through the gains from international trade in capital. The fact that countries are ageing at different rates means that they face different ageing-induced changes in saving and investment flows at any given time. This gives rise to opportunities for international trade in capital with attendant gains to both borrowing and lending countries. In particular, the interest rates facing lending countries will be higher than they would be in the absence of trade and, conversely, interest rates facing borrowing countries will be lower then they would be in the absence of trade. Hence for lending countries, the gains from trade in capital are the extra returns to domestic savers from higher interest rates over and above the higher cost to domestic borrowers. For countries borrowing capital, the gains from trade are the benefits to domestic borrowers from lower interest rates over and above the losses to domestic lenders. For a discussion of these and other open economy effects of demographic change see, for example, Bryant (2004), Bosworth *et al.* (2004) and Richardson (1997). There is no attempt here to calculate these potential gains.

9.3   Calculations for OECD Countries

The calculations are restricted to demographically-induced changes in the following: the working age population, LFPRs, aggregate labour productivity via age-specific productivity weights and the age composition of the workforce, and consumption possibilities via the open economy Solow effect and wealth deepening.

Table 9.1 reports projections of employment to population ratios ranging from the crudest measure, being the working-age population ratio (column 1), through to the support ratio given in (9.10) which allows for both age-specific LFPRs and age-specific productivity weights. The population data is from the United Nations, World Population Prospects, 2004 Revision. The LFPR data are from the OECD Labour Market Statistics by sex and age.[5] Column 2 is the working age population (Column 1) adjusted for age-specific LFPRs but without adjusting for age-specific productivity levels. This adjustment is done in Columns 3 and 4 which differ in that Column 3 uses the age-specific productivity weights in Miles (1999) and Column 4 uses those in Skirbekk (2004); both sets of weights are plotted in Figure 9.1. Values in column 3 are taken as the base case for comparison with the later retirement case (Column 5) and also for calculating the effect of various potential dividends discussed above.

Column (5) in Table 9.1 captures the effect of later retirement by assuming that the LFPRs of workers for each of the age groups over 55 have increased by 2050 to equal the LFPRs in 2004 for the next older age group in 2004. For example the LFPRs of 55–59 year olds (male and female) in 2050 are set

---

[5]Available at http://www1.oecd.org/scripts/cde/DoQuery.asp

Table 9.1: Projected Employment to Population Ratios: Alternative Measures

	(1) Working age pop share 2006	(2) LFPR age 15-74 2050	age 15-74 2006	(3) base case age 15-74 2050	age 15-74 2006	(4) Weighted LFPR age 15-74 2050	age 15-74 2006	(5) (later ret) age 15-74 2050	age 15-74 2050
Australia	0.746	0.707	0.477	0.421	0.519	0.456	0.522	0.455	0.492
Austria	0.769	0.678	0.464	0.367	0.518	0.406	0.527	0.408	0.451
Belgium	0.749	0.688	0.398	0.335	0.449	0.376	0.456	0.380	0.412
Canada	0.765	0.697	0.510	0.428	0.559	0.462	0.560	0.460	0.500
Czech R.	0.793	0.708	0.462	0.351	0.517	0.391	0.520	0.386	0.443
Denmark	0.742	0.702	0.505	0.460	0.553	0.500	0.550	0.496	0.534
Finland	0.755	0.696	0.450	0.388	0.499	0.428	0.493	0.426	0.469
France	0.734	0.682	0.407	0.349	0.458	0.392	0.459	0.392	0.433
Germany	0.777	0.679	0.446	0.367	0.497	0.404	0.499	0.404	0.448
Greece	0.778	0.707	0.413	0.336	0.462	0.373	0.471	0.371	0.410
Hungary	0.779	0.722	0.397	0.318	0.446	0.357	0.454	0.355	0.400
Iceland	0.726	0.700	0.565	0.521	0.607	0.552	0.607	0.542	0.582
Ireland	0.751	0.715	0.463	0.394	0.510	0.431	0.523	0.429	0.464
Italy	0.765	0.642	0.384	0.287	0.433	0.320	0.439	0.319	0.354
Japan	0.768	0.640	0.484	0.382	0.522	0.406	0.516	0.400	0.434
Korea	0.788	0.680	0.480	0.389	0.527	0.407	0.533	0.396	0.430
Luxem.	0.748	0.718	0.433	0.381	0.489	0.426	0.501	0.431	0.463
Mexico	0.675	0.730	0.408	0.430	0.437	0.454	0.456	0.451	0.470
Netherl.	0.755	0.692	0.489	0.419	0.538	0.456	0.541	0.457	0.493
New Z.	0.731	0.704	0.495	0.454	0.538	0.490	0.535	0.483	0.525
Norway	0.728	0.692	0.496	0.449	0.544	0.487	0.540	0.481	0.520
Poland	0.786	0.731	0.371	0.293	0.416	0.326	0.424	0.328	0.362
Portugal	0.766	0.693	0.470	0.388	0.518	0.421	0.526	0.418	0.453
Slovak R.	0.787	0.731	0.415	0.313	0.466	0.350	0.477	0.349	0.400
Spain	0.774	0.662	0.429	0.310	0.480	0.344	0.494	0.344	0.376
Sweden	0.741	0.693	0.477	0.434	0.524	0.474	0.517	0.468	0.509
Switz.	0.761	0.671	0.524	0.436	0.575	0.471	0.570	0.466	0.508
Turkey	0.694	0.751	0.310	0.312	0.337	0.336	0.353	0.341	0.348
UK	0.746	0.705	0.485	0.441	0.528	0.476	0.529	0.475	0.512
US	0.733	0.717	0.475	0.448	0.516	0.482	0.517	0.481	0.508
Average	0.754	0.698	0.453	0.387	0.499	0.422	0.504	0.420	0.457

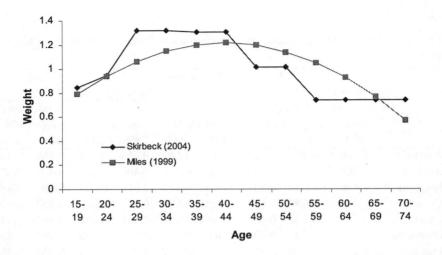

Figure 9.1: Age-Specific Productivity Weights

equal to the LFPRs of 50–54 year olds that applied in 2004. This is a way of allowing for the effect of forces discussed above that will tend to increase LFPRs of older workers between now and 2050.

Table 9.2 reports the percentage changes between 2006 and 2050 in each of the five measures of employment to population ratios that are reported in Table 9.1. In the base case the L/N ratio declines by 15.5 per cent on average over all OECD countries, with the range from -28.4 per cent (Spain) to 3.9 per cent (Mexico). At 12.1 per cent Australia is below the average, while western European countries are generally above the average. These declines would amount to the demographically-induced decline in living standards, in the absence of any other effects. A decline in living standards of 15.5 percent between 2006 and 2050 amounts to an annual reduction of 0.17 percent from an assumed annual growth of 1.75 percent in the absence of demographic change – that is, a reduction from 1.75 per cent to 1.58 per cent. The formula used for this calculation is: $g^* = \left[(1 + g)^{44} - x\right]^{1/44} - 1$, where $g = 0.0175$, $x = 0.155$, $g*$ is the growth of labour productivity after the effect

Table 9.2: Percentage Change in Labour Force Ratios: 2006 to 2050

	(1) Working age pop share	(2) LFPR age 15-74	(3) base age 15-74	(4) age 15-74	(5) (later ret) age 15-74
			Weighted LFPR		
Australia	-5.20	-11.63	-12.12	-12.75	-5.23
Austria	-11.85	-20.81	-21.67	-22.63	-12.99
Belgium	-8.14	-15.66	-16.31	-16.55	-8.29
Canada	-8.84	-16.18	-17.23	-17.75	-10.58
Czech R.	-10.72	-23.88	-24.33	-25.81	-14.28
Denmark	-5.43	-8.76	-9.62	-9.80	-3.49
Finland	-7.79	-13.77	-14.24	-13.60	-6.05
France	-7.10	-14.21	-14.45	-14.54	-5.48
Germany	-12.59	-17.58	-18.64	-19.01	-9.81
Greece	-9.19	-18.60	-19.19	-21.18	-11.22
Hungary	-7.38	-19.72	-20.01	-21.72	-10.32
Iceland	-3.61	-7.79	-9.10	-10.68	-4.14
Ireland	-4.84	-15.04	-15.49	-17.96	-9.00
Italy	-16.04	-25.27	-26.12	-27.34	-18.31
Japan	-16.70	-21.13	-22.22	-22.61	-16.82
Korea	-13.65	-18.89	-22.85	-25.77	-18.43
Luxem.	-4.02	-12.02	-12.87	-13.91	-5.42
Mexico	8.17	5.32	3.90	-1.19	7.64
Netherl.	-8.29	-14.24	-15.23	-15.53	-8.34
New Z.	-3.65	-8.21	-8.85	-9.79	-2.30
Norway	-4.98	-9.61	-10.48	-11.00	-4.30
Poland	-6.94	-20.87	-21.57	-22.78	-12.94
Portugal	-9.49	-17.56	-18.87	-20.50	-12.68
Slovak R.	-7.08	-24.51	-24.84	-26.71	-14.13
Spain	-14.47	-27.90	-28.35	-30.20	-21.62
Sweden	-6.39	-9.03	-9.49	-9.48	-2.76
Switz.	-11.76	-16.85	-18.00	-18.31	-11.53
Turkey	8.19	0.61	-0.08	-3.49	3.48
UK	-5.50	-9.13	-9.85	-10.08	-3.04
USA	-2.25	-5.77	-6.65	-6.89	-1.61
Average	-7.25	-14.62	-15.49	-16.65	-8.47

of demographic change, and $44 = 2050 - 2006$. A rate of growth of 1.75 per cent in the absence of demographic change was used by the Productivity Commission (2005) for Australia and is close to the 1.6 per cent adopted by Martins *et al.* (2005). This is argued here to be the worst case scenario because it assumes that all of the policies and other forces to increase LFPRs of older workers fail, and that all of the potential dividends discussed here are zero. These numbers are very similar to those found in other studies such as Productivity Commission (2005) for Australia and Martins *et al.* (2005) for a sample of OECD countries. Next the three potential consumption dividends are reported in Table 9.3.

9.3.1   The Open Economy Solow Dividend

From (9.5), C/N is higher for a given W/L ratio the lower is the employment growth rate, n, in 2050 relative to that in 2006. The proportional increase in C/N is the open economy Solow dividend, given by:[6]

$$\text{Solow dividend} \simeq - \left(\frac{W}{C} \right)_{2006} \Delta n \qquad (9.12)$$

This gives the proportional increase in consumption per capita arising from the reduction in the accumulation of wealth in 2050 compared with 2006, required to maintain the 2006 W/L ratio, as a result of a reduction in employment growth, n.

The W/C ratio was calculated as $(W/Y)(Y/C)$, where $W/Y = K/Y + F/Y$. The values for K/Y for 2006 were assumed to be the values for 2001 given in Kamps (2004)[7] and values for F/Y were those for 2004 in Lane, P. and Milesi-Feretti, G. (2006). Values for Y/C were obtained from the

---

[6]The approximation sign is used in the formulas for the various dividends because second-order terms in the derivations are ignored.

[7]Values of K/Y for a few smaller OECD countries were not available in this publication. These countries were assumed to have the average value of K/Y for the other OECD countries.

Table 9.3: Percentage Effects of Potential Dividends From Population Ageing: 2006 to 2050

	Solow dividend	Saving	Imp subst of L High	Imp subst of L Low	Net effect on C/N Worst	Net effect on C/N Best	Effect on growth Worst	Effect on growth Best
Australia	2.27	1.28	0.90	46.23	-12.12	-0.79	-0.134	-0.008
Austria	2.59	2.45	0.99	44.85	-21.67	-6.96	-0.246	-0.076
Belgium	0.34	1.57	0.66	25.69	-16.31	-5.72	-0.183	-0.062
Canada	2.19	1.40	0.62	45.86	-17.23	-6.37	-0.193	-0.070
Czech R.	4.47	3.48	2.11	54.74	-24.33	-4.21	-0.278	-0.046
Denmark	-1.38	0.58	-0.37	26.84	-9.62	-4.66	-0.106	-0.051
Finland	-0.69	0.73	0.44	32.55	-14.24	-5.57	-0.159	-0.061
France	0.46	1.63	0.78	35.77	-14.45	-2.62	-0.161	-0.028
Germany	1.56	1.43	-0.16	22.57	-18.64	-6.98	-0.210	-0.076
Greece	3.47	3.28	1.92	38.90	-19.19	-2.54	-0.217	-0.028
Hungary	2.54	2.62	2.31	44.06	-20.01	-2.85	-0.226	-0.031
Iceland	2.96	1.84	0.46	35.11	-9.10	1.12	-0.100	0.012
Ireland	4.15	0.99	3.05	53.47	-15.49	-0.81	-0.173	-0.009
Italy	1.51	2.48	1.46	39.17	-26.12	-12.86	-0.300	-0.143
Japan	1.46	2.64	0.53	16.83	-22.22	-12.19	-0.253	-0.135
Korea	10.37	4.66	-0.96	20.85	-22.85	-4.36	-0.260	-0.047
Luxem.	4.24	1.58	1.42	34.96	-12.87	1.82	-0.143	0.019
Mexico	8.56	4.46	5.22	50.82	3.90	25.89	0.042	0.264
Netherl.	0.18	1.53	0.10	36.83	-15.23	-6.53	-0.170	-0.071
New Z.	2.93	1.54	0.52	32.23	-8.85	2.68	-0.097	0.029
Norway	1.54	1.40	0.03	32.08	-10.48	-1.34	-0.116	-0.014
Poland	5.51	4.20	2.76	42.29	-21.57	-0.47	-0.245	-0.005
Portugal	1.65	1.47	1.31	28.14	-18.87	-8.26	-0.213	-0.091
Slovak R.	7.24	4.64	3.23	62.13	-24.84	0.98	-0.284	0.011
Spain	3.03	3.38	2.78	82.44	-28.35	-12.43	-0.327	-0.138
Sweden	0.38	0.48	-0.16	17.27	-9.49	-2.05	-0.105	-0.022
Switz.	1.22	1.96	-0.55	29.42	-18.00	-8.90	-0.202	-0.098
Turkey	3.72	1.91	5.33	56.14	-0.08	14.44	-0.001	0.151
UK	0.90	0.82	-0.03	19.92	-9.85	-1.35	-0.109	-0.015
USA	1.53	1.06	0.53	24.43	-6.65	1.51	-0.073	0.016
Average	2.70	2.12	1.24	37.75	-15.49	-2.41	-0.17	-0.03

OECD statistical database on line,[8] using the 2005 values which were the latest available.

As reported in Table 9.3, the average magnitude of this dividend for all countries is 2 percent per annum by the year 2050 with a range from minus 1.4 percent to 10 percent. As a check, the value for the United States of 1.5 percent is close to the value calculated in Cutler et al (1990) of 1.7 per cent for the period 2000 to 2050, assuming a closed economy. No comparison is available with Martins *et al.* (2005) because they are only interested in effects of demographic change on output per capita and hence do not report a Solow effect.

9.3.2   The Saving Dividend

The saving or wealth deepening dividend is the result of a changing proportion of high savers in the workforce. This could be measured by simulating a full overlapping generations CGE model, as do Mason and Lee (2004) for Taiwan for example. However a more modest model that captures the main features of the OLG model, the age composition effect, is adopted.

First a lifecycle wealth pattern for a representative worker in all countries is specified, as shown in Figure 9.2, using a Poisson distribution. This path is characterised by a rapid accumulation of wealth in the 40s and 50s, peaking at the age of 65 after which it is run down but not to zero. Then the aggregate ratio, W/L, is calculated as a weighted average of age-specific wealth, with the labour force shares as weights. This is calibrated for each country so that it equals actual W/L in 2006 by shifting the life cycle wealth pattern upward or downward by a fixed proportion for all age groups. Actual W/L in 2006 is calculated as $W/L = (W/Y)(Y/L)$, where W/Y is calculated as described in the previous section and Y/L is derived from the values for K/Y using

---

[8]Available at http://www.oecd.org/topicstatsportal

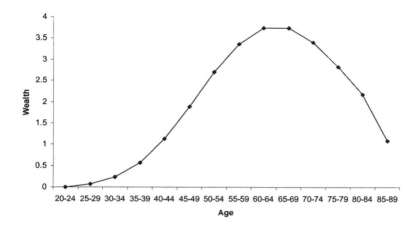

Figure 9.2: Wealth of Representative Worker over Life Cycle

the assumptions underpinning (9.11) yielding:

$$\frac{Y}{L} = \left(\frac{K}{Y}\right)^{\frac{\alpha}{1-\alpha}} \tag{9.13}$$

Labour is measured in efficiency units in order to net out the effect of technical progress on the W/L ratio.[9] Aggregate W/L for 2050 is similarly calculated as a weighted average using the labour force shares in 2050 as the weights, giving values for $(W/L)_{2006}$ and $(W/L)_{2050}$.

The saving dividend is then calculated from (9.4) as the change in C/N with respect to a change in the long run W/L ratio from 2006 to 2050:

$$\text{Saving Dividend} \simeq \left(\frac{L}{C}\right)(r-n)\Delta\left(\frac{W}{L}\right) \tag{9.14}$$

Column 2 in Table 9.3 indicates that the average saving dividend is 2.1 percent and the range is from 0.5 to 4.7 per cent. This is the result of an average increase in W/L of 17 per cent between 2006 and 2050. These

---

[9]Labour in efficiency units is equal to $A^{\frac{1}{1-\alpha}}L$.

outcomes are broadly consistent with the simulation results in Martins et al (2005) for their sample of four large OECD countries using a closed economy OLG model. In their simulation that is closest to the base case here, they found percentage increases in the K/L ratio over the period 2000 to 2050 for their four countries as follows (approximately): the United States 12; Japan 15; Germany 6; and France -6. The corresponding increases in the W/L ratio calculated here are 11; 9; 6 and 9 per cent. Hence only the outcomes for France are very different.

9.3.3   The Imperfect Labour Substitutability Dividend

Here we apply the idea, discussed in Section 9.2, that imperfect substitutability of workers by age implies that a change in the age distribution of workers can change average labour productivity. We can think of this as a change in the effective labour force, $A^{\frac{1}{1-\alpha}} L$, through changes in the productivity parameter, A. It is a separate effect from the impact of the age-specific productivity weights, α_i, in (9.12).

The method for calculating this effect is described as follows. Effective labour is assumed to be a CRESH function of labour inputs in natural units:

$$\sum_{i=1}^{k} \alpha_i \left[\frac{L_i}{f(L^*)} \right]^{\rho_i} = 1 \qquad (9.15)$$

where α_i is the productivity weight of labour of age i, k is the number of age groups, L_i is the number of workers of age i, L^* effective labour, and ρ_i is a parameter that represents the flexibility, or versatility, of L_i, meaning the degree to which L_i can substitute for any other input, L_j. All labour inputs are substitutes to some degree, which restricts ρ_i such that $-\infty < \rho_i < 1$. The larger the absolute value of ρ_i, the more easily L_i is substitutable for any other labour input with a given value of ρ_j. This implies that two labour inputs with high absolute values of ρ_i are good substitutes and two inputs with low absolute values of ρ_i are poor substitutes.

With $\rho = 1$, (9.15) gives the additive function for which the elasticity of substitution is infinite:

$$L^* = \sum_{i=1}^{k} \alpha_i L_i \tag{9.16}$$

The elasticity of substitution, σ_{ij}, between L_i and L_j is given by Hanock (1971, p.699):[10]

$$\sigma_{ij} = \frac{a_i a_j}{\sum_{m=1}^{k} s_m a_m} \tag{9.17}$$

where $a_i = 1/(1 - \rho_i)$ and s_m is the factor share of L_i.

Restrictions exist on the range of values of the σ_{ij} that yield a unique solution for the CRESH function (Hanoch, 1971). The binding restriction in the present application is that $\alpha_i \rho_i$ must be of the same sign for all i, assuming that all $a_i > 0$, which implies that all labour inputs are substitutes to some degree. Given all $\alpha_i > 0$ by definition, we must have, for all i, either $0 < \rho_i < 1$ $(a_i > 1)$ or $\rho_i < 0$ $(0 < ai < 1)$.

In applying the CRESH function, the degree of flexibility of workers varies with age. In particular, middle age workers are more flexible than either young or older workers. The particular values for a_i are:

Table 9.4: Values of Parameters, a_i

i	15-19	20-24	25-29	30-34	35-39	40-44
a_i	1.0	1.5	2.0	2.0	3.0	3.0
i	45-49	50-54	55-59	60-64	65-69	70-74
a_i	3.0	3.0	2.0	1.5	1.0	1.0

The parameters in the CRESH function are chosen so that the elasticity of substitution between workers of different ages is less than perfect. The parameters are assumed to be the same for all countries. There are two simulations: one where the elasticities of substitution between workers of different ages are relatively high (between 2 and 4) and another where the elasticities

---

[10]This is the Allen-Uzawa pairwise elasticity of substitution, which is the n-factor analogue of the two-factor Hicks ES of substitution.

are low (between 0.4 and 0.8). The high elasticity case is more realistic and is closer to the standard modelling assumption of perfect substitutability. Hence this case is adopted in calculating the 'best case' scenario. The low elasticity case is reported as a theoretical possibility and is interesting if only because it shows the large gains that could occur if the elasticity were low enough. The low elasticity case also indicates that the results are sensitive to the size of the elasticity.

As Table 9.3 indicates, the size of this dividend (for the high elasticity case) averages 1.24 percent – about half the size of each of the other two dividends. The highest gain is 5 percent and the lowest is minus 1 percent, indicating that this dividend is not universally positive, although negative values occur for only 6 out of the 30 countries (and the gains are universally positive for the low elasticity case). The outcomes for the G7 countries are very close to those reported for G7 countries in Prskawetz, Fent and Guest (2006), using the same CRESH model but slightly different data parameters. These results suggest that population ageing is moving countries a little closer to their optimum age workforce age distributions, at least according to the CRESH index. The apparent sensitivity of the size of this dividend to the value of the elasticity suggests scope for further investigation of this potential phenomenon including the need to obtain reliable econometric estimates of the elasticities.

9.4   Conclusion

The title of this chapter echoes the question asked by Disney (1996), 'can we afford to grow older?' His conclusion, that fears of an 'ageing crisis' were unfounded, is supported by the calculations presented here. This view has been supported by the balance of evidence published in academic economics journals, starting with the seminal work by Cutler *et al.* (1990) for the U.S. economy. However, this view is not as widely shared by commentators from different perspectives. The Washington-based Centre for Strategic and International Studies claims that 'global ageing ... may ultimately mean stagnating or declining living standards' (Jackson, 2003). The influential *Foreign Affairs* journal published a piece titled 'Gray Dawn: The Global Aging Crisis' (Petersen, 1999); the World Bank (1994) called for policies to avert an 'old age crisis' that is 'looming'.

According to the calculations for all OECD countries presented in this chapter, the worst that can be expected, even for countries that age the most, is a retardation in the rate of growth of living standards in the order of 0.3 per cent per year. The best case is no slow down at all, on average across all OECD countries, with some countries deriving positive net gains from demographic change.

This is not to deny that population ageing poses challenges and will have important macroeconomic effects. There will be fiscal effects, changes in international capital flows, and changes in relative prices of labour and capital. However, these amount mainly to income transfers from some groups in society to others rather than significant effects on national living standards. It is true that fiscal effects – in particular, the effects on pensions and health care costs – imply a loss of consumption possibilities, mainly through the disincentive effects of tax rates on work effort. But evidence presented elsewhere suggests that these deadweight losses will be small to modest (Cutler *et al.*, 1990; Davis and Fabling, 2002) and are swamped by the other effects considered in this chapter.

With respect to policy implications, if concerns about the costs of population ageing spur the implementation of policies to promote growth, that might be seen as a favourable outcome – the end justifying the means. On the other hand, if such policies involve income transfers within or between generations, the justification is less clear cut especially if the policy is argued on the grounds of a concern about population ageing. For example, tax smoothing through vehicles such as the Future Fund in Australia, fall into this category. Tax smoothing imposes a higher tax burden on current generations in order to lower the tax burden on future generations. The net gain in terms of intertemporal social welfare is an empirical question that must encompass implications for intergenerational equity and economic efficiency. Other examples where the net welfare gains may or may not be positive are tax expenditures to encourage higher labour force participation of older workers and higher retirement saving, and pro-fertility policies. Empirical analyses of the intertemporal social welfare effects of these policies would be helpful, not least because they are usually argued on the grounds of concern about population ageing – a concern that this chapter suggests is exaggerated.

Chapter 10

Capital Intensity and Productivity

The effect of population ageing on labour productivity is a critical relationship because labour productivity growth could potentially offset – indeed swamp – the economic burden caused by a falling employment to population ratio. This chapter explores a link between population ageing and labour productivity that has received little attention – that is, the effect on labour productivity via capital intensity which in turn is affected by sectoral shifts in demand in response to population ageing. The method is to apply a calibrated simulation model using data for two OECD countries, the United States and Australia. Although the two countries have common features there are also obvious differences. One is a large Northern hemisphere country with moderate population ageing and a large manufacturing base, while the other is a small Southern hemisphere country with a somewhat higher degree of population ageing and a smaller manufacturing share of output.

Broadly speaking there are two sources of labour productivity growth: technical progress and increases in the average capital–labour ratio. With respect to the former, the magnitude and direction of the effect of demographic change on technical progress remains an elusive question – it is unresolved in theory and empirically; see for example Birdsall *et al.* (2001) and Mason (2001). For this reason most empirical studies take an agnostic view in assuming that the net effect of demographic change on technical progress is zero; see, for example, Martins *et al.* (2005) for the OECD and Productivity Commission (2005) for Australia.

The other source of labour productivity growth – increases in the average K/L ratio – can be affected by demographic change in two ways. The first is a mechanical effect as capital takes time to adjust to changes in labour for any equilibrium ratio. This implies a short-run rise in the K/L ratio in response to population ageing. The second effect is a change in the equilibrium average ratio. The average ratio is affected by shifts in demand between sectors that have different K/L ratios. This link is analysed here.

Labour productivity affects economic welfare via consumption. In Chapter 9 the following identity for an open economy was introduced in order to link with consumption and productivity:

$$\frac{C}{N} \equiv \frac{L}{N}\left(w + r\frac{W}{L} - \frac{S}{L}\right) \tag{10.1}$$

In order to focus on labour productivity, the following closed economy version of the above equation is more helpful:

$$\frac{C}{N} \equiv \frac{L}{N}\frac{C}{Y}\frac{Y}{L} \tag{10.2}$$

where Y/L is average labour productivity. Population ageing lowers L/N which implies lower living standards C/N for a given level of labour productivity and consumption share of output C/Y. But neither Y/L nor C/Y are unaffected by ageing. Ageing can Y/L via capital intensity, as suggested above. Ageing also increases C/Y via lower capital widening requirements; and, in an open economy, an analogous effect on foreign assets per worker increases C/Y if foreign assets are positive and decreases C/Y if foreign assets are negative. Hence ageing is likely to affect all three of the ratios on the right-hand side of (10.2).

Section 10.1 discusses the relationship between ageing and labour productivity illustrating with data from the two countries: the United States and

Australia. Section 10.2 describes the simulation model, including behaviour of firms and consumers. Section 10.4 explains the simulation results.

10.1 Capital Intensity and Expenditure

Consider Tables 10.1 and 10.2 which, for the U.S. and Australia respectively, give household consumption shares in 2004.[1] For the U.S. the categories that vary most with age are the following primarily non-traded services: utilities, transport, finance-related services, education and health. For Australia, a similar set of non-traded services are relatively age sensitive in household expenditure: domestic fuel and power, housing, health care, transport and miscellaneous (which includes education). Of these, the most age-sensitive is health which increases in share of household expenditure for households with persons over 65 years of age.

The aim here is to account for the effect of prospective population ageing on the composition of demand for goods and services. First, two composite goods for each country are formed. Good 1 is the composite of the more age-sensitive goods identified above and which is also assumed to be a non-traded good – a reasonable assumption for the data in Tables 10.1 and 10.2. Good 2 is a composite of all the other goods and is assumed to be a traded good, which is also reasonable given that this good includes manufacturing, mining, agriculture, wholesale trade, and information. Following the model in Obstfeld and Rogoff (1996) it is also assumed that all capital goods are traded goods and therefore belong to the composite traded good (good 2).[2] Hence good 1 is a consumer good and good 2 is both a consumer good and

---

[1] Source: U.S. Department of Labour, Bureau of Labour Statistics, Consumer Expenditure Survey, Table 47, at www.bls.gov; and the Australian Bureau of Statistics, Cat. No. 6530.0, Table 19, Household Expenditure Survey.

[2] This avoids the need to decide how new capital goods of type 1 and 2 are allocated between each of the two production sectors; that is how the proportion of both non-traded and traded capital goods are allocated to the traded and non-traded sectors. Instead it is assumed that all capital goods are traded goods.

a capital good.

The next step is to consider the capital intensity of the two composite goods. Tables 10.3 and 10.4 give the capital intensities and GDP shares by major industry classification for, respectively, the United States in 2005 and Australia in 2004.[3] Output, X_i, is the gross output of industry i. Capital intensity is defined here as the industry's capital output ratio, $(K/X)_i$. The industries are sorted into the two composite goods. The far right-hand column gives the total capital employed as a ratio to total output of all industries combined, which is calculated by multiplying the capital intensity by the output share. The total of this column for all industry sectors would give the weighted average capital intensity of the economy. We are interested in the relative capital intensity of the two composite goods. This is given in both Tables 10.3 and 10.4 and is also summarised in Table 10.5. For the U.S. $(K/X)_1 = 3.21$ and $(K/X)_2 = 0.58$. For Australia $(K/X) = 3.11$ and $(K/X)_2 = 1.80$. Hence for both countries good 1 is much more capital intensive than good 2. This may seem a little counter-intuitive since non-traded services are usually thought to be more labour intensive than traded goods. While this is true for some services it is not true for the age-sensitive services which comprise our good 1. The implication is that a shift of expenditure toward good 1 due to an ageing population would raise the average capital intensity of the economy.

In order to calibrate the magnitude of this effect, the input-output coefficients for the two goods are needed. These were calculated from industry input-output tables for the two countries (the detailed tables are not reproduced due to space constraints).[4] The coefficients are reported in Table 10.5. For both countries the input of good 2 into industry output of good 1 $(a_{2,1})$ is greater than the input of good 1 into industry output of good 2 $(a_{1,2})$.

---

[3]The sources are *Australian Bureau of Statistics*, Catalogue 5204.0, and *Bureau of Economic Analysis*, at http://www.bea.doc.gov/bea/dn/FA2004/TableView.asp#Mid

[4]Source: For the US Bureau of Economic Analysis and for Australia, the data were obtained on application to the OECD.

Table 10.1: Consumer Expenditure Shares for the U.S. from 2004 Survey

	All units	<25	25-34	35-44	45-54	55-64	65-74	75+
		Age of reference person						
Housing	32.1	31.2	33.7	33.3	30.6	30.3	30.5	36.4
Transportation	18	19.2	19.9	18.2	17.7	17.8	17.8	12.8
Food	13.3	15.1	13.4	13.4	13.3	12.5	13.3	13.7
Utils, fuel, pub service	6.7	5.8	6.3	6.6	6.5	6.8	7.9	8.9
Health care	5.9	2.7	3.6	4.5	5.1	6.9	10.4	15.5
Entertainment	5.1	4.8	5.0	5.0	5.1	6.0	5.1	3.8
Apparel and services	4.2	5.6	5.0	4.2	4.2	3.9	3.3	2.3
Education	2.1	7.4	1.7	1.6	3.0	1.5	1.0	0.8
Miscellaneous	1.6	1.2	1.4	1.5	1.5	1.7	2.0	2.1
Housekeeping supplies	1.4	1	1.2	1.3	1.4	1.4	1.6	1.7
Personal care	1.3	1.4	1.3	1.3	1.3	1.3	1.4	1.6
Alcoholic beverages	1.1	2.0	1.2	1.1	1.0	1.0	0.9	0.7
Tobacco products	0.7	1.0	0.7	0.7	0.7	0.6	0.5	0.4
Reading	0.3	0.2	0.2	0.2	0.3	0.4	0.4	0.5
No cons units (000s)	116,282	8,817	19,439	24,070	23,712	17,479	11,230	11,536
Income before tax: $	54,453	22,840	52,484	65,515	70,434	61,031	42,137	28,028
Income after taxes	52,287	22,507	50,819	63,202	66,761	58,043	41,126	27,142
Age of ref person	48.5	21.4	29.7	39.7	49.3	59.1	69.3	81.2
Average no in unit:								
Persons	2.5	1.9	2.9	3.2	2.7	2.1	1.9	1.5
Children under 18	0.6	0.4	1.1	1.3	0.6	0.2	0.1	<0.05
Persons 65 and over	0.3	<0.05	<0.05	<0.05	<0.05	0.1	1.4	1.3
Av expenditure	43,395	24,535	42,701	50,402	52,764	47,299	36,512	25,763

Table 10.2: Consumer Expenditure Shares for Australia from 2004 Survey

	All units	<25	25-34	35-44	45-54	55-64	65+
		\multicolumn{6}{c}{Age of reference person}					
Housing costs	16.1	21.3	21.7	17.7	13.1	11.1	13.4
Domestic fuel and power	2.6	2.1	2.2	2.6	2.6	2.9	3.5
Food and non–alcohol bev	17.1	14.8	15.0	17.3	17.4	17.6	20.0
Alcoholic beverages	2.6	3.7	2.6	2.3	2.8	3.0	2.1
Tobacco products	1.3	1.8	1.3	1.3	1.3	1.5	0.8
Clothing and footwear	3.9	4.2	3.8	4.1	4.1	3.9	3.3
Household furn and equip	5.8	6.5	5.6	6.1	5.4	6.3	5.7
Household services	6.1	5.4	6.1	6.4	5.5	5.8	6.9
Medical and health	5.1	2.2	3.5	4.2	5.5	6.9	8.0
Transport	15.6	15.2	15.8	14.4	16.4	17.7	13.7
Recreation	12.8	11.8	11.8	12.5	13.8	12.9	13.8
Personal care	1.9	1.8	1.8	1.7	2.0	2.2	2.1
Misc goods and services	8.9	9.2	8.7	9.3	10.0	8.2	6.8
Total goods and services	100	100	100	100	100	100	100
Av age of reference person		22	30	40	49	59	74
Employed persons		1.4	1.5	1.5	1.8	1.1	0.2
Dependent children		0.3	0.8	1.4	0.8	0.2	-
Persons							
Under 18 years		0.3	0.8	1.4	0.7	0.1	-
18 to 64 years		1.9	1.8	1.8	2.2	1.9	0.2
65 years and over		-	-	-	0.1	0.1	1.4
Total		2.2	2.6	3.3	2.9	2.1	1.6
Households	'000	334.7	1405.1	1730.8	1568.1	1155.4	1541.7
Persons	'000	737.5	3706.7	5632.6	4566.0	2456.3	2507.6

Table 10.3: Capital–Output Ratios, K/X, for the US Private Sector in 2005

	K/X	X share	K/X
Composite good 1			
Utilities	3.22	0.02	0.07
Transportation and warehousing	1.32	0.04	0.05
Finance, insurance, real estate. et al.	4.48	0.20	0.88
Educ., health, social services	0.84	0.08	0.07
K/X Good 1	3.21		
Composite good 2			
Agriculture, forestry, fishing, and hunting	1.65	0.02	0.03
Mining	2.54	0.02	0.05
Construction	0.19	0.06	0.01
Manufacturing	0.43	0.22	0.10
Wholesale trade	0.39	0.05	0.02
Retail trade	0.68	0.06	0.04
Information	0.81	0.06	0.05
Professional and business services	0.37	0.11	0.04
Arts, ent., rec., accomm, food services	0.76	0.04	0.03
Other services, except government	0.83	0.03	0.02
K/X Good 2	0.58		

Table 10.4: Capital–Output Ratios, K/X, for the Australian Private Sector in 2004

	K/X	X share	K/X
Composite good 1			
Electricity, gas and water supply	8.08	0.03	0.24
Transport and storage	5.07	0.06	0.31
Finance and insurance	1.95	0.07	0.14
Education	1.98	0.06	0.11
Health and community services	1.33	0.07	0.09
K/X Good 1	3.11		
Composite good 2			
Agriculture, forestry and fishing	3.13	0.04	0.12
Mining	4.81	0.05	0.25
Manufacturing	1.22	0.16	0.20
Construction	0.60	0.07	0.04
Wholesale trade	1.36	0.06	0.08
Retail trade	1.03	0.08	0.08
Accommodation, cafes and restaurants	2.13	0.03	0.06
Communication services	2.81	0.04	0.11
Property and business services(a)	1.61	0.14	0.23
Cultural and recreational services	4.20	0.02	0.07
Personal and other services	1.50	0.02	0.03
K/X Good 2	1.80		
Excluded			
Ownership of dwellings	11.83	0.11	1.27

Table 10.5: Input–Output Parameters and K/X Ratios

	U.S.	Australia
$a_{1,2}$	0.08	0.11
$a_{2,1}$	0.19	0.17
$(K/X)_1$	3.21	3.11
$(K/X)_2$	0.58	1.80

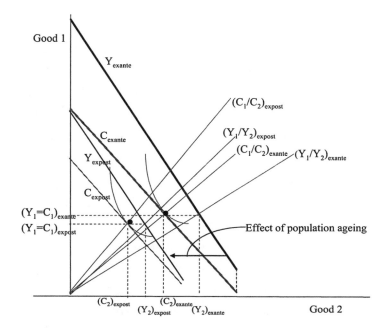

Figure 10.1: Effect of Population Ageing on Long Run Output and Consumption Ratios

This means that a shift of final goods expenditure toward good 1 would be less than the shift in total demands for industry output of good 1, and this would tend to dampen down the effect on the average capital intensity of the economy.

The change in output and consumption shares is illustrated diagrammatically in Figure 10.1. Good 1 (the relatively age sensitive, non-traded good) is represented on the vertical axis and Good 2 (the traded good) is on the horizontal axis. Ex ante and Ex post denote values before and after the occurrence of population ageing which is modelled as a shock (see Section 10.3.5). The Y line is a production possibility frontier, the slope of which is greater than 1 under the assumption that good 1 has a higher capital intensity than good 2. The C line is the consumption possibilities trade-off and lies below the GDP line to the extent of investment which consists exclusively of T goods. The assumption here is that long-run foreign assets are zero. Linearity of the Y and C loci is implied in an open economy model given perfect capital mobility.[5] The slope of the C line is less than the slope of the Y line because good 1 is more capital intensive than good 2 and therefore the investment share of output is greater the greater the good 1 share of output. The assumption that all capital goods are traded goods (good 2) means that good 1 consists entirely of consumption goods, that is, $Y_1 = C_1$. This level of C_1 is determined at the point of tangency of the indifference curve with the C_1/C_2 line.

Population ageing in represented as a reduction in employment which shifts the Y and C lines to the left. The shift in consumer preferences toward good 1 shifts the consumer indifference curve shifts downwards to the left and the consumption expansion path skews upwards to $(C_1/C_2)_{ex\ post}$. This in turn skews Y_1/Y_2 upwards which results in an increase in aggregate labour productivity due to the higher capital intensity of good 1.

10.2   The Simulation Model

10.2.1   Firms

The distinguishing feature of the model in this chapter is that the representative firm produces two composite goods defined as above, rather than a single good. This avoids the need to decide how new capital goods of type 1 and 2 are allocated between each of the two production sectors; that is, how the proportion of both non-traded and traded capital goods are allocated to the traded and non-traded sectors. Instead we assume that all capital goods are traded goods. Labour and capital are combined according to Cobb-Douglas

---

[5]The simulation model assumes an open economy but does not assume perfect capital mobility. This would imply a small degree of concavity in the Y and C loci, but the qualitative results would carry over.

technology. Each good is used in the production of the other in fixed proportion to the total output of the industry. Hence the input-output technology
is of the Leontief type. The final demand for each good is the total output of
the good minus the input of that good required to produce the other good.
This simple production set up follows Vanek (1963) and is represented as
follows:

$$X_{1,t} = A_1 K_{1,t}^{\gamma_1} L_{1,t}^{1-\gamma_1} \tag{10.3}$$

$$X_{2,t} = A_2 K_{2,t}^{\gamma_2} L_{2,t}^{1-\gamma_2} \tag{10.4}$$

$$Y_{1,t} = X_{1,t} - a_{1,2} X_{2,t} \tag{10.5}$$

$$Y_{2,t} = X_{2,t} - a_{2,1} X_{1,t} \tag{10.6}$$

where X, Y, K, L and X denote total output, final output, capital and
labour, respectively. The subscripts 1 and 2 refer to the two goods. The
parameter $a_{m,n}$ is the input of good m in the total industry output of good
n. In order to keep the technology as simple as possible there is constant returns to scale and no technical progress. Zero technical progress implies that
demographic change does not influence the technology of producing either
goods or intermediate inputs, which is justified on the basis of uncertainty
in the literature on this issue and the fact that it is not important for the
central aim of this chapter.

Aggregate final output is $Y_t = Y_{1,t} + Y_{2,t}$. Assume that capital and labour
can move freely between the production of goods. Firms therefore equate
the marginal value-added products of capital and labour in each sector with,
respectively, the user cost of capital, $r_t + \delta$, and the real wage, w_t, implying,
dropping time subscripts and defining k as capital per worker:

$$\frac{\partial X_1}{\partial K} \left(1 - pa_{2,1}\right) = A_1 \gamma_1 k_1^{\gamma_1 - 1} \left(1 - pa_{2,1}\right) = r + \delta \tag{10.7}$$

$$\frac{\partial X_2}{\partial K} \left(p - a_{1,2}\right) = A_2 \gamma_2 k_2^{\gamma_2 - 1} \left(p - a_{1,2}\right) = r + \delta \tag{10.8}$$

$$\frac{\partial X_1}{\partial L} \left(1 - pa_{2,1}\right) = A_1 \left(1 - \gamma_1\right) k_1^{\gamma_1} \left(1 - pa_{2,1}\right) = w \tag{10.9}$$

$$\frac{\partial X_2}{\partial L}\left(p - a_{1,2}\right) = A_2 \left(1 - \gamma_2\right) k_2^{\gamma_2} \left(p - a_{1,2}\right) = w \qquad (10.10)$$

where p is the price of good 2 in terms of the numeraire, good 1, which implies that the price of good 1 is equal to one.

Equations (10.7) to (10.10) is a system of four equations in four endogenous variables. Values of parameters $\gamma_1, \gamma_2, a_{1,2}, a_{2,1}$ are calibrated using data, as discussed in section 10.3.

The interest rate, r_t, which is endogenous but predetermined at time t, is specified as a function of foreign liabilities as follows:

$$r_t = \bar{r} + \lambda \left(\frac{D_{t-1}}{Y_{t-1}}\right) \qquad (10.11)$$

where D is foreign liabilities. This is a flexible specification that can apply to both a small and large open economy. In the small economy case (such as Australia) it implies imperfect capital mobility ($\lambda \neq 0$) which is consistent with widespread evidence (see Gordon and Bovenberg, 1996). In the large economy case (the U.S.) it implies monopsony power in the market for foreign capital since the economy is large enough to affect the world interest rate. In both large and small economies (10.11) can also be interpreted as allowing for a risk premium in the interest rate where the premium depends on their level of foreign debt.[6]

10.2.2   Consumers

Unlike the models in Chapters 7 and 8, there are no overlapping generations. Instead the one person households have finite lives but dynastic utility functions – they regard an infinite number of future generations as an extension of themselves. Consumers differ only in that their consumption demands are age-specific. Hence a representative consumer at time t can be defined

---

[6]Another feature of this specification is that the steady state level of foreign liabilities is constant as a ratio of GDP. This means that, following a shock, the foreign liabilities to GDP ratio eventually returns to its original steady state level, which in turn means that wealth is held constant in comparing one steady state to another.

as having the weighted average age of the population at time t, the weights being the population shares of each age group, $N_{i,t}/N_t$, where $N_{i,t}$ is the number of consumers aged i in year t and N_t is the population at time t.

An innovation in this chapter is the assumption that although all households are intratemporal optimizers not all households are intertemporal optimisers. Rather 30 per cent of consumers are rule-of-thumb consumers, meaning that they always consume a fixed proportion of their labour income. This is a common assumption in applied economy-wide models; in the context of population ageing; see, for example, the application of the MSG3 model in McKibbin and Nguyen (2001) and the OECD's MINILINK model in Turner *et al.* (1998).

A further difference in the model here is that the two consumption goods consist of good 1 and good 2 rather than a consumption good and leisure. Hence there is no explicit modelling of leisure.

The intertemporal optimising consumers solve the following model: the model and its solution method presented below is similar to that in Obstfeld and Rogoff (1996). Each cohort, i, maximises an intertemporal utility function, dropping the i subscripts:

$$U = \sum_{t=1}^{\infty} c_t^{1-\beta} \frac{(1+\theta)^{1-t}}{1-\beta} \tag{10.12}$$

where θ is the pure time preference rate and β is the representative agent's elasticity of marginal utility of consumption; c_t is an index of consumption of goods 1 and 2 defined by:

$$c_t = \left[\mu_t^{1/\Psi} c_{1,t}^{\Psi-1/\Psi} + (1-\mu_t)^{1/\Psi} c_{2,t}^{\Psi-1/\Psi} \right]^{\Psi/\Psi-1} \tag{10.13}$$

where μ_t is the expenditure share for good 1, the calculation of which is explained in section 10.3.

The intertemporal utility function is maximised subject to the budget constraint given by:

$$\sum_{t=1}^{\infty} \left(c_{1,t} + p_t c_{2,t} \right) \left(1 + r_t \right)^{1-t} = q_0 + \sum_{t=1}^{\infty} w_t l_t \left(1 + r_t \right)^{1-t} \tag{10.14}$$

where p_t is the price of good 2 in terms of good 1, r_t is the interest rate, q_0 is initial assets, and l_t is the consumer's labour supply which is assumed to be exogenous.

There is no government sector in the model and hence no government spending or taxation. The consumer's financial asset accumulation identity is:

$$q_t = \left(1 + r_t \right) q_{t-1} + w_t l_t - c_{1,t} - p_t c_{2,t} \tag{10.15}$$

The consumer's intertemporal problem is solved by maximising the utility function in (10.12) subject to the budget constraint (10.14). This yields the following relation between consumption of goods and leisure:

$$\frac{\mu_t c_{2,t}}{\left(1 - \mu_t \right) c_{1,t}} = p_t^{-\Psi} \tag{10.16}$$

Solving (10.16) for $c_{2,t}$ and substituting into (10.13), yields:

$$c_{1,t} = c_t \mu_i \left[\mu_i + \left(1 - \mu_i \right) p_{i,j}^{1-\Psi} \right]^{1/1-\Psi} \tag{10.17}$$

and repeating for $c_{1,t}$ gives:

$$c_{2,t} = c_t \left(1 - \mu_i \right) p_{i,j}^{1-\Psi} \left[\mu_i + \left(1 - \mu_i \right) p_{i,j}^{1-\Psi} \right]^{1/1-\Psi} \tag{10.18}$$

Defining P_t as the minimum price that buys a unit of the consumption index, c_t:

$$P_t c_t = c_{1,t} + p_t c_{2,t} \tag{10.19}$$

Equations (10.17) and (10.18) can be simplified using (10.19) to give:

$$c_{1,t} = \mu_t P_t^{\Psi} c_t \tag{10.20}$$

$$c_{2,t} = \left(1 - \mu_t \right) \left(\frac{P_t}{p_t} \right)^{\Psi} c_t \tag{10.21}$$

To obtain the Euler equation, first use (10.20) and (10.21) to substitute for $c_{1,t}$ and $c_{2,t}$ in the budget constraint (10.14). Then maximise the utility function (10.12) with respect to c_t subject to the budget constraint, giving:

$$\frac{c_t}{c_{t-1}} = \left[\frac{1+r}{1+\theta} \left(\frac{P_{t-1}}{P_t} \right) \right]^{1/\beta} \tag{10.22}$$

For rule-of-thumb consumers, c_t is determined by $c_t = \phi w_t l_t$ for all t where ϕ is the constant proportion of labour income consumed.

The labour allocated to good 1, $L_{1,t}$, is determined using the assumption that for good 1 output equals consumption (see the following section). Then $L_{2,t}$ is given by $L_{2,t} = L_t - L_{1,t}$ where L_t is exogenous. Labour productivity in the two goods can be determined as:

$$\frac{Y_{1,t}}{L_{1,t}} = A_1 k_{1,t}^{\gamma_1} - a_{1,2} A_2 k_{2,t}^{\gamma_2} \frac{L_{2,t}}{L_{1,t}} \tag{10.23}$$

$$\frac{Y_{2,t}}{L_{2,t}} = A_2 k_{2,t}^{\gamma_2} - a_{2,1} A_1 k_{1,t}^{\gamma_1} \frac{L_{1,t}}{L_{2,t}} \tag{10.24}$$

and aggregate labour productivity is:

$$\frac{Y_t}{L_t} = \frac{Y_{1,t} + p_t Y_{2,t}}{L_t} \tag{10.25}$$

Aggregate foreign liabilities, D_t, are then given by:

$$D_t = D_{t-1} (1 + r_t) + C_{1,t} + I_{1,t} - Y_{1,t} + p_t (C_{2,t} + I_{2,t} - Y_{2,t}) \tag{10.26}$$

where C_t is aggregate consumption which is equal to $N_t c_t$.

10.2.3 Living Standards

A given change in labour productivity, Y/L, caused by a change in capital intensity does not imply a commensurate change in long-run living standards, C/N. This is because first, an increase in long-run capital intensity requires an increase in long-run saving to maintain it when the workforce is growing – saving provides the necessary capital to equip new workers with the same capital as existing workers; and second, a higher capital per worker implies a higher loss of capital through depreciation.[7] Both of these effects lower the consumption share of output (C/Y) in the long run. A lower C/Y would at least partially offset the effect of an increase in Y/L on C/N as seen from the decomposition of living standards in (10.2). The simulations provide the magnitudes of these effects.

10.3   Calibration and Solution Method

10.3.1   Allocating Labour Between the Two Goods

The composition of demand determines the output mix because one of the goods is non-traded. For good 1, the non-traded good which is age-sensitive in consumption, output must equal consumption since capital goods can consist only of traded goods. Hence:

$$Y_{1,t} = C_{1,t} \tag{10.27}$$

Output of good 1 is also given by the production function:

$$Y_{1,t} = A_1 k_{1,t}^{\gamma_1} L_{1,t} \left(1 - a_{1,2}\right) \tag{10.28}$$

Equating (10.27) and (10.28):

$$L_{1,t} = \frac{C_{1,t}}{A_1 k_{1,t}^{\gamma_1} \left(1 - a_{1,2}\right)} \tag{10.29}$$

where the right-hand side variables are predetermined. The aggregate employment constraint implies that $L_{2,t} = L_t - L_{1,t}$. Investment, $I_{j,t}$, can be expressed in per worker units, $i_{j,t}$:

$$I_{j,t} = i_{j,t} L_{j,t} \tag{10.30}$$

---

[7]To see this, consider the well-known result for a steady state saving rate in the Solow growth model, $s = (z + \delta)(k/y)$ where s is the saving rate, z is the growth of workers, δ is the depreciation rate, k is capital per worker and y is output per worker (where workers are in measured in efficiency units).

where $i_{j,t}$ is given by the evolution of the capital stock:

$$i_{j,t} = k_{j,t} - k_{j,t-1}(1-\delta)\frac{L_{j,t-1}}{L_{j,t}} \qquad (10.31)$$

10.3.2 Age-dependent Preferences for the Two Goods

Recalling that the representative consumer has the weighted average age of the population, the consumer's preference for good 1 over time, μ_t is measured as the age-weighted expenditure share for good 1 of the population at time t. A projected time series for μ_t is constructed using the demographic projections from 2006 to 2050 holding constant the age-specific expenditure shares for each expenditure category given in Tables 10.1and 10.2. Hence:

$$\mu_t = \sum_i \sum_g w_{i,g,t}\frac{N_{g,t}}{N_t} \qquad (10.32)$$

where $w_{i,g,t}$ is the expenditure share of a household with reference person of age g on expenditure category i in year t.[8] The time series for μ_t is plotted in Figure 10.3 for both countries.

10.3.3 Other Parameter Values

The values of base case parameter values that were not given in the text are as follows. The intertemporal elasticity of consumption, $1/\beta$, is equal to 0.67; the elasticity of substitution between traded and non-traded goods in consumption, Ψ, is equal to 1.0. These values are in the range of estimates in the literature, as cited by Kenc and Sayan (2001). The values of other parameters are: $\bar{r} = 0.05$; initial debt to GDP, $D_0/Y_0 = 0$ and hence $r_0 = 0.05$; technical progress, $\dot{A}/A = 0.01$; depreciation, $\delta = 0.05$; and the interest rate parameter, $\lambda = 0.01$. The parameters γ_1, γ_2 are calibrated as follows. For the initial steady state, solve equations (10.7) to (10.10) by setting $p = 1$ and, given the Cobb-Douglas form of the production function, $k_j = \left(A_j\frac{K_j}{X_j}\right)^{1/1-\gamma_1}$

---

[8]No adjustment was made for the age composition of households using equivalence scales. This a source of approximation in the calculations.

for industry j, where data are given for the capital share of industry output, (K_j/X_j). This gives: $\gamma_1 = \left(\frac{r+\delta}{1-a_{2,1}}\right)\left(\frac{K}{X}\right)_1$ and $\gamma_2 = \left(\frac{r+\delta}{1-a_{1,2}}\right)\left(\frac{K}{X}\right)_2$.

A steady state implies, $d_t - d_{t-1} = 0$, $y_t - y_{t-1} = 0$, $c_t - c_{t-1} = 0$ and $P_t - P_{t-1} = 0$ which yields the following condition on the rate of time preference in a steady state (recalling the assumption of zero technical progress): $\rho = r_t$.

10.3.4   Demographic Projections

The medium fertility scenario is chosen for both the United States and Australia using the United Nations (2004) projections for both countries for the period 2006 to 2050. For years after 2050 population for each age group is assumed to asymptote to a constant by the year 2100. A productivity-weighted employment series is calculated, using labour force participation rates by age for males and females, which are assumed to be constant at their 2005 levels.[9] Labour productivity weights by age group were calculated from earnings for full-time workers.[10]

The support ratios, defined as productivity adjusted employment as a ratio to population, are plotted for the two countries in Figure 10.2. The support ratio for Australia is projected to fall by 13 per cent for Australia but only by about 5 per cent for the U.S. The projected degree of population ageing for the U.S. is somewhat less than has been projected in earlier studies such as Cutler *et al.* (1990). This is due to data revisions by the United Nations but also to assumptions about increasing labour force participation rates of older workers which, given the age specific productivity levels, tend to moderate the effect of the raw population shares. The raw population share of 15–65 years olds is projected by the United Nations to fall by 7.4

---

[9]Given by the US Bureau of Labour Statistics available at http://www.bls.gov/emp/emplab1.htm; and the Australian Bureau of Statistics Catalogue 6291.0.55.001 available at http://www.abs.gov.au/ausstats.

[10]The U.S. Census Bureau 2004 Population Survey, available at http://www.census.gov/population/www/socdemo/education/cps2004.html; and the Australian Bureau of Statistics, Employee Earnings, Catalogue 6310.0.

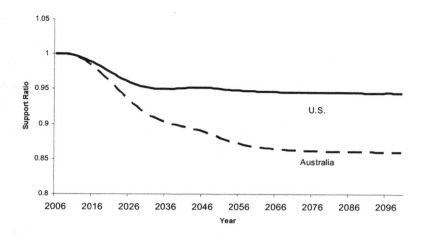

Figure 10.2: Support Ratios for the US and Australia

percent between 2006 and 2050. Once we allow for increases in labour force participation rates of older workers (which are quite modest) and labour productivity levels by age, the figure of 7.4 percent implies a drop of only 5 per cent in the employment to population ratio.

10.3.5 The Solution Method

The economy is assumed to be in a steady state in 2006 at which time it is subject to the unanticipated ageing shock. Once the ageing shock occurs, agents are assumed to know the future demographic structure with certainty. The optimal adjustment path in response to the shock is determined by finding the new initial value of the consumption index that leads to the steady state. In order to ensure that the economy converges to a new steady state, the demographic projections are applied only up to the year 2050, after which the rate of growth of employment and population are assumed to remain constant and equal to the rate of employment growth in the year 2100. A shooting algorithm is applied to find the initial value of consumption that leads to the new steady state following the shock, as follows. Specify a trial value of C_{t-1}, then solve forward for C_t according to the Euler equation. Then calculate $C_{1,t}$ and $C_{2,t}$, followed by investment, I, output, Y, and foreign liabilities, D. The model is solved forward until D_t/Y_t reaches a steady state value which is ensured provided that the process starts from an initial steady state and provided that the exogenous variables eventually stabilise at constant growth rates following the initial shock.

10.4   Simulation Results

The series for aggregate labour productivity (10.25) are plotted in Figure 10.4 for the U.S. and Figure (10.5) for Australia. There are two series for each country. The base case series is the case where consumers' preferences for the two goods change as they age. Hence the representative consumer, who has the average age of the population, has time varying preferences given time varying average age of the population (population ageing). These time varying preferences are reflected in the parameter μ_t in 10.13, discussed in subsection 10.3.2. The series for μ_t is plotted in Figure 10.3 for both countries. The second labour productivity series in Figures 10.4 and 10.5 represents the case where μ_t is constant – that is, consumers' preferences for the two goods are assumed to be invariant with respect to age and therefore the representative consumer's preferences are invariant with respect to time.

The most obvious observation from these results is that labour productivity increases in both countries and for both series. Note that labour productivity increases even when consumers' preferences are constant (constant μ_t). This is due to the Solow effect which in this case implies lower capital requirements (that is, lower investment) due to a more slowly growing labour force. This effect can be explained in terms of the diagram in Figure 10.1, where investment is the gap between the Y and C line. The Solow effect implies that this gap is smaller following population ageing (the *ex post*

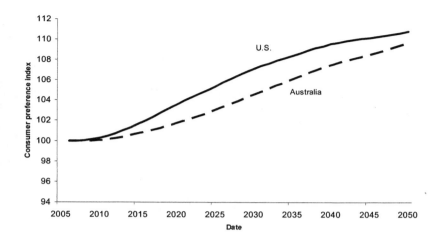

Figure 10.3: Index of Consumer Preferences Parameter, μ_t

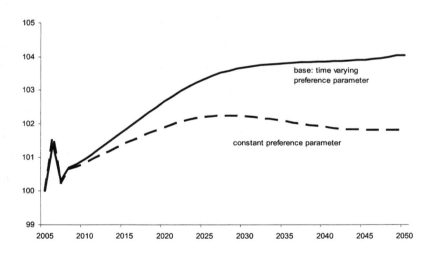

Figure 10.4: US Labour Productivity

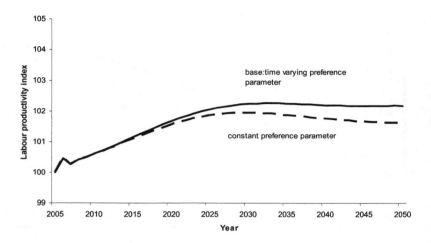

Figure 10.5: Australian Labour Productivity

case) than before population ageing (the *ex ante* case). Because all capital goods are included in good 2, this shifts the Y_1/Y_2 line upwards implying that good 1 has a higher share of output. Since good 1 is more capital intensive than good 2, average capital intensity rises and so too does aggregate labour productivity. The size of this boost to labour productivity between 2005 and 2050 is about 2 per cent for the U.S. and 1.5 per cent for Australia. The difference in magnitude for the two countries is because the difference in the capital intensities of the two goods for the U.S. is greater than that for Australia and because the change in employment growth is different.[11] The difference in capital intensities means that a given shift in expenditure (investment or consumption) has a greater effect on aggregate capital intensity in the U.S. than in Australia. The difference in employment growth implies different impacts on investment expenditure.

---

[11]It is also due to the difference in input-output coefficients for the two countries, because it is the effect on total outputs rather than final demands that accounts for aggregate capital intensity and therefore aggregate labour productivity in the economy.

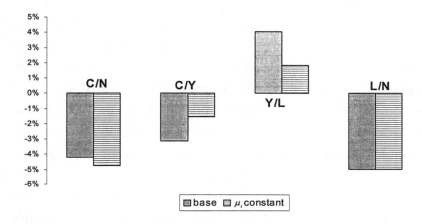

Figure 10.6: Decomposition of Effect of Ageing on Living Standards in the US from 2005 to 2050

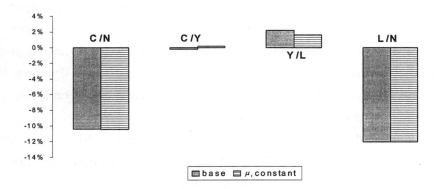

Figure 10.7: Decomposition of Effect of Ageing on Living Standards in Australia From 2005 to 2050

As Figures 10.4 and 10.5 show, the rise in labour productivity in the base case is greater than in the constant μ_t case. The effect of the time varying μ_t applying in the base case is to boost labour productivity a further 2 per cent in the U.S. and a further 0.5 per cent in Australia. This is a quantification of the effect illustrated in Figure 10.1 as an upward shift of the C_1/C_2 line caused by consumer preferences shifting toward good 1. This change in the consumption mix causes a change in the output mix and therefore a change in aggregate capital intensity and labour productivity. In summary, there are two sources of shift in the expenditure share toward good 1 as the population ages: a drop in investment which implies a drop in expenditure on good 2; and an increase in consumption preferences for good 1.

Working partially to offset the difference between the U.S. and Australia in the impacts of expenditure shifts on labour productivity is the relative degree of projected population ageing in the two countries. The support ratio – the ratio of employment to population – is projected to fall by 13 per cent for Australia but only about 5 per cent for the US. This reflects more extreme population ageing in Australia which in turn implies a more marked slowing in employment growth causing a larger Solow effect, and a more marked shift in consumer expenditure towards good 1 causing a larger shift in the parameter μ_t. Both of these effects imply a greater shift in labour productivity in Australia than the U.S. which partially offsets the differences in relative capital intensities of the two goods between the two countries. The offset is only partial – the net result remains a bigger impact on labour productivity in the U.S. than in Australia.

Turning finally to the effect on living standards, Section 10.2.3 showed that higher labour productivity arising from an increase in capital intensity does not imply a commensurate increase in living standards. Higher capital widening requirements with a growing workforce and higher depreciation both mitigate the boost to living standards, reflected in a lower consumption share of output. This is illustrated in Figures 10.6 and 10.7. For the U.S. in

Figure 10.6, the effect on living standards, C/N, of the 2 per cent boost to labour productivity, Y/L, from a time varying μ_t is offset by 1.5 per cent due to a lower C/Y. This leaves only a net 0.5 per cent boost to living standards from the 2 per cent increase in labour productivity. For Australia, the 0.5 per cent boost to Y/L due to the time varying μ_t is offset almost completely (by 0.4 per cent) leaving a tiny 0.1 per cent net increase in living standards.

Consider the overall effect of ageing on living standards for the U.S. and Australia. For both countries and for both scenarios about consumption patterns, ageing has a negative effect on living standards – by a little over 4 per cent for the U.S. and 10 per cent for Australia. The possibility that this loss could be substantially offset by the effect on labour productivity of a higher capital intensity due to shifts in demand patterns is not supported by the empirical analysis in this study.

10.4.1 Sensitivity

The two parameters driving labour productivity in each sector are the cost of capital (the interest rate plus the depreciation rate) and the capital–output ratio. In this subsection, a sensitivity analysis with respect to these variables is reported. In particular an alternative value of the interest rate of 6 per cent is chosen instead of the base case of 4 per cent. Furthermore, the difference in the labour productivity for the two goods is reduced from approximately 2.5 to 0.5, which is a considerable reduction. Results are reported for the U.S. only as the effect for both countries was similar. The higher interest rate made little difference: the increase in labour productivity for the varying μ_t and constant μ_t cases respectively was 5 per cent and 2.3 per cent, compared with 4 per cent and 2 per cent for the base case. The smaller gap in the capital intensities of the two goods is clearly expected to matter because this is the very source of differences in labour productivity between the sectors.

With respect to capital intensity, reducing the gap in capital intensities from 2.5 to 0.5 resulted in a reduction in the gain in labour productivity from 4 per cent to 1.3 per cent for varying μ_t and from 2 per cent to 0.5 per cent for a constant μ_t . Hence the change in labour productivity is approximately proportional to the change in the gap between capital intensities which accords with intuition.

There is a more fundamental assumption that, although supported by the data for both countries, could be questioned. The assumption that population ageing shifts expenditure towards the capital intensive good depends on both consumer expenditure and investment expenditure shifting towards the capital intensive good. The assumption regarding investment expenditure depends in turn on the assumption that capital goods are less capital intensive than consumer goods. The data for both countries support this result – manufactured goods are of relatively low capital intensity. If however, due to problems in data aggregation and so on, capital goods turn out to be of higher than average capital intensity then the Solow effect would tend to lower average capital intensity. In that case the consumer effect would work in the opposite direction to the Solow effect and the net effect on capital intensity would be ambiguous. If, at the same time, shortcomings in the consumer data mean that consumer expenditure shifts away from the capital intensive good, then we would have both the Solow effect and the consumer effect working together but opposite to the effect found in the simulations. This would reverse the effects on labour productivity – it would decline rather than increase with population ageing. The point of this discussion is that the effect on labour productivity depends crucially on capital intensities of various goods and on consumer expenditure patterns as the population ages. Such alternative scenarios are not simulated here because they are not supported by the data; nevertheless they are acknowledged as possible outcomes.

10.5 Conclusion

The effect of ageing on labour productivity is crucial in determining the economic burden of ageing. Yet little is known about this key relationship. One potential effect of ageing on labour productivity is through shifts in demand between sectors of the economy that have different long-run capital intensities. This chapter has applied a simulation model to investigate the order of magnitude of such effects based on data for two countries: Australia and the United States. Although both are English speaking OECD countries, they have quite different industrial structures, different projected patterns of population ageing, and are of vastly different sizes.

The empirical results indicate that this particular channel could boost labour productivity by 4 per cent for the U.S. and 2 per cent for Australia in total over the 45 year period 2006 to 2050. Clearly this is small when considered on an annual basis (less than 0.1 per cent compound per annum). It would, for example, reduce the annual rate of economic growth from say 3 per cent to no less than 2.9 per cent. Moreover, the effect on living standards of the small boost to labour productivity is even smaller, due to higher depreciation and higher capital widening requirements associated with higher capital intensity.

Taking another perspective, it could be argued that the annualised effect on living standards of ageing is modest in the first place, especially for the U.S. but even for Australia: a 10 per cent drop in living standards over 45 years amounts to 0.23 per cent per annum. It may not be surprising therefore that a second order effect of ageing on living standards via capital intensity is likely to be small – and so it turns out. Even so, the simulation analysis plays a role in providing empirical support for such intuition.

The discussion of sensitivity of these results pointed to the importance of data and assumptions. Potential shortcomings in the data due to aggregation and interpretation, and other assumptions in the model, could alter magnitudes and even direction of the effects on labour productivity. Nevertheless the main point is that ageing-induced shifts in expenditure between sectors with different capital intensities can be expected to have implications for labour productivity, but the magnitudes are likely to be small.

Chapter 11

Extensions and Sensitivity Analyses

In the analyses of population ageing in Chapters 8, 9 and 10, various non-conventional assumptions were adopted. The purpose of this chapter is to revisit these assumptions in order to investigate the sensitivity of the results to variations in the key parameters. Four assumptions are chosen for the sensitivity analysis: the CRESH parameters in modeling imperfect elasticity of workers by age (Chapter 9); sectoral capital intensities and the effect of ageing on sectoral demands (Chapter 10); rule-of-thumb consumers (Chapter 10); and an upward sloping supply price of foreign capital (Chapter 8);

Section 11.1 outlines the way in which the above assumptions are modelled. The demographic projections and simulation method are outlined in Section 11.4 and the results are given in Section 11.5.

11.1 Two Effects of Ageing on Labour Productivity

This section considers imperfect substitutability of workers by age, in subsection 11.1.1, and the role of different capital intensities, in 11.1.3.

11.1.1   Imperfect Substitutability of Workers by Age

Following Chapter 9, the CRESH function of labour inputs distinguished by age is given by:

$$\sum_{i=1}^{k} \alpha_i \left[\frac{L_i}{f(L^*)} \right]^{\rho_i} = 1 \tag{11.1}$$

where α_i is the distribution parameter of labour of age i, k is the number of age groups, L_i is the number of workers of age i, L^* is the index of composite labour inputs and ρ_i is a parameter that determines the flexibility, or versatility, of L_i, meaning the degree to which L_i can substitute for any other input, L_j. It is assumed here that all labour inputs are substitutes to some degree, which restricts ρ_i such that $-\infty < \rho_i < 1$. See the subsection 11.1.2 for details about the application of the CRESH function.

Returns to scale are assumed to be constant which implies $f(L^*) = L^*$. If $\rho_i = \rho$ then (11.1) becomes CES:

$$L^* = \left[\sum_{i=1}^{k} \alpha_i L_i^{\rho} \right]^{1/\rho} \tag{11.2}$$

when $\rho = 0$, (11.1) is Cobb–Douglas, for which the elasticity of subsitution is unity:

$$Y = \prod_{i=1}^{k} L_i^{\alpha_i} \tag{11.3}$$

As ρ approaches ∞, the elasticity of substitution approaches zero, in which case the function is of the Leonteif form:

$$Y = min_{i=1,..,k} \frac{L}{a_i} \tag{11.4}$$

where the a_i are constants. Finally, if $\rho = 1$, the elasticity of subsitution is infinitely large and:

$$Y = \sum_{i=1}^{k} \alpha_i L_i \tag{11.5}$$

In (11.5) the index of labour inputs is a sum of labour inputs by age, weighted by age-dependent productivity levels. The implication of (11.5) is that effective units of labour of different ages, $a_i L_i$, are infinitely substitutable. In other words, once workers of different ages are adjusted for their productivity differences they become identical inputs in economic terms. The age distribution of the labour force, in the case of infinite substitutability (11.5), affects output only if workers have different age-dependent productivity levels, α_i. In that case an optimal age distribution – that which maximises the index value of labour inputs – would be one in which all workers were the age of the most productive workers. But that is not true if workers of different ages are imperfect substitutes, in which case the optimal age distribution is given in Prskawetz and Fent (2004), citing Lam (1989), as:[1]

$$\frac{\pi_j}{\pi_i} = \left(\frac{\alpha_j}{\alpha_i} \right)^{\sigma} \tag{11.6}$$

where the π's are the shares of the labour force in age groups denoted by i and j, the α's are the productivity weights and σ is the elasticity of subsitution between labour inputs i and j. This is found by equating the marginal products of labour of each age group.

If the productivity weights in (11.6) are equal then $\alpha_i = \alpha_j$ and the optimal age shares are equal no matter what the value of α. If, on the other hand, older workers are more productive than younger workers, then their optimal labour force share is higher than for younger workers by a factor given by σ. The lower is σ, the less variation in optimal labour shares for any given productivity weights. Intuitively, a low σ implies that different types of labour are very complementary – they cannot be easily substituted. Therefore small adjustments to the type of labour employed cause relatively

---

[1] This derivation requires the assumption, adopted throughout the analysis, that workers are paid (the value of) their marginal products. In that case the marginal rate of substitution is equal to the relative prices of labour i.e. $\frac{w_i}{w_j} = \frac{\alpha_i}{\alpha_j} \left(\frac{\pi_j}{\pi_i} \right)^{1/\sigma}$. Equality of marginal products implies $w_j = w_i$ and therefore $\frac{\pi_j}{\pi_i} = \left(\frac{\alpha_j}{\alpha_i} \right)^{\sigma}$.

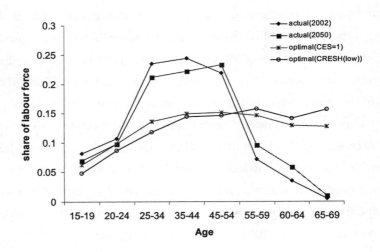

Figure 11.1: Age Distribution of the Labour Force

large changes in marginal products, and hence relatively small adjustments in labour shares are required to equate marginal products.

The significance of this is that population ageing implies a shift in the age distribution relative to the optimal distribution. Figure 11.1 shows the optimal and actual distribution of the labour force for Australia. It is apparent from inspection that the actual distribution in 2050 is projected to be closer to the optimal than it was in 2002. This can be expected to generate a dividend in terms of labour productivity and therefore living standards. The magnitude of this dividend will be investigated below using the simulation model.

11.1.2   Applying the CRESH Function

This subsection describes the method of applying the CRESH function of labour inputs (11.1). As discussed in the previous subsection, the CRESH function allows for an assumption that middle-aged workers are more flexible than young workers or older workers. The degree of flexibility is a hump-shaped function of age, rising to middle-age then falling to old age. The intuition for this is that middle-aged workers, defined here as workers in the 35 to 54 age group, are more substitutable for young workers than are workers; and they are more substitutable for older workers than are younger workers.

Table 11.1 gives the matrix of values of σ used in the simulations. These values satisfy the restrictions on the range of values of the σ_{ij} in order to yield a unique solution for the CRESH function (Hanoch, 1971). The binding restriction in the present application is that $\alpha_i \rho_i$ must be of the same sign for all i, assuming that all $a_i > 0$, where $a_i = 1/(1 - \rho_i)$, which implies that all labour inputs are substitutes to some degree. Given all $\alpha_i > 0$ by definition, we must have for all i, either $0 < \rho_i < 1$ $(a_i > 1)$ or $\rho_i < 0$ $(0 < a_i < 1)$. This restricts values of the σ_{ij} to values which are all relatively high or relatively low.

Males and females are distinguished in terms of their age-dependent productivity weights but their productivity-adjusted labour units are assumed to be infinitely substitutable at any given age. Hence:

$$(\alpha L)_i = (\alpha L)_{i,males} + (\alpha L)_{i.females} \tag{11.7}$$

and therefore α_i is a weighted average of the productivity weights for males and females:[2]

$$\alpha_i = \frac{(\alpha L)_{i,males} + (\alpha L)_{i.females}}{L_i} \tag{11.8}$$

In the simulations, the productivity weights by sex were proxied by the age distribution of full-time average weekly earnings by sex at August 2003,

---

[2]It is of course possible to treat females as a separate labour group with age dependent ES but this creates additional anomalies of the kind illustrated in Tables 10.1 and 10.2. The assumption of infinite elasticities between males and females of any given age is preferred in order to avoid these anomalies.

Table 11.1: Parameters Used in Applying the CRESH Function

High elasticity of substitution

a_i	ρ	s_i		15-19	20-4	25-34	35-44	45-54	55-9	60-4
3	0.667	0.043	15-19							
3.6	0.722	0.084	20-24	2.34						
4.2	0.762	0.237	25-34	2.73	3.28					
4.8	0.792	0.273	35-44	3.12	3.74	4.37				
5.4	0.815	0.260	45-54	3.51	4.21	4.91	5.62			
4.8	0.792	0.072	55-59	3.12	3.74	4.37	4.99	5.62		
4.2	0.762	0.028	60-64	2.73	3.28	3.82	4.37	4.91	4.37	
3.6	0.722	0.003	65-69	2.34	2.81	3.28	3.74	4.21	3.74	3.28

$\sum a_i s_i = 4.61$

Low elasticity of substitution

a_i	ρ	s_i		15-19	20-4	25-34	35-44	45-54	55-9	60-4
0.45	-1.222	0.043	15-19							
0.54	-0.852	0.084	20-24	0.35						
0.63	-0.587	0.237	25-34	0.41	0.49					
0.72	-0.389	0.273	35-44	0.47	0.56	0.66				
0.81	-0.235	0.260	45-54	0.53	0.63	0.74	0.84			
0.72	-0.389	0.072	55-59	0.47	0.56	0.66	0.75	0.84		
0.63	-0.587	0.028	60-64	0.41	0.49	0.57	0.66	0.74	0.66	
0.54	-0.852	0.003	65-69	0.35	0.42	0.49	0.56	0.63	0.56	0.49

$\sum a_i s_i = 0.69$

obtained from Australian Bureau of Statistics (ABS) Catalogue 6310.0. The labour force (in persons, not hours worked) and the labour force participation rate by age and sex were obtained from ABS Cat 6291.055.001. The population projections by age and sex, 2002–2100, were obtained from ABS Cat 3222.0, Series B. Of the three series of population projections published by the ABS, Series B is based on assumptions for international migration, fertility and mortality which yield population levels that are in between those of Series A and C.

Table 11.2: Capital–Output Ratios for Australia in 2002

	K/Y	GDP share	K/GDP
Sector			
Manufacturing	1.41	0.14	0.20
Property and business services	1.27	0.10	0.13
Ownership of dwellings	12.11	0.09	1.10
Construction	0.68	0.07	0.05
Wholesale trade	1.08	0.06	0.06
Retail trade	1.24	0.06	0.07
Health and community services	1.51	0.06	0.08
Transport and storage	5.49	0.05	0.29
Agriculture, forestry and fishing	2.12	0.05	0.11
Finance and insurance	1.45	0.05	0.07
Mining	3.80	0.05	0.18
Education	2.73	0.04	0.12
Govt admin and defence	2.56	0.04	0.10
Electricity, gas, water supply	7.68	0.04	0.27
Communication services	3.62	0.03	0.10
Personal and other services	1.23	0.02	0.02
Accomm, cafes and restaurants	2.76	0.02	0.05
Cultural, recreational services	1.72	0.02	0.03
Total			3.03

11.1.3 Sectors with Different Capital Intensities

In order to simulate the effect of sectoral shifts in demand on average capital intensity and labour productivity we need a model of production with a high capital intensity sector and a low capital intensity sector. The two sectors in the model consist of a tradable, T, and non-tradable, N, sector, where T goods are assumed to have a higher capital intensity than N goods. Whether population ageing increases or decreases the average capital intensity of the economy depends on two empirical questions. One is whether T goods are more or less capital intensive than N goods. The other is whether population ageing will shift demand from T goods to N goods or vice versa. Table 11.2 summarises the four possible combinations of these two factors.

In the previous chapter these two empirical questions were answered by analysing data on sectoral household expenditures, sectoral capital intensity ratios, and input–output tables for Australia and the United States. This chapter investigates the sensitivity of the results to variations in the relevant parameter values.

The base case is the scenario in which population ageing shifts demand from T to N goods and T goods are more capital intensive than N goods. This is considered here to be the most plausible scenario. The result is that the average capital intensity of the economy decreases. In none of the three other possible cases can we be sure that the average capital intensity of the economy will decrease. The two ambiguous cases in the right hand column of Table 11.2 arise because the two types of demand shifts between T and N goods work in the opposite direction. On the one hand, lower investment lowers, due to lower capital widening requirements, demand for T goods relative to N goods, but on the other hand, the assumption in these cases is that relative consumer demand for T goods increases. All four possible cases indicated in Table 11.2 are simulated and the results briefly reported.

11.2   Ageing and Consumption Bundles

Following chapter 10 shifts in consumer preferences are modelled by specifying a variable, μ_t, that defines relative preferences for traded and non-traded goods where these preferences are a function of age. In chapter 10 this variable was calibrated using household expenditure data by age and then future values were determined using demographic projections. The aim here is to investigate the sensitivity of this variable to the age structure of the population. A simple and convenient way of capturing this is to assume that the preference for traded goods decreases as the employment to population ratio decreases. Hence μ_t is defined as:

$$\mu_t = \mu_0 \left(\frac{L}{N} \right)_t^{\phi} \tag{11.9}$$

The value of μ_0 is set by calibration, as described in chapter 10, and the base case value of ϕ is equal to 1.0; results are reported for values of ϕ equal to -1 and 4.

Again, it is assumed that a proportion, $1 - \xi$, of consumers are intertemporal optimisers and ξ are rule-of-thumb consumers who consume a constant proportion of their income. The rule-of-thumb consumers have the same consumption as the optimising consumers in the initial steady state but hold that level fixed as a proportion of their income. Hence the ageing shock only affects their consumption only insofar as it alters their level of income, which is the same for all consumers. The base case value of ξ is 0.3 and is compared with alternative values of zero, 0.5 and 0.7. Total consumption is the sum of consumption of intertemporally optimising consumers and rule-of-thumb consumers.

11.3 Imperfect Capital Mobility

It is common in modelling population ageing to adopt either the small open economy assumption or the closed economy assumption, or perhaps a comparison of both (Elmendorf and Sheiner, 2000). Yet neither assumption is entirely satisfactory in a world of imperfect international capital mobility. The small country or perfect capital mobility assumption is unsatisfactory because ageing affects the saving-investment balance which impacts on a country's interest rate unless capital is perfectly mobile. The closed economy assumption is unsatisfactory, even for very large economies such as the US, because increasingly globalised capital markets mean that even a large country's interest rate is not completely determined within its borders.

With a perfect world capital market (and hence a constant interest rate) and a constant rate of time preference, the path of output is disconnected from the consumption path. This is not the case, however, with imperfect capital mobility which is modelled here by specifying the interest rate as a positive function the ratio of foreign liabilities to GDP lagged one period:

$$r_t = \bar{r}_t + \lambda \left(\frac{d}{y}\right)_{t-1} \tag{11.10}$$

Here the marginal cost of borrowing increases as foreign liabilities increase. A demographic shock therefore affects output via its effect on consumption, because consumption affects foreign liabilities ceteris paribus, which therefore affects the interest rate and investment. The strength of this affect depends on the value of λ which in the base case is set equal to 0.02, implying that a 10 percentage point increase in the ratio of foreign liabilities to GDP increases the interest rate by 0.2 of one per cent.

11.4   Demographic Projections

Demographic projections for Australia are adopted as being typical of projections for ageing OECD populations. Following chapter 8, the population projections by age and sex, 2002–2100, were obtained from the Australian Bureau of Statistics (ABS) Cat 3222.0, Series B. Of the three series of population projections published by the ABS, Series B is based on assumptions for international migration, fertility and mortality which yield population levels that are in between those of Series A and C. The productivity weights by sex were proxied by the age distribution of full-time average weekly earnings by sex at August 2003, obtained from ABS Catalogue 6310.0. The labour force (in persons, not hours worked) and the labour force participation rate by age and sex were obtained from ABS Cat 6291.055.001.

Steady state labour productivity growth, driven by neutral technical progress, is assumed to be exogenous and equal to 1.5 per cent per year in both sectors. This implies that there is no influence of demographic change on technical progress, which is a reasonable assumption given the uncertainty in the literature on this issue and the fact that it is not important for the central aim of the chapter.

The assumed difference in capital intensities of the N and T sectors is crucial for the analysis. Using the notation above, it is assumed that:

$$\left(\frac{\bar{k}}{\bar{y}}\right)_T = a \left(\frac{\bar{k}}{\bar{y}}\right)_N \tag{11.11}$$

where $a > 0$. The base case value of a is 2.0 and results are reported for alternative values.

The production function is calibrated for a given capital intensity, where these vary between the T and N sectors. The calibration implies that in the T sector the capital elasticity of output higher than in the N sector. Given the first order condition for investment and the condition that output and capital are in an initial steady state, the capital elasticty is given by $\gamma_{T,N} = (r + \delta) \left(\frac{k_0}{y_0}\right)_{T,N}$. The values of $(k/y)_0$ for the T and N sectors were calculated by assuming the following: an economy-wide value of $(k/y)_0$ equal to 3.0, a in (11.11) equal to 2.0 in the base case, and that the initial shares of GDP of the T and N sectors are both equal to 0.5. An economy-wide capital–output ratio of 3.0 was used by Kenc and Sayan (2001) for an aggregate of four large European countries: Germany, France, Italy and the UK. The assumption that the capital intensity of traded goods is twice that of non-traded goods is roughly consistent with data from developed economies; and the assumption that the GDP shares of T and N sectors is 50 per cent is also plausible if we add to mining, agriculture and manufacturing, the tradable proportion of the output of other industries such as finance and education.

The remaining base case parameter values adopted in the model are as follows. The intertemporal elasticity of consumption, $1/\beta$, is equal to 0.67; the elasticity of substitution between traded and non-traded goods in consumption, Ψ, is equal to 1.0. These values are in the range of estimates in the literature, as cited by Kenc and Sayan (2001). The values of other para-

Table 11.3: Possible Scenarios Determining the Effect of Population Ageing on Average Capital Intensity

	Decreases demand for T relative to N	Increases demand for T relative to N
$(K/Y)_T > (K/Y)_N$ in steady state	Base case ave K/Y decreases	Case (2) Effect on ave K/Y ambiguous
$(K/Y)_T < (K/Y)_N$ in steady state	Case (3) ave K/Y increases	Case (4) Effect on ave K/Y ambiguous

meters are: $\phi = 1$, r in a steady state $= 0.05$, $g = 0.015$, $\delta = 0.05$, $\xi = 0.3$, and $\lambda = 0.02$.

11.5   Simulations and Results

The solution procedure including calibration of an initial steady state is the same as in previous chapters. The approach is to take each of the innovations separately. Hence in order to determine the effects of sectoral shifts in demand, the effect of the workforce age distribution is ruled out by adopting the additive function (11.5). Similarly, in simulating the effect of the workforce age distribution the effect of sectoral shifts in demand is ruled out by assuming that the capital intensities of T and N goods are equal.

Four age distribution simulations are conducted: (1) Additive function of labour inputs; (2) CRESH function with low values of σ; (3) CRESH function with high values of σ; and (4) CES function with an elasticity of substitution equal to 1 (the Cobb-Douglas case).

The empirical estimates of σ in the literature are closer to the values used in the 'high' simulation (although there appear to be no estimates for the CRESH functional form). Card and Lemieux (2001) estimate constant elasticities between different age groups for the US, UK and Canada in the range of 4 to 6. Estimates from earlier literature are surveyed in Stapleton and Young (1988) and range from 2 for highly educated workers to very high

Table 11.4: Effects and Labour Productivity: Percentage Change Relative to No Demographic Change

| | Effects of workforce age distrib | | | | Effects of sectoral shifts in demand | | | | |
	Add've	CRESH (low)	CRESH (high)	CES =1	$a = 2$ $\phi = 1$	$a = 3,$ $\phi = 1$	$a = 2,$ $\phi = 4$	$a = 0.7$ $\phi = 1$	$a = 2$ $\phi = -1$
2002	0.00	0.00	0.00	0.00	0.00	0.00	0.00	0.00	0.00
2010	0.21	12.72	1.01	6.51	1.26	1.29	0.82	-0.37	1.58
2020	0.85	25.43	2.05	11.72	0.66	0.44	-2.28	0.83	2.90
2030	1.63	32.59	2.85	14.25	-0.09	-0.89	-5.37	2.41	4.64
2040	1.76	35.21	3.04	15.16	-0.82	-2.07	-7.17	3.03	5.45
2050	1.67	38.23	3.23	16.87	-1.50	-3.07	-8.50	3.21	5.84
2100	1.23	39.27	2.78	16.79	-2.74	-4.64	-10.48	3.28	6.15

Table 11.5: Ageing and Living Standards: Percentage Change Relative to No Demographic Change

| | Effects of workforce age distrib | | | | Effects of sectoral shifts in demand | | | | |
	Add've	CRESH (low)	CRESH (high)	CES =1	$a = 2$ $\phi = 1$	$a = 3$ $\phi = 1$	$a = 2$ $\phi = 4$	$a = 0.7$ $\phi = 1$	$a = 2$ $\phi = -1$
2002	0.00	0.00	0.00	0.00	0.00	0.00	0.00	0.00	0.00
2010	-3.55	5.51	-3.02	0.80	-2.71	-2.10	-2.39	-3.86	-2.95
2020	-4.89	13.99	-3.93	3.58	-4.55	-4.43	-5.42	-5.12	-4.00
2030	-7.55	17.42	-6.47	3.00	-8.48	-9.03	-11.40	-7.25	-6.16
2040	-10.03	17.74	-8.93	1.32	-11.82	-12.74	-16.01	-9.25	-7.99
2050	-11.73	17.96	-10.50	0.51	-13.91	-15.01	-18.65	-10.71	-9.20
2100	-14.77	17.47	-13.45	-1.55	-17.60	-18.93	-23.05	-13.32	-11.35

Table 11.6: Percentage Change in Consumption per Person Relative to No Demographic Change

| | Base: $\xi = 0.3$ | $\xi = 0.3$ | | | $\lambda = 0.02$ | | |
	$\lambda = 0.02$	$\lambda = 0$	$\lambda = 0.005$	$\lambda = 0.04$	$\xi = 0$	$\xi = 0.5$	$\xi = 0.7$
2002	0.00	0.00	0.00	0.00	0.00	0.00	0.00
2010	-3.55	-6.28	-4.23	-3.34	-3.36	-3.77	-4.20
2020	-4.89	-6.28	-5.13	-4.84	-4.80	-4.99	-5.20
2030	-7.55	-6.28	-6.91	-7.81	-7.71	-7.38	-7.10
2040	-10.03	-6.28	-8.89	-10.34	-10.31	-9.70	-9.05
2050	-11.73	-6.28	-10.59	-11.93	-11.97	-11.40	-10.66
2100	-14.77	-6.28	-14.47	-14.81	-14.83	-14.69	-14.40

elasticities (as high as 79) for workers with low education. Clearly, differences in human capital among workers is an important factor determining the value of σ, and the simulation model here does not control for this factor. However, the average value of σ between workers will be lower the faster is technological change, because there will be bigger differences in the types of human capital between younger and older workers (Boockmann, 2000) – young workers will embody the latest computer skills and so on. Since technological change has been more rapid in the period since that covered by the empirical studies cited above, we might expect the elasticities now and in the future to be somewhat lower than those cited – perhaps closer to the $CES = 1$ case, but not as low as the CRESH(low) case.

There are five simulations of the effect of sectoral shifts in demand. In each case one of the two key parameters are varied while the other is held constant at the base case value. The combinations of the two parameters are:

(a) $a = 2$, $\phi = 1$ (the base case)

(b) $a = 3$, $\phi = 1$ (T goods are even more relatively capital intensive than in the base case)

(c) $a = 2$, $\phi = 4$ (consumer demand shifts even more to N goods than in the base case)

(d) $a = 0.7$, $\phi = 1$ (T goods are less, rather than more, capital intensive than N goods)

(e) $a = 2$, $\phi = -1$ (consumer demand shifts toward T goods, rather than N goods, as consumers age)

The simulated percentage changes in labour productivity are reported in Table 11.4 and changes in living standards are in Tables 11.5 and 11.6 relative to the case of no demographic change, where living standards are defined as consumption per person. The first column in each table, labelled 'Additive', is the case where neither of the innovations is applied – that is, it assumes an additive labour index and equal capital intensities of T and N goods. In this case labour productivity increases slightly following the ageing shock, due to capital deepening; and by 2050 living standards are about 12 per cent lower than they otherwise would be, due to the falling employment to population ratio which is offset somewhat by lower capital widening requirements; see Culter *et al.* (1990) for a discussion and decomposition of these effects. The next three columns give the effects of varying the workforce age mix holding constant the capital intensities between T and N goods. The columns labeled CRESH(high) and CRESH(low) refer to high and low elasticities of substitution with a CRESH labour index. The final column, $CES = 1$, refers to constant values of σ for all pairs of age groups, where the value of 1 is in between the average values in the 'low' and 'high' scenarios. Hence this is a middle case.

The results therefore suggest that the workforce age distribution effect is probably not large but may not be trivial. It is only large in the very unlikely CRESH(low) case. On the other hand, the CRESH(high) case may be toward the other extreme if the conjecture about the effect of technological change is borne out. Outcomes may be expected to be somewhere in between these two cases, perhaps such as values around $\sigma = 1$ which makes the $CES = 1$ case of interest. In the $CES = 1$ case the boost to labour productivity from the age distribution effect is sufficient to roughly offset the effect of the lower employment to population ratio on living standards. In this case the net effect of ageing on living standards is negligible. Further empirical investigation of the range of magnitudes of σ would therefore be a useful topic of future research.

The five columns on the right-hand side of Tables 11.4 and 11.5 refer to the effects of sectoral shifts in demand relative to the case of no demographic change. The first of these columns gives the base case assumption for which labour productivity in 2050 is 1.5 per cent lower as a result of demographic change. Comparing this with the 'Additive' case, in which neither of the modelling innovations applies and in which labour productivity is 1.67 per cent higher in 2050, gives a turnaround of about plus 3 per cent in both labour productivity and living standards as a result of the base case modelling innovations combined. This must be interpreted as a small magnitude in the context of technical progress driving steady-state labour productivity growth of 1.5 per cent per annum. For example, a 3 per cent decrease in labour productivity is equivalent to a loss of about 2 years of typical labour productivity growth spread out over a 50 year period.

The next two columns labelled $a = 3$, $\phi = 1$ and $a = 2$, $\phi = 4$ refer to cases (b) and (c) described above. In both of these cases the theoretical results are also borne out, in the sense that labour productivity declines by more than in the base case. However, the magnitudes are still not very large when one considers the period of time over which they are occurring in the presence compounding technical progress. The same conclusion applies to the effects on living standards. The final two columns refer to cases (d) and (e) above. Although these two cases are less likely, they cannot be ruled out in the absence of a more thorough empirical analysis of capital intensities and consumer preferences. In these two cases the direction of the effect on labour productivity was found to be ambiguous in theory. However, the simulations reveal that, for the parameter values chosen, the net effect is positive but small.

11.6   Conclusion

This chapter has examined the sensitivity of earlier results to changes in the modelling of demographic change. Attention is focused on two in particular – sectoral shifts in demand and complementarities among workers of different ages – both of which have been shown to influence the impact of ageing on labour productivity. The importance of the effect on labour productivity was motivated by the controversy that exists about the effect that population ageing has on aggregate labour productivity growth.

A simulation analysis was conducted in order to gauge the likely orders of magnitude of the effects of these modifications on both labour productivity and living standards. A difficulty in conducting this exercise is the paucity of recent empirical estimates of the important parameters that drive the results. These parameters are the elasticities of substitution between workers of different ages, and the effect of ageing on the shifts in demand between sectors with relatively high and low capital intensities, respectively. This chapter has not attempted an empirical investigation of these parameters. Rather, a range of values is simulated.

The results suggest that the effects of sectoral shifts in demand are not likely to be large – in all cases the effects on labour productivity were less than 10 percent over a 50 year period. A 10 per cent change over 50 years can be regarded as small in the context of compounding technical progress driving growth of labour productivity in the order of 1 or 2 per cent per annum. For example, 1.5 per cent per annum compound growth per annum increases labour productivity by 110 per cent over 50 years. So a 10 per cent loss would imply that labour productivity would increase by only 100 per cent instead of 110 per cent over 50 years.

The effect of allowing for imperfect substitutability of labour inputs by age is potentially of larger magnitude, especially if the elasticities of substitution between workers of different ages are smaller than the empirical estimates in the literature due to faster technological change in the recent past.

Bibliography

[1] Aghion, P. and Howitt, P. (1998) *Endogenous Growth Theory*. Cambridge, MA: MIT Press.

[2] Amiel, Y. and Cowell, F.A. (1992) Inequality measurement: an experimental approach. *Journal of Public Economics*, 47, pp. 3-26.

[3] Amiel, Y. and Cowell, F.A. (1994) Income inequality and social welfare. In *Taxation, Poverty and Income Distribution* (ed. by J. Creedy), pp. 193-219. Aldershot: Edward Elgar.

[4] Amiel, Y., Creedy, J. and Hurn, S. (1999) Measuring attitudes towards inequality. *Scandinavian Journal of Economics*, 101, pp. 83-96.

[5] Arrow, K. and Hurwicz, L. (1972) An optimality criterion for decision-making under ignorance. In *Uncertainty and Expectations: Essays in Honour of G.L.S. Shackle* (ed. by C.F. Carter and J.L. Ford). Oxford: Basil Blackwell.

[6] Arrow, K.J. and Fisher, A.C. (1974) Environmental preservation, uncertainty, and irreversibility. *Quarterly Journal of Economics*, 2, pp. 312-319

[7] Atkinson, A.B. (1970) On the measurement of inequality. *Journal of Economic Theory*, 2, pp. 244-263.

[8] Atkinson, M., Creedy, J. and Knox, D. (1996) Alternative retirement income strategies: a cohort analysis of lifetime redistribution. *Economic Record*, 72, pp. 97-106.

[9] Auerbach, A.J. and Kotlikoff, L.J. (1987) The effects of a baby boom on stock prices and capital accumulation in the presence of social security. *Econometrica*, 71, pp. 551-578.

[10] Australian Government (2002) *Intergenerational Report. 2002-2003 Budget Paper No. 5.* Canberra: Commonwealth of Australia.

[11] Australian Government (2006a) A plan to simplify and streamline superannuation. 9 May 2006, available at http://www.budget.gov.au/2006-07/overview2/download/ overview2.pdf

[12] Australian Government (2006b) A plan to simplify and streamline superannuation; A detailed outline. May 2006, available at http://simplersuper.treasury.gov.au/documents/outline/download/ simpler_super.pdf.

[13] Banks, J. and Johnson, P. (1994) Equivalence scale relativities revisited. *Economic Journal*, 104, pp. 883-890.

[14] Barro, R.J. (1974) Are government bonds net wealth? *Journal of Political Economy*, 82, pp. 1095-1017.

[15] Barro, R. (1979) On the determination of public debt. *Journal of Political Economy*, 87, pp. 940-971.

[16] Barro, R. and Sala-i-Martin, X. (1995) *Economic Growth.* New York: McGraw-Hill.

[17] Becker, G., Murphy, K. and Tamura, R. (1990) Human capital, fertility and economic growth. *Journal of Political Economy*, 98, pp. S12-37.

[18] Birdsall, N., Kelley, A. and Sinding, W. (2001) *Population Matters. Demographic Change, Economic Growth, and Poverty in the Developing World.* New York: Oxford University Press.

[19] Blanchard, O. and Fischer, S. (1989) *Lectures in Macroeconomics.* Cambridge: MIT Press.

[20] Bodie, Z., Merton, R.C. and Samuelson, W. F. (1992) Labour supply flexibility and portfolio choice in a life cycle model. *Journal of Economic Dynamics and Control,* 16, pp. 427-449.

[21] Boockmann, B. (2000) Cohort effects and the returns to education in West Germany. *Centre for European Economic Research Discussion Paper.*

[22] Bosworth, B., Bryant, R. and Burtless, G. (2004) *The Impact of Ageing on Financial Markets and the Economy: A Survey.* Chestnut Hill, MA: Centre for Retirement Research at Boston College.

[23] Brent, R.J. (1984) On the use of distributional weights in cost-benefit analysis: a survey of schools. *Public Finance Quarterly,* 12, pp. 213-230.

[24] Browning, E. K. (1987) On the marginal welfare cost of taxation. *The American Economic Review,* 77, pp. 11-23.

[25] Bryant, R. (2004) Cross-border macroeconomic implications of demographic change. *Brookings Institution Discussion Paper* No. 166.

[26] Calvo, G. and Obstfeld, M. (1988) Optimal time-consistent fiscal policy with finite lifetimes. *Econometrica,* 56, pp. 411-432.

[27] Campbell, J. and Mankiw, N.G. (1990) Consumption, income, and interest rates: reinterpreting the time series evidence. *National Bureau of Economic Research Working Paper,* No. W2924.

[28] Caplin, A. and Leahy, J.V. (2000) The social discount rate. *National Bureau of Economic Research Working Paper*, No. W7983.

[29] Card, D. and Lemieux, T. (2001) Can falling supply explain the rising return to college for younger men? A cohort-based analysis. *The Quarterly Journal of Economics*, May, pp. 705-746.

[30] Carter, R.M. *et al.* (2006) The Stern review: a dual critique. *World Economics*, 7, pp. 165-232.

[31] Chamley, C. (1986) Optimal taxation of capital income in general equilibrium with infinite lives. *Econometrica*, 54, pp. 607-622.

[32] Chichilnisky, G. (1997) What is sustainable development? *Land Economics*, 73, pp. 467-91.

[33] Christiansen, V. and Jansen, E.S. (1978) Implicit social preferences in the Norwegian system of social preferences. *Journal of Public Economics*, 10, pp. 217-245.

[34] Cowell, F.A. and Gardiner, K. (1999) Welfare weights. (Unpublished paper) STICERD, London School of Economics.

[35] Creedy, J. (1996) *Fiscal Policy and Social Welfare*. Cheltenham: Edward Elgar.

[36] Creedy, J. (2007) Policy evaluation, welfare weights and value judgements: a reminder. *Australian Journal of Labour Economics*, 10, pp. 1-15.

[37] Creedy, J. and Guest, R. (2008a) Discounting and the time preference rate. *Economic Record*, 84, pp. 109-127.

[38] Creedy, J. and Guest, R. (2008b) Population ageing and intertemporal consumption: representative agent versus social planner. *Economic Modelling*, 25, pp. 485-498.

[39] Creedy, J. and Guest, R. (2008c) The labour supply and savings effects of superannuation tax changes. *Australian Economic Papers*, (forthcoming).

[40] Creedy, J. and Guest, R. (2008d) Changes in the taxation of private pensions: macroeconomic and welfare effects. *Journal of Policy Modelling*, (forthcoming).

[41] Creedy, J. and Guest, R. (2008e) Sustainable preferences and damage abatement: value judgements and implications for consumption streams. *University of Melbourne Department of Economics Working Paper, no. 1026.*

[42] Creedy, J. and Scutella, R. (2004) The role of the unit of analysis in policy reform evaluations of inequality and social welfare. *Australian Journal of Labour Economics*, 7, pp. 89-108.

[43] Creedy, J. and Sleeman, C. (2005) Adult equivalence scales, inequality and poverty. *New Zealand Economic Papers*, 39, pp. 51-83.

[44] Cutler, D. M. and Katz, L. (1992) Rising inequality? Changes in the distribution of income and consumption in the 1980s. *American Economic Review*, 82, pp. 546-551.

[45] Cutler, D.M., Poterba, J.M., Sheiner, L.M. and L.H. Summers (1990) An Aging Society: Opportunity or Challenge? *Brookings Papers on Economic Activity*, 1, pp.1-74.

[46] Dalton, H. (1954) *Public Finance* (4th Edition). London: Routledge and Kegan Paul.

[47] Dasgupta, P. (2006) Comments on the Stern Review of Climate Change. University of Cambridge.

[48] Davidson, S. and Guest, R. (2007) The fiscal consequences of superannuation tax reform. *Agenda*, 14, pp. 5-15.

[49] Davis, N. and R. Fabling (2002) Population ageing and the efficiency of fiscal policy in New Zealand. *New Zealand Treasury Working Paper* 02/11.

[50] Day, C. and Dowrick, S. (2004) Ageing economics: human capital, productivity and fertility. *Agenda*, 11, pp. 3-20.

[51] Deaton, A. (1999) Saving and growth In *The Economics of Saving and Growth* (ed. by K.Schmidt-Hebbel and L.Serven), Cambridge: Cambridge University Press.

[52] Decoster and Ooghe (2003) Weighting with individuals, equivalent individuals or not weighting at all: does it matter empirically? In *Inequality, Welfare and Poverty: Theory and Measurement* (ed. by Y. Amiel and J.A. Bishop), pp. 173-190. New York: Elsevier.

[53] Disney, R. (1996) *Can We Afford to grow Older?* Cambridge: MIT Press.

[54] Doyle, S., Kingston, G. and Piggott, J. (1999) Taxing super. *University of New South Wales Retirement Economics Research Paper*, no. 12.

[55] Ebert, U. (1997) Social welfare when needs differ: an axiomatic approach. *Economica*, 64, pp. 233-244.

[56] Edgeworth, F.Y. (1897) The pure theory of taxation. *Economic Journal*. Reprinted in *Papers Relating to Political Economy*, 2, pp. 63-125. London: Macmillan.

[57] Elmendorf, D.W. and Sheiner, L.M. (2000) Should America save for its old age? Fiscal policy, population ageing and national saving. *Journal of Economic Perspectives*, 14, pp. 57-74.

[58] Evans, D.J. (2005) The elasticity of marginal utility of consumption: estimates for 20 OECD countries. *Fiscal Studies*, 26, pp. 197-224.

[59] Faruqee, H. and Muhleisen, M. (2001) Population ageing in Japan: demographic shock and fiscal sustainability. *International Monetary Fund Working Paper*, No. 01/40.

[60] Floden, M (2003) Public saving and public policy coordination in aging economies. *Scandinavian Journal of Economics*, 105, pp. 379-400.

[61] Foertsch, T. (2004) Macroeconomic impacts of stylized tax cuts in an intertemporal computable general equilibrium model. *Congressional Budget Office Technical Paper*, Washington, DC.

[62] Freebairn, J. (1998) Compulsory superannuation and labour market responses. *Australian Economic papers*, 37, pp. 58-70.

[63] Frisch, R. (1959) A complete scheme for computing all direct and cross demand elasticities in a model with many sectors. *Econometrica*, 27, pp. 177-196.

[64] Gauthier, A. (2000) Public policies affecting fertility and families in Europe: a survey of the 15 member states. *Paper prepared for the European Observatory on Family Matters, Annual Seminar, 15-16 September.* Sevilla, Spain.

[65] Gevers, L., Glesjer, H. and Rouyer, J. (1979) Professed inequality aversion and its error component. *Scandinavian Journal of Economics*, 81, pp. 238-243.

[66] Glesjer, J., Gevers, L., Lambot, Ph. and Morales, J.A. (1977) Professed inequality aversion among students. *European Economic Review*, 10, pp. 173-188.

[67] Glewwe, P. (1991) Household equivalence scales and the measurement of inequality: transfers from the poor to the rich could decrease inequality. *Journal of Public Economics*, 44, pp. 214-216.

[68] Gordon, R.H. and Bovenberg, A.L. (1996) Why is capital so immobile internationally? Possible explanations and implications for capital income taxation. *American Economic Review*, 86, pp. 1057-1075.

[69] Guest, R. (2005) A potential dividend from workforce ageing in Australia. *Australian Bulletin of Labour*, 31, pp. 135-154.

[70] Guest, R. (2006) Population ageing, fiscal pressure and tax smoothing: A CGE application to Australia. *Fiscal Studies,* 27, pp. 183-204.

[71] Guest, R. (2007a) Can OECD countries afford demographic change? *Australian Economic Review*, 40, pp. 1-16.

[72] Guest, R. (2007b) Innovations in macroeconomic modelling of population ageing. *Economic Modelling*, 24, pp. 101-119.

[73] Guest, R. and McDonald, I.M. (2004) The effect of world fertility scenarios on international living standards? *The Economic Record*, 80, 1, pp. S1-S12

[74] Guest, R. and Swift, R. (2008) Fertility, income inequality and labour productivity. *Oxford Economic Papers*, 60, pp. 1-22.

[75] Hanoch, G. (1971) CRESH production functions. *Econometrica*, 39, pp. 695-712.

[76] Harberger, A.C. (1964) Taxation, resource allocation, and welfare. In *The Role of Direct and Indirect Taxes in the Federal Revenue System.* NBER Other Conference Series No.3, University Microfilms.

[77] Heal, G. (1998) *Valuing the Future. Economic Theory and Sustainability*. New York: Columbia University Press.

[78] Higgins, M. and Williamson, J. (1997) Age structure dynamics in Asia and dependence on foreign capital. *Population and Development Review*, 23, pp. 261-293.

[79] Horne, J. (2002) Taxation of superannuation in Australia: An assessment of reform proposals. *Macquarie University Department of Economics Research Discussion Paper*, No. 212.

[80] Investment and Financial Services Association (2007) Essential Super Stats, Volume 1. available at http://www.ifsa.com.au/ documents/2%20Essential%20Super%20Stats%20January%202007.pdf

[81] Jackson, R. (2003) *Germany and the Challenge of Global Ageing*. Centre for Strategic and International Studies, Nationwide Global, March.

[82] Jenkins, S.P. and Cowell, F.A. (1994) Parametric equivalence scales and scale relativities. *Economic Journal*, 104, pp. 891-900.

[83] Kamps, C. (2004) New estimates of government net capital stocks for 22 OECD countries 1960-2001. *IMF Working Paper 04/67*, Washington, DC.

[84] Kelley, A.C. and Schmidt, R.M. (1996) Saving, dependency and development. *Journal of Population Economics*, 9, pp. 365-86.

[85] Kenc, T. and Sayan, S. (2001) Transmission of the demographic shock effects from large to small countries: an overlapping generations CGE analysis. *Journal of Policy Modelling*, 23, pp. 677-702.

[86] Kingston, G. and Piggott, J. (1993) A Ricardian equivalence theorem on the taxation of pension funds. *Economics Letters*, 42, pp. 399-403.

[87] Kirman, P. (1992) Whom or what does the representative individual represent? *Journal of Economic Perspectives*, 6, pp. 117-136.

[88] Knox, D. (1990) *A Review of the Options for Taxing Superannuation.* Sydney: Australian Tax Research Foundation.

[89] Koopmans, T.C. (1960) Stationary ordinal utility and impatience. *Econometrica*, 28, pp. 287-309.

[90] Koopmans, T.C., Diamond, P.A. and Williamson, R.E. (1964) Stationary utility and time perspective. *Econometrica*, 32, pp. 82-100.

[91] Kulish, M., Smith K. and Kent, C. (2006) Ageing, retirement and savings: a general equilibrium analysis. *Reserve Bank of Australia Research Discussion Paper*, No. 2006-06.

[92] Laibson, D. (1996) Hyperbolic discount functions, undersaving, and savings policy. *National Bureau of Economic Research Working Paper*, No. 5635.

[93] Lam, D. (1989) Population growth, age structure, and age-specific productivity. *Journal of Population Economics*, 2, pp. 189-210.

[94] Lane, P. and Milesi-Feretti, G. (2006) The external wealth of nations Mark II:revised and extended estimates of foreign assets and liabilities, 1970–2004. *International Monetary Fund Working Paper*, WP/06/69.

[95] Lewbel, A. (1989) Exact aggregation and a representative consumer. *Quarterly Journal of Economics*, 104, pp. 622-633.

[96] Li, C-Z. and Lofgren, K-G. (2000) Renewable resources and economic sustainability: a dynamic analysis with heterogenous time preferences. *Journal of Environmental Economics and Management*, 40, pp. 236-250.

[97] Lucas, R. (1988) On the mechanics of economic development. *Journal of Monetary Economics*, 22, pp. 3-41.

[98] Lucas, R.E. (1990) Supply-side economics: an analytical review. *Oxford Economic Papers*, 42, pp. 293-316.

[99] Marini, G. and Scaramozzino, P. (2000) Social time preference. *Journal of Population Economics*, 13, pp. 639-645.

[100] Martins, J., Gonad, F., Antolin, P., de la Maisonneuve, C. and Yoo, K (2005) The impact of ageing on demand, factor markets and growth. *OECD Economics Department Working Paper*, No. 420.

[101] Mason, A. (2001) Population, capital and labor. In *Population Change and Economic Development in Asia: Challenges Met, Opportunities Seized* (ed. by A, Mason), pp. 209-230. Stanford University Press, Stanford, California.

[102] Mason, A. and Lee, R. (2004) Reform and support systems for the elderly in developing countries: capturing the second demographic dividend. Paper presented at the Center for Health Aging and Family Studies and the China Centre for Economic Research, Peking University, Beijing, May 10-11. http://www2.hawaii.edu/~amason/Research/MasonLeeBeijing4a.pdf

[103] McKibbin, W.J. and Nguyen, J. (2004) Modelling global demographic change: results for Japan. *Australian National University Centre for Applied Economic Analysis Working Paper*, No. 4/2004.

[104] Mera, K. (1969) Experimental determination of relative marginal utilities. *Quarterly Journal of Economics*, 83, pp. 464-477.

[105] Miles, D., (1999) Modelling the impact of demographic change on the economy. *Economic Journal*, 109, pp. 1-36.

[106] Milligan, K. (2005) Subsidizing the stork: new evidence on tax incentives and fertility. *Review of Economics and Statistics*, 87, pp. 539-555.

[107] Moffitt, R. (1997) The effect of welfare on marriage and fertility: what do we know and what do we need to know? *Institute for Research on Poverty, Discussion Paper No 1153-97*.

[108] Moreh, J. (1981) Income inequality and the social welfare function. *Journal of Economic Studies*, 8, pp. 25-37.

[109] Nordhaus, W.D. (1994) *Managing the Global Commons: The Economics of Climate Change*. Cambridge: MIT Press.

[110] Nordhaus, W.D. (2006) The Stern review on the economics of climate change. *National Bureau of Economic Research Working Paper, no. 12741*.

[111] Obstfeld, M. and Rogoff, K. (1996) *Foundations of International Macroeconomics*. New York: MIT Press.

[112] Oksanen, H. (2003) Population ageing and public finance targets. *European Commission Economic Papers*, No. 193.

[113] Okun, A.M. (1975) *Equality and Efficiency: The Big Trade-off*. Washington: The Brookings Institution.

[114] Padilla, E. (2002) Intergenerational equity and sustainability. *Ecological Economics*, 41, pp. 69-83.

[115] Pearce, D. and Ulph, D. (1998) A social discount rate for the United Kingdom. In *Economics and Environment: Essays on Ecological Economics and Sustainable Development* (ed. by D. Pearce). Cheltenham: Edward Elgar.

[116] Petersen , P.G. (1999) Gray dawn: the global ageing crisis. *Foreign Affairs*, 78, pp. 42-55.

[117] Piggott, J. (1997) Taxation and pensions. *UNSW Retirement Economics Research Paper, no. 7.*

[118] Pigou, A. C. (1932) *The Economics of Welfare* (4th edition). London: Macmillan.

[119] Preinreich, A.D. (1948) Progressive taxation and sacrifice. *American Economic Review*, 38, pp. 103-117.

[120] Productivity Commission (2005) *Economic Implications of an Ageing Australia.* Commonwealth of Australia, Canberra.

[121] Prskawetz, A. and Fent, T. (2004) *Workforce Ageing and Economic Productivity: The Role of Supply and Demand for Labour. An Application to Austria.* Vienna Institute of Demography, Austrian Academy of Sciences.

[122] Prskawetz, A., Fent, T. and Guest (2006) *Workforce Ageing and Economic Productivity: The Role of the Demand for Labour.* In *Population Aging, Human Capital Accumulation, and Productivity Growth. A Supplement to Population and Development Review.*(ed. by A. Prskawetz, D. Bloom and W. Lutz. Population Council: New York.

[123] Ramsey, F. (1928) A mathematical theory of saving. *Economic Journal*, 38, pp.543-559.

[124] Rawls, J. (1971) *A Theory of Justice.* Harvard: Harvard University Press.

[125] Richardson, P. (ed.) (1997) Globalisation and linkages: macrostructural challenges and opportunities. *OECD Economic Studies*, No. 28.

[126] Richter, W.F (1983) From ability to pay to concepts of equal sacrifice. *Journal of Public Economics*, 20, pp. 211-229.

[127] Robbins, L. (1935) *An Essay on the Nature and Significance of Economic Science* (2nd Edition). London: Macmillan.

[128] Romer, Paul M (1990) Capital, labor, and productivity. *Brookings Papers on Economic Activity, Microeconomics*, pp.337-367.

[129] Samuelson, P.A. (1947) *Foundations of Economic Analysis*. Cambridge: Harvard University Press.

[130] Shilizzi, S. (2007) Discounting the distant future using short time horizons: investments with irreversible benefits. In *Economics and the Future: Time Discounting in Private and Public Decision Making* (ed. by D. Pannell and S. Shilizzi). Cheltenham: Edward Elgar.

[131] Shorrocks, A. F. (2004) Inequality and welfare evaluation of heterogeneous income distributions. *Journal of Economic Inequality*, 2, pp. 193-218.

[132] Skirbekk, V. (2004) Age and Individual Productivity: A Literature Survey. Paper delivered at the Symposium on Population Ageing and Economic Productivity. Vienna Institute of Demography,Vienna.Available at:http://www.oeaw.ac.at/vid/staff/fuernkranz/pdf_documents/ chapter_7/skirbekk.pdf

[133] Solow, R. (1992) An almost practical step toward sustainability. *Invited lecture on the occasion of the fortieth anniversary of Resources for the Future*, 8 October 1992.

[134] Solow, R. (2005) Sustainability: an economist's perspective. In *Economics of the Environment: Selected Readings* (ed. by R. Stavins). New York: Norton.

[135] Stapleton, D. and Young, D. (1988) Education attainment and cohort size. *Journal of Labor Economics,* 6, pp. 330-361.

[136] Stavins, R.N.. Wagner, A. and Wagner, G. (2003) Interpreting sustainability in economic terms: dynamic efficiency plus intergenerational equity. *Economics Letters,* 79, pp.339-343.

[137] Stern, N. (1977) Welfare weights and the elasticity of the marginal valuation of income. In *Studies in Modern Economic Analysis* (ed. by M. Artis and R. Nobay). Oxford: Basil Blackwell.

[138] Stern, N. (2007) *The Economics of Climate Change: The Stern Review.* Cambridge: Cambridge University Press.

[139] Turner, D., Giorno, C. DeSerres, A., Vourch, A. and Richardson, P. (1998) The macroeconomic implications of ageing in a global context. *OECD Economic Department Working Paper,* No. 193.

[140] United Nations (1987) *Our Common Future. Report of the World Commission on Environment and Development.* Oxford: Oxford University Press.

[141] United Nations (2004) *World Population Prospects: The 2004 Revision.* New York: United Nations.

[142] United Nations (2007) *World Population Prospects: The 2006 Revision.* New York: United Nations.

[143] van de Ven, J. and Creedy, J. (2005) Taxation, reranking and equivalence scales. *Bulletin of Economic Research,* 57, pp. 13-36.

[144] Vanek, J. (1963) Variable factor proportions: inter-industry flows in the theory of international trade. *Quarterly Journal of Economics,* 77, pp. 129-142.

[145] Varian, H.L. (2006) Recalculating the costs of global climate change. New York Times (14 December).

[146] Von Weizacker, C. (1965) Existence of optimal programs of accumulation for an infinite time horizon. *Review of Economic Studies*, 32, pp. 85-104.

[147] Weitzman, M.L. (2007) *The Stern Review of the Economics of Climate Change.* (Unpublished paper) Harvard University.

[148] Werner, R. and Veld, J. (2002) *Some Selected Simulation Experiments with the European Commission's QUEST model.* European Commission, Brussels.

[149] Whitehouse, E (1999) The tax treatment of funded pensions. *World Bank Social Protection Discussion Paper,* No. 9910.

[150] Woodward, R.T. and Bishop, R.C. (1997) How to decide when experts disagree: uncertainty-based choice rules in environmental policy. *Land Economics*, 73, pp. 492-507.

[151] World Bank (1994) *Averting the Old Age Crisis: Policies to Protect the Old and Promote Growth.* Oxford: Oxford University Press.

[152] Young, H.P. (1987) Progressive taxation and the equal sacrifice principle. *Journal of Public Economics*, 32, pp. 203-214.

Index

DATE DUE	RETURNED